Parish Churches

To our good friend, Ray, gentle
and enduring scholar, and his
lovely wife, Muriel.
   With good wishes for
the future.
         Sincerly,
      Malcolm & Hilda

Now, sadly, you have departed, Mac.,
How we wish you could come back!
         In memoriam,
 and Ray.

by the same author

*

ENGLISH ABBEYS
CATHEDRAL ARCHITECTURE
OLD ENGLISH HOUSES
AN INTRODUCTION TO ENGLISH
MEDIAEVAL ARCHITECTURE

Parish Churches

___

Their Architectural Development in England

___

HUGH BRAUN

FABER AND FABER
London

First Published in 1970
This edition published 1974
by Faber and Faber Limited
3 Queen Square London WC1
Printed in Great Britain by
Whitstable Litho Whitstable Kent

ISBN 0 571 10553 X

To the
parochial church councils
who care for them

Contents

Illustrations

Illustrations

Illustrations

I

The Study of Old Churches

Our old parish churches, scattered in their profusion in every nook and corner of the land, have long been objects of interest as well as veneration. Everywhere one finds the village churches, some humble, others stately, and their counterparts the churches hidden about our densely populated cities. Finest of all are the large town churches, packed with monuments of past worthies, presenting their Gothic splendours as the central features of market towns, and surrounded by churchyards which join with the marketplaces to defy encroachment upon the ancient meeting-places of our urban communities.

To its parishioners their church is the shrine of their history, where their forefathers came in their day to be baptized and married, and around whose walls, their roles fulfilled, they have slept down the centuries in the midst of the scenes they knew.

But to the nation as a whole each parish church is a record of the country's past, a monument to the days of which as children we read in the history books. Kings and bishops pass, and straggling armies, here and there sad battles sweep up to its walls. As poverty and pestilence stalk by, the generations repair and enlarge their churches, adding stone upon stone and spanning across the walls with beams from parish coverts. Fire and decay destroy the village homes, but the parish church survives down the centuries as nucleus for each renaissance.

A national interest in the parish church as a subject for research developed as a reaction from two aspects of life at the close of the eighteenth century. One of these was the Industrial Revolution, the commercial and materialistic nature of which was beginning to irritate the intelligentsia of the period and recreate an interest in what was regarded as the romance of the Middle Ages.

The other factor was the rapidly increasing wealth and political power of the nation and a resulting chauvinistic dissatisfaction with the imported architecture of the Italian Renaissance. Horace Walpole's Gothic Revival, known from the name of his house as 'Strawberry Hill', was in reality a patriotic revolution.

The practical requirements of the new industrial architecture, however, encouraged the less romantic Humanist element among the savants to launch the far more serious Classical Revival which reached its heyday during the railway boom of the second quarter of the nineteenth century. It may well have been the excesses of this architecturally grim era which turned the Englishman's thoughts once more towards his national building style, the familiar Gothic of his parish churches.

The first person to write authoritatively upon the subject of what he called 'English' architecture was a Liverpool architect, Thomas Rickman. His book was published as early as 1817. It has formed the basis of all subsequent literature on the subject. It was he who divided English Gothic into three periods according to the lowering of the pitch of arches from 'lancet' to 'debased'.

It will be realized from this that, notwithstanding Rickman's practical knowledge as an architect, his consideration of historical architecture was based solely upon aesthetic grounds, an attitude which has unfortunately bedevilled all subsequent study and paved the way for the ever-increasing host of amateur architectural historians who are apt to treat all architecture not as building construction but as pictorial design.

Rickman's interest was academic. But the immense problems presented by the arrears of maintenance discernible in our great cathedral churches forced the leading architects of the day to begin a serious study of the 'Gothick'. One of the first to do so was Sir Gilbert Scott, who after an apprenticeship as a designer of workhouses in 1847 became appointed as architect to Ely Cathedral and subsequently to many others. It was in this fashion that the impressive era of Victorian Gothic came into being, architects great and small following the trend and interpreting the medieval as best they could, helped in no small degree by the romantic revival launched by the Pre-Raphaelites.

The revival of interest in matters medieval quite naturally brought about a reaction against the many drastic alterations made to the interiors of old parish churches since the Reformation. The resulting wave of 'church restorations' did a very great deal of damage to the buildings by removing genuine and often charming period features and replacing them with bogus and only half-understood 'Gothic' substitutes. Nevertheless such regrettable excursions had the effect of stimulating national interest in what had come to be accepted as our 'national' architecture.

As the architect of the period was too busily occupied with the practical responsibilities of his profession to devote much time to academic research, it was left to laymen to develop the study of English medieval architecture. In 1849 an Oxford bookseller, J. H. Parker, published a book which extended the work done by Rickman a generation earlier, introduced more detailed illustration to the public, but continued to discuss the aesthetic and delved no deeper into the constructional aspect of architecture. Parker's book went into a number of editions and until the end of the century he remained the authority.

When recalling the work of such men as these early explorers it becomes us to remember the transport problems they had to face. In Parker's day the railways were novelties represented by a few main lines, while Rickman had to rely entirely upon the horse. All the same, they managed to extend their studies over the countryside to provide them with sufficient material to establish a history of Gothic architecture acceptable to the profession, and to discover most of the more remarkable examples known to us today, a fact which in itself is truly remarkable.

While Parker was sufficiently broadminded to carry his researches into the sphere of medieval domestic architecture, the popular interest at the time was probably in the Gothic as represented by the great cathedral and abbey churches, and, more intimately, by one's own parish church. For the upper classes the period was one of expansion in ritual, away from the Methody chapel and towards the medieval splendour of vestments and scenic colour. Thus in addition to the pictorial aspect of architecture, the clergy in particular were becoming interested in the original ritual use of the medieval churches of this country.

An interest began to develop in the historical growth of the church plan. In the same way that elevational architecture had been examined from the pictorial aspect, the plan came to be investigated from the point of view of its accommodation. Although neither exercise was able to take into account any structural considerations, this amateur research continued to explore the church plan and authoritative statements began to appear from the pens of antiquaries.

In addition to a lack of architectural experience, the writers on architectural history were hampered by two other deficiencies. One of these was the ignorance of any country save his own which was then the birthright of every Englishman. The other was the Victorian bias against everything taught in childhood as unworthy of the Englishman's consideration.

Thus, apart from the subject countries of his Empire, the Englishman of the period could accept as significant only France and—for the aesthete—Italy. Holland and Germany were still barbarous. Spain had had the Inquisition and had sent an armada against us. And all had impossible hotels!

Ancient Constantinople was the capital of a country whose inhabitants were unspeakable. They were moreover heathen Mussulmen, foreigners of the worst kind against whom we had fought for centuries in the Crusades.

Latin was a respectable language, especially as, being dead, it was only used by the best-educated people. Greek was certainly respectable, but deviations from the Classical form employed by such people as the Byzantines could only be ignored.

When studying the history of architecture, that of the land of Homer could hardly have been disregarded. Nor could the achievements of Imperial Rome be passed over.

The difficulty presented itself of how to find a link which would bridge the Dark Ages and account for the eventual appearance of an architectural style in this country. The only solution conceivable to the Victorian Englishman was that somehow there must be a direct connection spanning the thousand years between Imperial Rome and post-Conquest England. In other words, the architecture of the latter must be 'Romanesque'.

Thus by a stroke of the pen the glories of Byzantium are banished as though they had never existed.

Only fifteen years ago, the writer, visiting a London institute in which future architectural historians were being trained, and asking to see a book on Byzantine buildings, was told pityingly that the institute did not concern itself with *Oriental* architecture. Yet from the walls of many an English church the 'oriental' faces gaze down upon us today as from a Byzantine mosaic. Look at the great porch of Malmesbury in Wiltshire, or the tiny parish church of Kilpeck in Yorkshire, and you can see far Byzantium carved in English stone.

On page 241 of the *Larousse Encyclopedia of Byzantine and Medieval Art*, Professor Jean Hubert, discussing the Early Middle Ages, sets forth the situation with absolute clarity when he states 'Rome, five times conquered, was no more than a large city of ruins, its aqueducts in disrepair, its countryside a wasteland. The real capital was Byzantium, the only cultural centre . . .'.

When the huge monastic churches came to be built, these adopted the elongated nave flanked by aisles and might thus be considered to be vaguely basilican. Nothing else about them was Roman. Their architecture was, as indeed one might have expected, entirely a development of the Byzantine. Away from these huge buildings, the rural churches probably followed more closely the compact plans of their more easterly prototypes.

The misleading term 'Romanesque' which has for some time past been applied to the architectural style which was being introduced into this country towards the close of the first millennium may owe its origin to the French, who call it, with still less reservation, 'Roman'.

Our own particular brand of 'Romanesque' has been still further bedevilled by having been divided into two halves on either side of the Norman Conquest, as though the whole of the country's building trade had been exterminated and replaced from the Continent in 1066.

The mistake is not due to the eighteenth-century antiquaries, who were patriotic enough to call all round-arched, pre-Gothick, buildings 'Saxon'. It is true that the enormous wealth looted from the English by the Church following the Conquest enabled it to rebuild all the great Anglo-Saxon minsters so that none remained to bear witness to pre-Conquest achievement. But the builders were still the same as before, and had their works been called at the time 'Norman' it would have been nothing more than a political trick.

It is now too late to restore the use of the word 'Saxon', so the writer has fallen back upon the use of the term 'pre-medieval' to designate the English Byzantine style which preceded the Gothic in this country.

English architectural historians have become accustomed to dividing their Gothic era into three phases—early, middle and late. Since Rickman's day they have been known by the slightly ludicrous names of Early English, Decorated and Perpendicular. Any subdivision of a country's architectural styles is apt to be invidious, for there are no sudden changes of style even where revolutionary influences irrupt from abroad. We shall find later that the middle and late periods of Gothic are apt to interweave more than might at first be supposed.

The movements accompanying the Crusades towards the end of the twelfth century hastened the development of the Gothic style in England. The intermediate period, however, called by architectural historians the Transitional, has not been separately dealt with in this book, nor has the rapid deterioration of English Gothic under first Spanish and then Dutch pressure been accorded more than passing notice as it began to develop through considerable confusion into the English Renaissance.

The thirteenth century, however, a period which saw the aesthetic zenith of the early, purer Gothic which is represented by Salisbury and the Yorkshire abbeys but never really had a chance of achieving a place in the architecture of the parish church, is nevertheless given its own chapter under the heading Early Medieval.

Rickman's two other periods, those not easily separable middle and late divisions which are perhaps styles rather than historical periods, have been joined together under the designation High Gothic. The whole arrangement is of course very arbitrary as, regional tastes apart, it may take several generations to change the face of a country's buildings.

Shakespeare has explained to us how a building is designed—first the plot, then the model. What he meant was that the plan comes first, then its elevational presentation. There are two aspects of any building, its lay-out and its appearance. Both are of interest to the architectural historian, and in a very old building the changes and additions to the plan and the recurring evidences of ever-changing fashion are both endless subjects for investigation.

This book follows the Shakespearian precept by dealing first with the growth of the parish church as a building designed to accommodate a congregation of persons engaged in worship and changing through the centuries as new factors influence the plan. Then, after some consideration of the constructional methods used, we examine the architectural forms deriving from these and the whims of aesthetic fancy by means of which each building displays its face to the countryside it adorns.

In planning, as in architectural expression, the nineteenth-century student of parish church architecture has hitherto devoted his attention towards trying to consolidate a firm link with Rome. Without pausing to consider the realities of the situation he has taken as prototype the Roman basilica, slipping without difficulty into the belief that there could be no other link possible. Had he ignored this preconceived notion and examined the plans of village churches more carefully, he would have found that the link was to be found very much closer at hand.

It is useless to study the plan of a building without going back in time to find out for what purpose it was designed. If one is withdrawing to some distance it is of no use to consider present-day arrangements as identical with those obtaining at the time the building was being planned.

Protestant England could not pretend to a history reaching back more than four centuries. Thus it was important to take the study of the English church plan back over that distance and pick it up at the period just preceding the Reformation. In other words, one had to examine it not only from the point of view of a Roman Catholic, but a Roman Catholic of medieval days.

The difficulty is at once apparent. For the Victorian church, of whatever denomination, packed with pewing and comfortably be-hassocked, bears no resemblance whatsoever to the bare, absolutely unfurnished building of medieval days.

Nor could anyone familiar only with the Anglican parish service, read by a priest seated throughout it just beyond the chancel arch, imagine the same chancel being solely occupied by a priest stationed at a distant altar, far away from his congregation at the end of an empty chancel.

Anyone examining the situation by trying to adopt the viewpoint of a nineteenth-century Roman Catholic would probably have got no further than trying to equate it with an experience of a Mass attended in some church in France or Italy. For here he would have encountered the open 'Baroque' plan and a service still impossible to transfer to an English parish church of the Middle Ages with its long lonely chancel and its spreading transepts from which no one could have seen anything of what was taking place at the altar.

Confronted with this problem of trying to discover just how these churches were used, the writer has studied a number of recommended authorities but has utterly failed to discover any contemporary account of instructions issued to parish priests to assist them in regulating the performance of their rustic services, nor indeed any suggestions as to how these were organized with regard to the buildings themselves.

A vast amount of research has been undertaken and voluminous literature published on the nature of the 'Roman-Frankish' ritual employed during the performance of the Mass in a great church of what we would call our Anglo-Saxon period. All writers agree that even such highly organized worship followed a great variety of interpretations. By the Middle Ages there were in England at least five 'Uses'—of Sarum, York, Bangor, Hereford and Lincoln. And all these were designed for celebrating the Mass in a monastic choir, a long clear room having the altar at one end and fixed stalls at the other, and could hardly have been transferred to a parish church, administered by a single priest standing before a congregation crowding into a seatless hall, a rustic flock attending to the words of a pastor, far removed in every way from professionals assisting at an organized ritual.

When chancels were short Byzantine annexes and the altar was close at hand one could perhaps visualize the Mass performed as in the 'open' Roman Catholic churches of the present day. But the elongation of chancels which came about during the thirteenth century and the consequent removal of the altar fifty feet or so away from the congregation—where it remained until the Reformation—suggests that more of the service may have taken place at the chancel arch as in the Byzantine ritual, a possibility which is emphasized by the continued use of the transept in English parish church planning.

It appears that in Anglo-Saxon days there was a prelude to the service known as the 'Fore-Mass'; perhaps this took place at the chancel arch.

The writer has talked with priests, Catholic as well as Anglican, who find no difficulty in contemplating the possibility that the scene during Mass in an Anglo-Saxon parish church may not have appeared so very different from the more 'homely' service one sees today in the churches of Orthodoxy.

After all, the church vestments used today in an English church are Byzantine garments, and the Roman Church has never abandoned the use of the Greek appeal 'Kyrie eleison'—Lord, have mercy upon us.

To have talked in this fashion to a Victorian Protestant would have seemed to him the height of impertinence. Orthodoxy would have seemed to him a greater heresy than the Roman, and, in view of its geographical situation, little better than Mohammedanism. The life of Byzantium was known to have been notably immoral. Orthodoxy was the religion of the barbarous Muscovite.

The unravelling of the true history of the English parish-church plan requires the co-operation of two persons, the architect and the ecclesiastic. More than a century has passed since the day of the

Oxford bookseller, and our horizons have extended far beyond his. Yet no attempt has been made by historians to re-examine the tentative theories of Parker's day and reconsider the 'Romanesque' attitude towards English ecclesiastical origins. The writer hopes that this may now be done, and a more reasoned investigation undertaken.

When examining medieval ecclesiastical architecture it is essential to keep in mind the wide gulf separating the 'great' church from its poor parochial relation. At the turn of the millennium the monastic churches were quite enormous, while the parish churches were architecturally almost negligible. The great cathedral city such as Exeter, or the abbey town such as Wilton, had its inhabited area divided, like the countryside about it, into small and densely-packed areas each with its parish church, completely dominated by the great churches towering above them. So they remained throughout the Middle Ages.

But as time went on and market-towns developed independently of the ecclesiastical centres, the single parish church of a township which had hitherto known only a small population might have had to be developed with each generation as its congregation increased, until at the height of the medieval period it might have reached a scale where it could at least vie with many of the lesser monastic churches. Such large town churches might become multi-aisled and extend their transepts to an inordinate length. They would become cluttered with the tombs of rich merchants, and those who perhaps could not achieve right of interment among the noble families whose sepulchres lined some neighbouring minster.

But it is not with these great town churches that the following pages are concerned, rather with the smaller, more intimate buildings found in the country parishes.

2

Early Churches

The church as we have known it for many centuries is a building designed for the congregational worship of a unique God, omnipresent but at all times invisible. Christianity as a religion has been in existence for less than two millennia. But the buildings it uses for worship can trace their origins much further back in history, into the dim distances of the pagan eras of antiquity.

It was difficult for primitive men to feel much confidence in an invisible God whose lineaments they could not conceive. The deity they worshipped and at times appealed to had to be represented by some sculptured figure from which they could form some impression of a real personage and not merely a wisp of cloud or a borrowed voice. The statue had to be established in a becoming setting and attended by a retinue of priests. In this we find the beginnings of religious architecture, the provision of a house for the god.

The shrines of an even dimmer antiquity notwithstanding, the origins of our architecture may be said to stem from the Classical Age of Greece which produced such temples as the Parthenon at Athens. The temple of that day was a rectangular building the roof of which was supported upon sturdy columns of the 'Doric' Order within which light stone partitions surrounded the actual apartment inhabited by the god in the form of a votive statue.

From its primitive beginnings in Bronze Age Greece, temple architecture developed into a style having as its ordinance the 'Corinthian' Order, in which the slender column was crowned by a lovely capital, the 'bell' of which was ornamented by leaves of the acanthus fern, lapping it in tiers and springing out at each angle to form a 'volute' resembling a frond beginning to uncurl. Upon this Order was based the magnificent Hellenistic temple architecture which attended the birth of the Roman Empire.

Great builders though they were, the Roman engineers had no real architectural style of their own and displayed their wisdom by adapting the Hellenistic style to their own large secular buildings constructed in purely practical fashion of brick and concrete. With such sophisticated materials, however, they were able to develop the arcuated form of construction, new to the world of architecture. As Roman taste developed, the arch came to be employed not only as a structural device but as a feature to be displayed in elevations, either singly or as part of an arcade.

The principal ceremony connected with pagan worship was the sacrifice upon an altar, often accompanied by fire. Such altars had inevitably to be set up in the open air, so that the congregations attending upon the sacrifice were without shelter.

The altar was situated before the entrance façade of the temple, so that the statue representing the god was, if not actually visible, at least imaginable to the assembled worshippers. The line passing between the altar and the statue constituted an axis or orientation governing the lay-out of the temple enclosure.

The heyday of the Hellenistic era came at the beginning of the first century A.D. when the Western world was beginning to drift away from paganism, with the monotheistic religions—Judaism and, later, Christianity—bringing the curtain down upon the obsolescent architecture of Classical days. The huge temples of the period were being surrounded by spacious enclosures of ornamental walling designed as scenic architecture on a magnificent scale. The temple of Apollo at Didyma in Asia Minor had its congregational area before the altar laid out in this fashion as a sort of open-air nave, perhaps the first attempt to create an architectural area, not for the accommodation of the god, but for those who were engaged in worship. This fine achievement appeared, however, at the very end of the pagan Hellenistic era so that instead of launching a type of structure which might have soared to unimaginable heights, the Didymaean adventure followed the old gods into oblivion.

During the Imperial Roman period the stage was reached at which worshippers frequented the temple itself to view the votive statue. It therefore became desirable to endow this with a special architectural setting instead of merely placing it in the centre of the apartment.

The old gods of Babylonia had always been set in a niche formed in a wall, as though appearing in a doorway to receive the petitions of their suppliants. The statues were, however, quite small and in no way compared with the huge creations of the Hellenistic world.

One of the most remarkable features of historical architecture is the apse. At first glance it appears to be an incomplete building of which one half is missing. Its external appearance, as a somewhat clumsy bulge, is incidental to its internal function, which is to invite one to inspect some feature to which it forms a setting. In effect a horizontal arch, it may perhaps have had its origin as a revetment to earthwork, as would be necessary, for instance, when providing an entrance façade to a tumulus. The concave façade of the 'long barrow' is a feature well known to the archaeologist. The trilithons of Stonehenge, tomb of the sun, are arranged in a horseshoe formation which would seem to be analagous to an apse. It is possible that the introduction of the apse into the Roman temple as a setting for the cult statue may derive from some such prehistoric origin.

As the Roman engineers developed their new arcuated designs they discovered the tunnel vault and, eventually, the dome. By forming a semicircular recess and covering it with a half-dome they perfected the apse. Lofty apses or 'exedrae' were set in the architectural walling enclosing the wide courts of the Hellenistic temples where they made attractive settings as 'nymphaea' for fountains. Eventually they were brought inside the temple itself to provide an impressive background for the cult statue, setting it, not just in a doorway, but in a cavernous home.

From this period the apse became the recognized terminal feature for a religious building. In addition, the sophisticated

Romans provided an apse at the end of their hall of justice so as to introduce an atmosphere of awe surrounding the magistrates seated around its wall. These justice halls, and indeed any large building of exceptional merit, were designated by the Greek word 'basilica', this meaning, simply, a hall fit for a king. No other architectural period has produced an expression of this sort simply denoting the superlative in architectural excellence. The term 'basilica', therefore, has always remained in use to denote a building of incomparable majesty. To this day, the Baroque cathedral of St. Peter at Rome is called 'basilica'.

Contemporary with the Hellenistic temples were the synagogues of the Jews, the first people to worship an invisible god who needed no representation in sculptured form. Their buildings were designed from the first to accommodate their worshippers under cover. Although not large in area, they were planned to be as commodious as possible. Short rectangles in form, their lines were those of the lesser or provincial Roman basilica planned as a central structure with its walling carried on Classical columns and surrounded on all sides by an aisle with a lean-to roof. (Fig. 1.)

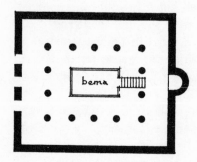

Fig. 1
Plan of early Synagogue
Based on that of the small provincial 'basilica'. A tall central structure carried on columns and surrounded by an aisle. A miniature apse enclosed by doors to provide a cupboard containing the sacred scrolls which are brought to a raised platform, the *bema*, to be read to the surrounding congregation.

The apse was there, but reduced in scale so as to form a cupboard closed by doors which when opened disclosed instead of a statue the scrolls of the Mosaic law, the whole feature designed more on the lines of the Babylonian cult niche rather than the large Roman apse or exedra. An interesting piece of furnishing was the raised platform provided in the centre of the synagogue to which the scrolls were brought for reading to the congregation. On the same platform a trained choir led the liturgy.

Christian worship was intended from the start to be conducted under cover, as befitted a religion opposed to 'pagan' ceremonial in which the sacrifice was attended in the open air.

The basic action in the Christian form of worship was the communal enjoyment of a sacramental meal, such, indeed, as could have been taken in an ordinary home.

Such research as has been found possible into the arrangements for Christian worship in the very early days has indicated that no recognized form of church existed and that the early Christians gathered in ordinary houses to affirm their creed, celebrate their Mystery, and say their prayers in as inconspicuous a fashion as possible. While large gatherings are known to have taken place in the underground caverns outside Rome, the church was not yet a recognizable building.

Thus with the sudden flight of the old gods from the Rome of Constantine in the first half of the fourth century, the architects of the imperial city found themselves completely taken by surprise.

Above three holy sites in Bethlehem and Jerusalem the emperor erected charming little memorial temples, basilicas in miniature. It is to the design of these buildings which, small though they might be, were intended to represent monumental architecture in its highest form, that we owe the origins of Christian church design; but Constantine's three temples were nothing more than monuments and could in no wise accommodate a host of worshippers.

The problems set by congregational worship on an imperial scale were new to architectural experience and the Roman architects were faced with having to design and build covered accommodation, without loss of time, to meet the new demand.

The buildings they ran up were very large, but of the flimsiest construction. They consisted of a long central structure covered with a simple roof and having its walls carried on rows of columns, sometimes salvaged second-hand from destroyed temples. Wide aisles flanked the central 'nave'. Their size and special dignity entitled them to be called 'basilica' but architecturally they were negligible when compared with their mighty Imperial predecessors. (Fig. 2.)

The apse was there, recalling both the pagan statue and the ring of dignified magistrates now replaced by clerics. Before it was set the raised platform of the Jews, also used to seat a choir. In the chord of the apse was the altar upon which was performed the Christian Mystery.

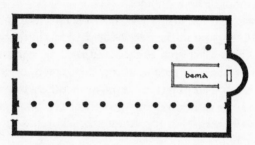

Fig. 2 *Plan of Christian 'Basilica'*
The type of church erected in the Rome of Constantine for Christian worship. A wide nave flanked by wide aisles beyond rows of columns. Covered with light timber roofs. An apse to accommodate the seats of the clergy. In the chord of the apse, the altar; before this the raised *bema* upon which a choir sang and the scriptures were read to the congregation.

Such were the great churches of Constantine's Rome before he moved his capital to the shores of the Bosphorus. It was in these vast bare barns that the Roman Church was established and in which it had to maintain its dignity for centuries to come while Christian architects were covering Europe with some of the most magnificent buildings the world had ever seen.

For soon the imperial city, seat of the Popes and headquarters of the Latin Church, was to decline into a ghost town, having to wait patiently for a thousand years until an architectural Renaissance could restore to it its lost glories.

Meanwhile the churches of both the Latin and Greek rites spread throughout Europe, North Africa and the Near East.

Christianity is believed to have reached Britain by way of Gaul during the third century. Early in the next, bishops are recorded as established in such cities as London, York and Lincoln. Of this period the only known remains of a church are those at Calleva, now Silchester in Hampshire, where the building appears to have been designed as a miniature reproduction of a Roman basilica.

Detached from Roman Britain and preserved from its eventual fate, Ireland is believed to have been originally converted by missionary monks making the long journey along the southern shores of the Mediterranean. Thus during the fifth century, when Christianity was becoming submerged in the stress of heathen invasion, Ireland was developing as the seat of a Celtic Church which was to maintain Christian worship in these islands throughout the Dark Ages closing in upon them.

The Celtic Church appears to have been based upon monastic settlements of humble huts surrounding chapels which were originally simple rectangles but later seem to have been provided with small square chancels. In due course the Celtic Church was able to establish itself to some degree in Britain, but none of its original churches has come down to us.

The Roman rural temple in this country was a small square room surrounded by a veranda, a feature common to all Romano-British domestic buildings and possibly introduced into the temple plan to serve as a rustic version of the Classical peristyle. It seems possible that some of these structures—perhaps even some of the larger ones in the cities—may have been preserved undamaged by subsequent invaders of the country.

When St. Augustine undertook his missionary expedition to Britain at the close of the sixth century, he appears to have been anxious to avoid any disrespect towards existing native customs. He erected several very well-built churches along the south-east coasts which were simple rectangular rooms with an apse at the end and had the remaining three sides surrounded with pillared verandas or porticos. The churches were lofty and must in their day have been most impressive even though they could hardly have stood up, architecturally speaking, to their predecessors the pagan temples in the Roman cities amongst the ruins of which they were built.

A handful of these churches of St. Augustine survived the Dark Ages and are with us today, the most notable example being that at Bradwell in Essex. But their provenance was too restricted for them to have had any influence on the future of English church design. In the simplicity of their plan, however, they must have accorded well enough with the taste of the Celtic Church which remained the only form in which Christianity held on to these islands during the period of the Dark Ages.

Such hold as the Latin Church retained in this country was due to the security of its tenure in Ireland. This was the Celtic Church, established in primitive monastic settlements each with a small chapel or oratory. Its Rite was 'Latin', and its culture strongly Celtic.

During the Dark Ages the Celtic Church in England had dwindled to two main sites. In the north-east the sea-girt rock of Lindisfarne and in the south-west the Isle of Avalon hidden in the Somerset marshes remained strongholds of Christianity surrounded by pagan England. While its buildings may have been too insignificant to be counted as architecture, the Celtic Church continued to maintain its spiritual links with the city of the Popes and by doing so assured the continuity of the Latin Rite in this country.

3

The Byzantine Church

====

The transfer by Constantine of the capital of the Roman Empire from Rome to Byzantium resulted not only in the building of a great new city on virtually a clear site, but the founding of a new metropolis provided from its inception with an entirely new state religion. As an architectural revolution it was unparalleled in history.

The known world was covered with the temples to a long-established pantheon, architecturally the most magnificent examples of contemporary culture. And all now suddenly become obsolete.

In their place, the votaries of the Hellenistic and Roman world were demanding an entirely new type of building—a Christian church.

In essence, the requirements of the plan were simple enough. What was wanted was a large building capable of accommodating a large congregation under cover.

The hastily-erected 'basilicas' of Rome had been but temporary expedients fulfilling this requirement. But architecturally they were contemptible successors to the glorious temple groups of the Hellenistic Age all of which were still very much in evidence.

Thus it was demanded of the architects of the day that they should apply their skill in designing, not only large buildings for Christian worship, but structures presented in such a fashion that they should represent the crowning architectural achievements of their Age.

The temples of the pagan era had relied for their effect upon row after row of tall columns crowned by masses of rich sculpture. But these costly features, no longer structural but become purely ornamental, had now been banished to the interiors of buildings. Here, in reduced condition, they were being employed to carry walling and by opening up the lower parts of this to enable the floor areas of buildings to be extended into lateral or circumambient aisles.

The early basilicas had been covered with open timber roofs. The latest structural discovery, however, was the vaulted ceiling of stone or concrete which had been developed into a truly monumental architectural feature, the dome.

It was the dome which came to be adopted by the architects of Byzantium as the architectural indication of a church.

A place of worship is usually aligned upon a sacred axis, as Christian churches are aligned upon Jerusalem. But a dome is unsuited as a form of roofing for a building having a pronounced axis; thus the Byzantine churches tended towards more centralized plans, concentrating worshippers into a compact area rather than forcing them to extend away from the altar as in the Roman basilicas.

With such a demanding form of roofing, the domed churches were unable to expand laterally to cover a wide area. But externally their architecture had produced something missing from major structures since the days of the Pyramids, an impression of which the principal element was a vertical one. From this time onwards, the Greek architects—and they were Greeks rather than Romans—no longer concentrated upon the Hellenistic passion for spreading their compositions over vast areas but exercised their structural capabilities in raising them ever higher towards the heavens. This established the form of the Christian church as a lofty structure piling up towards a central crowning feature.

In Rome itself, Ravenna, and other towns of Latinism the basilican halls continued to be built out of the ruins of paganism. But in the Byzantine regions in which a new world culture was taking root, the church form in process of development was adopting the compact centralized plan.

The feature continued from basilican architecture was the use of columns to support walling and the lateral expansion of a main structure by means of aisles. And by employing heavy masses of stonework, legacy from the imperial engineers of Rome, in place of the slender columns of the past, the Byzantines were able to lift their structures to a considerable height before crowning them with the desired dome.

An innovation introduced by the Byzantine architects was the division of the aisles into two stories: the vaulted floors—again a Roman device—of the galleries being carried upon a lesser arcade springing from turned columns of Classical type. This 'duplex' principle of alternating heavy piers and slender columns plays a large part in Byzantine ordinance and may be found echoed even in some English parish churches of the twelfth century displaying in their aisle arcades pillars alternating with piers.

But architectural detailing apart, the spirit of Byzantine church architecture was undoubtedly born in the three little memorial temples erected by Constantine over the holy sites in Bethlehem and Jerusalem. These little shrines, most venerated in all Christendom, were not aligned in the normal fashion upon a sacred axis but were actually focused upon the shrine itself and could thus concentrate upon an effect, not of length or breadth, but of verticality.

The three memorial temples were not, however, quite the first of their kind. Circular temples were not uncommon in the Hellenistic world. And the last great temple of all, which bade farewell to all the gods of Olympus, was the mighty dome of the Roman Pantheon, perhaps after all the real progenitor of the churches of Christendom.

But away from Jerusalem the alignment upon the city as a sacred axis had to be maintained. Thus in its final form the Christian Church, even the cathedral in Constantinople itself, had to adopt this axis and abandon the perfect circular plan. Nevertheless the vertical element remained, announced without any chance of misapprehension by the dome, great or small, crowning every Byzantine church.

Thus the structural nucleus of every Byzantine church is a central turriform structure with four semicircular—later to become pointed—arches rising from four tall and massive piers. The tower rises high enough above the surrounding roofs to carry a low dome, usually with a ring of small windows round its base, and often covered with a low-pitched conical roof. (Fig. 3.)

The visible part of the central nucleus becomes circular or octagonal to help carry the dome. The ring of small windows lighting the 'crossing' below is the origin of the English lantern tower.

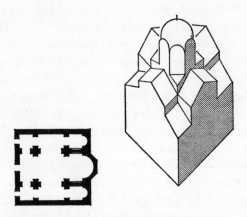

Fig. 3   *Byzantine Church*
A tall building centralized upon a crossing covered by a dome, four short projections supporting this to give a cruciform plan. The whole enclosed within a square. Often two-storied beyond the cruciform portion. Of no great extent when compared with the 'basilican' church, but structurally and aesthetically a building of far greater architectural merit.

The four arches of the crossing lead into four short but tall projections covered with low-pitched roofs which abut against the side of the tower. The cruciform mass thus produced is common to the normal Byzantine church.

The complete circular plan of Constantine's three buildings which had a central feature surrounded by an aisle was retained for special buildings only. Charlemagne's palace chapel at Aachen was so designed—it remains to this day. An early church at St.

Augustine's abbey at Canterbury was of the same form. The Knights Templar retained it throughout their history in recognition of their special interest in Jerusalem. A number of their churches remain to this day, notably the Temple in London.

But the standard plan of the Byzantine church was the central tower surrounded by four short 'wings'.

While Rome remained the political capital of the Latin Church —the liturgical language of which continued, however, to be Greek in some regions as late as the sixth century—Byzantine power and culture ignored it to spread its far more powerful influence into Western Europe. As the Holy Roman emperors shifted their interest away from Italy into the Rhineland, the Western empire, while accepting the Pope of Rome as its spiritual head, was in every other respect a western counterpart to Byzantium and followed the fashion set by the great metropolis.

In architecture, however, the western regions could not compete. They could not raise a dome. So while subscribing to the principle of building churches round and up to a central feature, they had to translate the dome into a tall timber roof. Thus the central domed nucleus of the Eastern Byzantine church is represented in the contemporary West by a towered nucleus capped with a timber steeple. (Fig. 4.)

The building materials of the ancient world were stone and brick. The West had field-stone for rubble walling but as yet no freestone for mason-work. The craft of brickmaking had almost entirely vanished with the Legions.

But the forests of the West could produce quantities of good building timber. So it was towards this material that its architects turned for the construction of important buildings. Western Byzantine timber architecture has so far attracted the attention of few students, but in Scandinavia, Central Europe and Russia there are well-known examples which have managed to avoid the conflagrations of the passing centuries.

The churches of the middle of the first millennium in Western Europe were planned mainly in accordance with the structural requirements of raising a building which would show itself above the humbler roofs about it and to some extent hold its own amongst the trees, hills and other natural features in the immediate neighbourhood. Such buildings would of necessity be much cluttered up with structural elements connected with this desire for height.

Where materials permitted they had an eastern apse. Where not, they compromised with a square recess.

In their simplest form they were a single square tower. The first development would be the addition of the four 'wings' supporting the nucleus. Lastly would come the addition of aisles filling in the four corners.

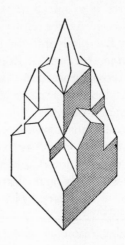

Fig. 4
Western Byzantine
Sketch based upon the ninth-century church of Germigny-des-Prés near Poitiers, but omitting its apsidal terminations. Plan similar to Eastern Byzantine but central feature raised to form a tower. A timber 'broach' is indicated to suggest original form of tower roof.

At the present time there has been no research into how these churches were used. The Orthodox congregations pressed upon the entrance to the apse indicated by the screen or iconostasis. Possibly the Western churches were utilized in much the same manner.

In the Greek church of today the priest stands before the iconostasis while the congregation gather round him, taking turns to hold his heavy missal and joining far more intimately in the service than a Western congregation seated sedately in its pews could do today.

It may be that in the early days of the Latin Church in this country the same kind of intimacy prevailed in the humble seat-less village churches.

4

The Anglo-Saxons

By the second half of the first millennium Rome, seat of the Popes and religious capital of the 'Frankish' Church, had become a ghost-town of imperial memories haunting mile after mile of ruins already overgrown. Culturally it had ceased to exist. Byzantium, now Constantinople, was the capital of a rich empire, founded upon Christianity, and covering with its churches the whole of the Ancient World and all south-eastern Europe. In the Rhineland the Western Emperors adopted Christianity to the extent that they called themselves 'Holy' and 'Roman'. But such culture as they had assimilated was derived from Constantinople, not from the ruins of Classical Rome.

The Eastern and Western Churches each employed its own Rite. The latter had several of these. During the fourth century when the 'Roman' emperors were still in Italy the 'Gallic' Rite is thought to have been carried thence to Africa and onwards to these islands, there to establish the 'Celtic' Church which continued to be the acceptable form of worship until the middle of the seventh century.

The Celtic Church, based for practical purposes in the security of the Irish zone, was probably an 'official' church, patronized by the nobility and centred upon monastic settlements. It was administered by bishops of native origin but maintaining loyal though tenuous contact with Rome. Scattered about Britain within the Celtic orbit were the monastic houses, later to become harassed and destroyed by various Continental invaders. Lack of resources would have precluded the erection of churches for ordinary folk.

The missionary expedition of St. Augustine was an isolated incident, and the pressure from the East forced the British Church to retreat into its two strongholds of Lindisfarne and Avalon. Nevertheless when Christianity finally became established in the Anglo-Saxon England of the seventh century, it was in accordance with the Latin Rite and under the aegis of the Celtic Church that it did so.

For practical purposes, however, Anglo-Saxon England was an appendage of Western Byzantinism, a culture which had progressed along different lines from that which had founded the Celtic Church some three centuries earlier. In Western Europe the form of the Latin Rite in use was the 'Gallican' and it was in the 'Roman-Frankish' form of this that the ritual employed in Anglo-Saxon England came to be established.

During the latter part of the eighth century, church organization had come to be sufficiently well established for the country to be divided into dioceses. But parish development probably followed at a very leisurely pace. The Heptarchy was an uneasy confederation and it was not until 829 that a central government came into being. It may have been well into the tenth century before the parochial organization of England became an established fact.

But by this time Anglo-Saxon England had become a country in its own right. On the perimeter of the sphere of Western Byzantinism, it was particularly free to develop along its own lines as befitted an island nation. Thus, the Danish attacks notwithstanding, the country's monastic houses developed and in doing so provided architectural leadership, until by the tenth century their churches had attained a high degree of architecture. And in their shadow the parish churches at last began to rise.

At the end of the tenth century Archbishop Dunstan was classifying churches as head-minsters, middling-minsters, and lesser-minsters. It sounds as though all these classes represented churches of monastic origin; the term may, however, have been in general use for all churches. A fourth class, churches with no burial ground, he calls field-churches.

The first buildings in which village worship took place may well have been domestic structures as in the early days of Christianity.

But when proper churches came to be built, they would most probably have been founded on the Byzantine model, in its Western form, this of course very far removed from its Constantinople origins.

In architecture there are two primary dimensions, length and breadth. If a roof be needed to protect occupants from climatic conditions, and the third dimension be thus incorporated, this need be no larger than required to enable those below it to stand upright. To increase the vertical element in a building is to approach the monumental.

With this element becoming the primary factor in the design of the Christian church it can be appreciated that, however extensive the plan of a church might be, it was essential that it should be seen to rise above all surrounding structures.

In Eastern Byzantium it was the dome; in the West it was the tower with the steepled roof. Thus we can be fairly certain that the first real parish churches to be built in this country—perhaps in the middle of the ninth century—would have either been very simple structures on the Celtic plan or designed as turriform naves with a small excrescence on the east to contain the altar. (Fig. 7*d*.) And humble though they might be, their religious status would at once have been advertised by virtue of their height.

The area of the turriform nave would have been governed structurally by the walling material available, in particular the lengths of timbers available for spanning the roof. With posted construction, a timber tower could easily have been surrounded by an aisle in imitation of a large Byzantine church. (Figs. 5 and 6. Plate 1.) The outer walling of such an aisle could be of timber framing or of stone. In some cases the aisle wall could have attained the height of a tower in its own right, with the posted structure remaining concealed within.

A stone-walled building, however, could not have been expanded by means of aisles, as the local builders of those days would have lacked the skill to carry the walling above openings by systems of arches carried on pillars. Thus the only way to extend the accommodation of early stone buildings was to build on adjuncts of stone or timber and make openings through the nave

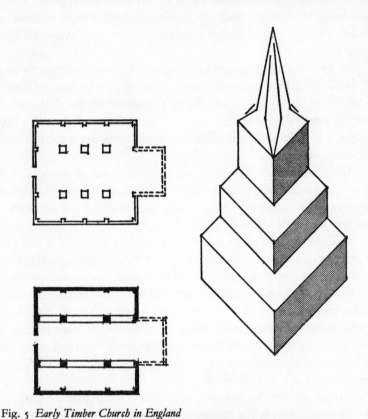

Fig. 5 *Early Timber Church in England*
Based upon a square tower carried upon four great posts but
occasionally six as at Blackmore in Essex, upon which building the
sketch is based. Surrounded, as in its prototype sketched in Fig. 4,
by an aisle. No chancels now remain, as most of the surviving
timber churches have been preserved only to serve as bell-towers at
the west end of later stone naves. It will be noted that there is an
intermediate stage forming a lean-to carried upon the aisle roof
which may serve to indicate the system upon which the elaborate
timber steeples of contemporary great churches were assembled.

walls to effect connection with each. As the early builders seem to
have been unable to turn arches of any but very small spans, such
openings would have been very narrow; they could, however,
have been quite high.

The side walls of the nave being only half the distance from the altar of that at the west end, the most useful situations for such adjuncts were in those side walls. Thus the lateral 'wing' came to be an established feature of the stone turriform church, joining with the chancel—and perhaps a western extension as well—to imitate the cruciform mass of the contemporary Byzantine church. (Fig. 7*a*. Plate 4.)

There are many indications that the east wall of the nave with the chancel entrance there situated was the focus of the nave plan. The nave of an early church at North Elmham in Norfolk actually runs north and south so that the apse is set in a long east wall. (Fig. 8.) In larger and later churches, such as that at Milborne Port in Dorset, the 'transept' arches of what has become a central tower are set tight up to the east wall so that this runs almost unbroken from the end of one transept to the other.

The majority of turriform naves were probably extended westward by means of a 'wing' on this side so as to produce the Byzantine effect of a cruciform pile of structures supporting a central feature. (Fig. 7. Plate 2.)

It will be seen that all these turriform churches set out on a centralized plan, whatever their system of construction, were purely Byzantine in concept and owed nothing to the long 'basilican' plan originating in the Rome of Constantine.

But the Byzantine plan never made any headway in the old Hellenistic regions of Syria and the North African littoral. Those areas of Christendom remained loyal to the Roman basilica, building wide churches with their naves flanked by Classical columns or Roman arches and covered with timber roofs, low-pitched in the Classical fashion.

North Africa in particular was a region which would have nothing to do with the centralized plan which it would clearly have regarded as 'un-basilical', possibly 'oriental', and certainly barbarous. And it was by way of these regions that the Celtic Church found its way to Britain.

When the Dark Ages came to an end with the spread of Christianity through Anglo-Saxon England during the eighth century, the Celtic Church had two bases from which to expand. Of these the Northumbrian, in the Anglian sphere, would have been by far the most accessible to Continental civilization. Hence it is along our eastern littoral, from Northumbria to the East Saxon border, that we find the earliest churches. These followed, however, the Celtic plan of nave and chancel, both raised in height to monumental degree. (Fig. 13.) By the end of the millennium the Celtic Church form had taken over all the eastern dioceses of Durham, York, Lincoln and Elmham in East Anglia.

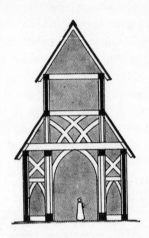

Fig. 6
Section through a 'four-poster' church
Showing the four posts carried on their sleeper foundations and the manner in which they are braced together by curved struts and braces. The surrounding aisle can also be seen.

In Saxon Wessex, however, progress from the Glastonbury base seems to have been much slower. There is no evidence that the Celtic Church plan made any headway at all. It seems probable that Wessex had to wait until the ninth century at the earliest before any kind of parish church plan became accepted, and that when it did, the model was not the Celtic, but the Byzantine plan, emanating from the Rhineland, which came to be adopted.

A building of extraordinary interest is the church which appears to have been built by St. Aldhelm at the beginning of the eighth century at Bradford-on-Avon in Wiltshire. It is built of stone and must have been one of the first stone buildings to be erected since Roman days. The walling is extremely primitive and owes nothing to mason-craft. Its plan comprises a rectangular nave set east and west with a small chancel projecting from its east wall. It displays the proper element of height but there is no sign of any tower.

Thus it is basically a Roman type of church of Celtic origin. But on each side of the nave a small 'wing' projects to introduce a cruciform element into the plan which must certainly represent Byzantine influence.

Perhaps the best-known example of the Western Byzantine type of church—though unfortunately rebuilt—remaining today is that at Germigny-des-Prés near Orleans dating from about the year 810. It has a towered nucleus flanked by the typical four short arms which are in this case extended by apses in their end walls. The exterior illustrates the Byzantine device of piling up a system of features towards a central climax, in this case the central tower, the focus of the interior being the space surrounded by the four great piers of the crossing below. (See Fig. 4.)

Scattered about Western Europe are small square or circular buildings called today 'baptisteries' which are in fact almost certainly early churches supplanted by later buildings and relegated to their present use. Ecclesiologists have become so accustomed to regarding an axial plan as essential to a church that they cannot conceive a church as having a centralized form unless it should be a building of the Templars, with whom it was inevitable.

Even as late as the twelfth century a great Byzantine church such as that of St. Mark at Venice was being followed by another, lavishly be-domed, at Périgueux. During the previous century, however, the octagonal central tower had become the crowning feature of the Western great church.

An early record of exceptional importance is that giving an account of the erection in 878 by Alfred the Great of a church at Athelney in Somerset—ancient Avalon—as a memorial of his victory over the Danes. The description of the building states clearly that it was founded upon four great piers and goes on to say that it was the first to be built upon this plan. This gives a date for the introduction of the standard Byzantine plan into this country.

This was however an important church. The parish church would not have been raised upon piers and arches. The central nucleus would have had to be content with narrow arched openings leading into the adjacent 'wings' and chancel.

When such early adjuncts to an ancient church were retained into the medieval period the arches leading into them had to be widened.

Western adjuncts are not always present to complete the cruciform arrangement. When these are eventually built they are often larger than the others and may have a wide arch joining them to

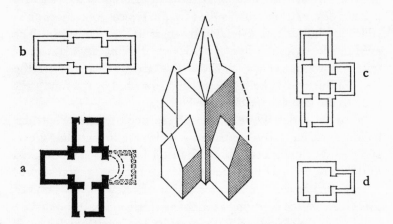

Fig. 7 *Stone tower-nave*
    The 'turriform' type of church, representing the Western
    Byzantine style in England. Various types of plan are shown.
    (a) is represented by Netheravon in Wiltshire, (b) by
    Barton-on-Humber in Lincolnshire, (c) by Hemyock in
    Devon, (d) by Barnack in Northamptonshire. No chancels
    remain today; they may have been square or apsidal. Various
    ways in which the tower might be roofed are shown in Fig. 23.
    See also Plates 23 and 24.

the central area. That at Netheravon in Wiltshire is an impressive example now lacking its 'west nave'.

Fig. 7 illustrates the various ways in which the tower-nave could be extended in order to increase accommodation. The completely cruciform plan, as at Breamore in Hampshire, is shown at 7*a*. The 'axial' arrangement is shown in 7*b*: the church at Barton-upon-Humber in Lincolnshire would appear to have been on this plan, which survives into the twelfth century. The nave with wings only may be seen illustrated in 7*c*. Hemyock church in Devonshire may have been of this class which is seen without its tower at North Elmham in Norfolk. (Fig. 8.) There must also have been churches consisting of a nave only, as in 7*d*; such still exist on the Continent. No chancels attached to turriform naves now remain. They may have been apses or square-ended, long or short as suggested in the illustration.

Discussion of this type of plan cannot, however, be complete without an examination of the twelfth-century 'axial' plans with central towers some of which may be found to have originated as turriform naves still retaining original chancels. (See Fig. 10, also Plate 8.)

It seems strange to find a Christian church properly orientated as regards its apse but with its architectural axis running north and south, defying not only Roman usage but the much nearer Celtic association. Such churches may however have been uncommon. There can be no doubt that the route of future development was indicated by the 'west nave'.

The 'Romanizing' of parish church plans and the abolition of the obstructive turriform nucleus eventually led to the western arch being omitted and the whole nave being covered with one roof passing from west to east.

This is in fact the stage reached by the parish church plan at the end of the first millennium. Rectangular nave and chancel are set out on the simple 'Celtic' plan. But the transverse element west of the chancel arch is not abandoned, the two 'wings' remaining to form what may be called the 'pseudo-cruciform' plan. (Fig. 9. Plates 5 and 6.)

In many an old church we may discover the remains of an arch which once led into an early wing. Sometimes such arches have been enlarged. Often some variation in the eastern arch of a medieval arcade may recall a vanished wing. Frequently the wing itself has been rebuilt as an expanded end to a later aisle. (Figs. 15, 16, 17.)

While there is no doubt that the plans of the eleventh century on the whole indicate that the designers of the English parish church were abandoning the Byzantine form and turning towards the long Roman plan, there are plenty of indications that the

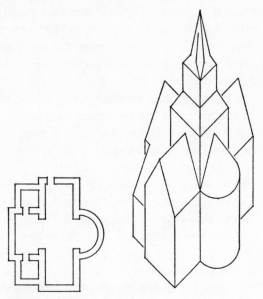

Fig. 8 *Elmham Church*
This remarkable building of which remains exist at
North Elmham in Norfolk, is believed to be of
eleventh-century date. Its nave runs north and south
(compare Fig. 7c) with the apse in the east wall
and a 'west nave' flanked by miniature aisles
to balance this and complete the cruciform plan.
As it seems probable that some kind of central feature
would have existed, the sketch indicates a wooden steeple.

transept was to be retained and that a cruciform or pseudo-cruciform plan had come to stay. During the twelfth and thirteenth centuries some of the smallest churches will be found to have sprouted some kind of broadening-out at one or both sides of the east end of the nave.

As late as the fifteenth century the aisle-less pseudo-cruciform plan with a western bell-tower is still normal practice for parish church builders, clearly indicating the desire to concentrate the accommodation upon the chancel arch. (Fig. 17*b*.)

Returning to the eleventh century, there can be no doubt as to the Byzantine affinities of Anglo-Saxon England. The prestige of

Constantinople was such that many of the survivors of Harold's army enlisted in the forces of the Emperor of the East, preferring to do this rather than undertake the much shorter journey to join their cousins in the Rhineland.

There may well have been plenty of eleventh-century church builders who were continuing to build turriform naves, in stone as well as timber. And some of these stone naves which were raised above adequate arches may today be central towers.

In the Western Byzantine world every building had to be covered with a high-pitched roof to shed snow and prevent its blowing into the shingled covering. And most square buildings, such as those of turriform character, had to be covered with something in the nature of a timber steeple. Thus the steeple must have become as common an architectural feature in the West as the dome with its low conical cap was in the East.

The central lantern tower, derived from the Byzantine dome with its ring of small windows, had become firmly established as an appropriate and indeed desirable crowning feature of the great monastic church set out on the long Roman plan.

In order to be able to appreciate the importance of stylistic pressures upon the church architects of the period it is necessary to recall the vast extent of the Empire of Holy Church. For today the great minsters which for so long loomed over the land are gone. St. Edmundsbury, once the largest church in the world, is represented by a shapeless mass of masonry, Evesham by a single small archway. Mitred Cirencester is as though it had never been. And in addition to such huge establishments there were scores of smaller ones, the priories, their sites all gone back to cattle-pastures. All these places had their churches, each with its central tower rising above its choir.

While it would seem most unlikely that either the finances or the architectural potential of the parish would have enabled it to emulate the ordinance, internal or external, of a neighbouring priory church, it would seem quite likely that an enterprising township might like to have gone as far as raising a parish church with a central tower rising above transepts, the whole in rubble stone instead of expensive masonry. Cruciform parish churches are found in close association, as in Wessex. And, stylistic pressures apart, there can be little doubt as to the aesthetic appeal of the central tower as a crowning feature to any church, large or small, once the Byzantines had introduced this feature as the external symbol of a religious edifice.

In some cases existing turriform naves provided the nucleus of

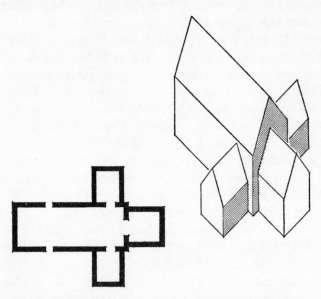

Fig. 9 *Pseudo-cruciform church*
 The type of plan developed from that shown in Fig. 7*a* by
 dispensing with the turriform nucleus and combining its
 area with that of the 'west nave'. The lateral wings remain;
 the arches leading to them are often very narrow. This type
 of church plan was common during the eleventh and twelfth
 centuries. See also Plates 5 and 6.

a central tower. And there are known examples of a pseudo-cruciform church being converted to cruciform by the erection of a central tower at the east end of the nave between the wings. (See Fig. 12*a*.) Careful examination and detailed measurement can sometimes produce surprising results.

The thirteenth century was the period for central tower developments in the parish church plan. It should be noted that the central towers of parish churches were rarely lantern towers such as had been raised over the crossings of great churches to light them. The parish church tower was simply a bell-tower, usually with only its belfry stage rising above the roof. The ringing-floor would be contrived immediately below the belfry, sometimes projecting downwards into the church. Thus the crossing arches of parish churches, especially in the case of early towers, are often quite low, similar to those in aisle arcades.

During the twelfth century one finds small churches which seem to combine both types of plan by setting a central tower between nave and chancel but dispensing with wings. This type of plan is called by antiquaries the 'axial'. (Fig. 10. Plate 8.)

It should be emphasized that during the eleventh century the plans of the parish church and the minster had been developing along entirely different lines. The great monastic churches had been expanding their monumental plans on a vast and extravagant scale, rivalling each other in their lengths until they had become the largest edifices in the world of their day. Though begun as compact centralized structures of Byzantine form, for a century past they had been reaching eastwards in emulation of the basilican type of church. They had built new eastern terminals to their choirs, incorporating a transept with a lantern tower over the crossing.

It was not until the end of the twelfth century that some of their flimsy lanterns, most of which fell through ignorance of structural design, were to soar anew above their crossings as lofty central towers, restoring to the great church of the Middle Ages the focal feature abandoned through over-concentration upon planning extent. Thus it may be to the development of the central towers of parish churches that we owe the beginnings of Lincoln or Canterbury.

While the cruciform village church is limited in its distribution to certain areas, it is the western bell-tower, rising through the centuries towards great architectural glories, which is the crowning feature of by far the majority of English parish churches.

The origin of the western bell-tower is interesting. When the great abbey churches of the tenth century were beginning to

expand eastwards from their original Byzantine turriform beginnings, these remained as western towers. Their retention was inevitable, as the new lanterns over the crossings were too light in
construction to be able to carry bells. As the fashion for spreading
frontispieces, twin-towered, took over the development of the
western façade of the great church, most of the great west towers
were swept away, that of Ely remaining as one of the latest and

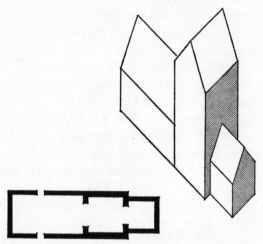

Fig. 10 *Church with 'axial' tower*
A twelfth-century type of plan probably developed
from that shown in Fig. 7*b*. Various alternative
types of tower-roofs are shown in Fig. 23. See also
Plate 8.

most magnificent. But the western bell-tower had by this time
come to be established as a standard feature in any parish church
which was able to afford such a luxury.

Extension eastwards from one of the tall early churches was a
practice also followed by the parish churches. Stone turriform
naves can be found now serving as bell-towers. Some of the early
timber churches of Essex remain at the ends of later naves. (Plates
1 and 2.) Sometimes the tower framework was incorporated within
the west end of a stone nave. Some examples of timber framing
carrying bells above the west end of a nave. hitherto believed to

be late medieval, will be found in fact to be earlier than the walling about them, this often of the thirteenth century. Late towers raised within the west ends of naves may represent a rebuilding of a timber predecessor.

Where naves attached to the eastern side of an early timber church have been subsequently extended with aisles it will be found that their arcades have half-bays at their western ends indicating where the aisles have been extended there to absorb the eastern aisle of the timber church.

One of the most interesting examples of the development of a medieval church from a turriform ancestor may be seen at South Brent in Devonshire where at the west end of the large nave is the original tower standing upon all four arches and retaining its southern wing.

The Byzantine church began by having no chancel other than the Classical apse containing the altar. The cathedral at Constantinople lacked any kind of chancel. But by the seventh century the development of the ordinary 'four-poster' plan resulted in the creation of an aisle, east of the crossing, the centre bay of which provided a short chancel preceding the apse. Thus the sanctuary became as long as it was broad.

To both the Eastern and Western churches, the apse remained the only acceptable termination. The Celtic Church, however, never seems to have subscribed to the Classical plan in this respect, possibly because the construction and roofing of an apse would have been beyond its capabilities. Thus it had become understood from the start in this country that the square-ended chancel could be accepted instead of the traditional apse. As most of the Anglo-Saxon parish churches were of timber construction, unsuited to circular planning, the normal timber-framed chancel was square on plan. The masonry apse, however, continues well into the twelfth century in the parish church, as may be seen in fine form at Steetley in Derbyshire. (See also Plate 6.) Notwithstanding Continental insistence upon the traditional form, however, England retained the square end to its chancels, supported by the choirs of the great churches.

An interesting variant of the normal semicircular apse is the polygonal one with three sides, a common Byzantine form, which from its incidence in this country might be called the 'Mercian apse'. That at Wing in Buckinghamshire is a well-known example from the eleventh century in which each face is ornamented with an arch in low relief clearly indicating its Byzantine origins. The polygonal apse actually continues in use right into the Gothic era and thus outlasts the older form. Externally it appears most attractive but it was possibly inconveniently planned.

The strongest support to the square-ended plan came from the twelfth-century Cistercians, who seem to have regarded it as a manifestation of austerity and a kind of visible protest against the contemporary Benedictine terminal feature of a great apse surrounded by an aisle. Not to be thought of as inferior designers, the Cistercians would on occasion employ the eastern aisle in connection with the square-ended presbytery, a pleasant example of the growing individuality of the English church-builder.

This was despite the powerful pressures emanating from the Continent which must have borne heavily upon the great establishments.

The parish churches, however, free from such influences, were able to develop even more independently.

5

Medieval Churches

The eleventh century saw the consolidation of the English Church under the aegis of a host of rich and powerful monasteries which absorbed virtually the whole of the Anglo-Saxon building potential and converted this to its use. Building mystique was derived from Western Byzantinism with its political headquarters in the Rhineland. Scandinavian influences had endowed the Anglo-Saxon style with many and varied forms of lavish ornament, all of which continued in use notwithstanding the change in supervision consequent on the change of ownership. It is probably quite wrong to attribute this ornament to the appearance of the Normans, who came to this country not to civilize but to seize. It is true that one finds certain forms of Classical ornament appearing after the Conquest but such would probably have drifted over from the Continent in the normal course of progress.

It is doubtful whether any Continental influences affected to any large extent the actual building craftsman. It was probably contributions by travelled amateurs which played the greater part in introducing new ideas into architecture. Among these would have been, in course of time, those who had taken part in the then spectacular expeditions to the Crusades, visiting on the way many parts of Europe, the Eastern Byzantine world, and the ancient lands of Hellenism. Such travellers, besides encountering undreamed-of architectural marvels, would have been able to appreciate for the first time the Roman church in regions nearer its heart-land, and compare its manifestations with corresponding

English versions. It was probably the Crusading expeditions which finally brought about the end of Byzantine England.

The twelfth—Crusading—century was the period which saw the transition from Anglo-Saxon to medieval England. The parish church nave settled down to its final rectangular form, elevated as high as possible but no longer turriform. The early-medieval nave was usually about twenty feet wide and perhaps sixty feet long for the normal parish church. Two doors were set facing each other at a point about two-fifths or three-eighths of the length of the nave from its western end.

While in these days many north doors have been blocked up to defeat the north wind, in medieval days they were important for processions, especially that held on Palm Sunday when the congregation left the nave by the north door. The procession passed round the east end of the church and halted at the churchyard cross which was usually somewhere on the south side of the church. The procession should properly speaking have re-entered the church by its west door. But English climatic conditions did not favour west doors. Not until the late-medieval bell-towers were being added to the west ends of naves did the west door come to be accepted. Processions used therefore to re-enter the church by the south door.

The south or sunny side of the church was usually its entrance front. In some situations, however, the position of the village—or perhaps the manor house—might determine otherwise.

The nomenclature of the adjuncts to a church have become muddled in the course of translation from the Latin. The pillared 'veranda' surrounding the little church of St. Augustine's day was called a *porticus*, which is of course simply 'portico'. If the outer side of a *porticus* became wholly or in part built up as a solid wall it still retained its designation, which was confusing as the built-up part no longer served as a porch. A structure projecting at right angles to the main building was called an *ala* or 'wing'. With the provision of openings leading out of the nave into a *porticus* this appendage began to share with the wing the same designation of *ala*. Hence the modern word 'aisle'.

Except in small churches where the parish may have failed to expand its population, the nave seldom omitted to develop its plan as the Middle Ages approached. Perhaps the most striking introduction into the form of the twelfth-century parish church was the arcade of semicircular—later pointed—arches carried upon a series of either piers or pillars beyond which the width of a nave could be increased by perhaps even half as much again. Single arches had long been used in parish churches, especially at the entrances to chancels, but a series of arches each supporting its neighbour was a feature only employed hitherto in the greater buildings. The embellishment of these arcades, in particular the capitals crowning their supports, was to provide carvers with pleasurable exercises for centuries to come. (Plate 10.)

Those who would assign to the English medieval church plan a 'basilican' origin see evidence of this in aisled construction. But this is a basic architectural device found even in the most primitive timber buildings and is an obvious method of widening a plan. The great West Mercian churches of Gloucester, Tewkesbury, and vanished Pershore, lined with gigantic circular piers, would seem to illustrate crude attempts to copy the basilican model, but such structures belong to a sphere far removed from that of the contemporary parish church.

Architectural students know that in order to achieve a stable elevation one's interest should be directed to a central opening rather than a solid support. The medieval church designers seem to have developed this rule of design to the extent that they avoided central openings in lateral treatments to which attention was not to be diverted. Certainly most church arcades, whatever their length, are usually set in an even number of bays. In parish churches the number is usually four, in very small naves, two. In the great churches the arrangement may be due to the use of the duplex bay in which piers and pillars alternate, but this would be unlikely to affect the parish church.

The first aisles were always very narrow, usually less than eight feet wide. The reason for this was that they had to be roofed by extending the nave roof downwards to cover them before its eaves came too near the ground to allow for windows in the aisle walls. (Fig. 14.)

The addition of side-aisles to the nave indicates the first stage towards extending the accommodation of the basic parish church plan. This by the end of the twelfth century had established itself in two main sizes. The larger parish churches were either pseudo-cruciform with lateral wings near the east end of the nave (Fig. 9), or, less frequently, fully cruciform with a central tower. (Fig. 11.) Such churches could easily be enlarged by the addition of aisles to the nave.

The small parish church was usually on the 'Celtic' plan of small nave and chancel (Plate 7)—the former probably too short for widening, so that the building would either survive the centuries unaltered, as at Barfreston in Kent, or be pulled down entirely and rebuilt. The churches with 'axial' towers (Fig. 10)—relics probably of early turriform types—could have their naves widened by aisles or even extended lengthwise away from the tower. For the western bell-tower, which was to be so common a feature in the years to come, was then a rarity and any existing towers would have been too valuable to lose.

The belfries of that period, where no central tower existed, would probably have been timber turrets, either carried on heavy tie-beams spanning the nave or perhaps a wing, or supported by timber posts from within the building in the fashion of an early timber church.

The chancels of churches prior to the end of the twelfth century were either apses or square-ended adjuncts of little projection. But this was about to be changed.

The eastern arms of the great minsters had not originally been given any great projection, for the monastic choir had been sited at the eastern end of the long nave and had the lofty crossing immediately to the east of this so that a short presbytery was all that was needed to give internal dignity to the monks' part of the building. But the fashion was appearing for longer eastern arms to augment the dignity of this part of the building and give a better balance externally to the greatly-extended naves.

It may have been partly due to the increased length of the choir of the great church that the thirteenth century saw the chancels of parish churches similarly extended.

But the functions of the two structures were in fact entirely different. The monastic choir had become a spacious apartment, enclosed by screens to form a church on its own. At the west end were the fixed stalls of the community; at the opposite end, separated from them by a wide area of pavement, was the high altar. But the long parish chancels were simply long empty halls with the altar at the east end and the chancel arch at the west. The only occupant of such an apartment would presumably have been the priest, celebrating the ritual of the Mass at the altar, far away from his congregation except when they actually drew near to communicate.

There seems to be no explanation for the sudden elongation of the medieval chancel, nor any description as to just how it was utilized with regard to the congregation. But from the beginning of the thirteenth century onwards the long chancel was a permanent part of every English parish church and it remained so for more than three centuries. Common to all sizes of churches, they were well-designed structures lit at first by lancet windows and later by fine traceried ones. Each had its own 'priest's door' in its south wall.

It will be found that many of these extravagant chancels were added originally to parish churches having some connection with a rich monastic house. Such chancels may have appeared during the course of an architectural competition between a number of such establishments having responsibilities for churches in neighbouring parishes.

But a desire for architectural dignity, especially in comparison with the eastern arm of the great church, could account for only one aspect of the innovation. Was there a change in parish church ritual requiring a longer chancel? Conversely, how did the new situation affect the conduct of the services? There seems to be no literature throwing light on the matter, the service books of the Middle Ages being concerned with the scene in the minster choir.

It may be that the chancel extension was intended to enhance the dignity of the altar by removing it farther away from the laity. The revised prayer book of 1552 envisages the communicants separating themselves from the main body of the congregation by approaching the altar, men on one side, women on the other. Is this perhaps a recognition of a practice to be continued from medieval days, the entry into the chancel only of those actually communicating? The Reformed prayer book of course refers to the altar as being in the 'body' of the church, *or* in the chancel.

Bearing in mind that the chancels of the Middle Ages, like the naves to which they were attached, were entirely empty of furniture, and not packed with seating as today, it is possible to imagine the parish chancel capable of comparison with the contemporary monastic choir without, of course, the latter's seating arrangements. Thus one might see the parish chancel as a spacious apartment designed to welcome the communicants when their time came to approach the altar. A hint of this is given when one discovers that the eastern faces of the chancel screens are often as elaborately decorated as those facing the nave.

In default of explanations connected with ritual one must take account of the fact that intra-mural sepulture must have been a greatly appreciated status symbol during the Middle Ages when the eastern arms of the great minsters were being lengthened partly so as to provide more space for the interment of important personages. Thus it is conceivable that the chancels of parish churches were extended to provide places of sepulture higher up the social scale than could be achieved by those whose relics were assigned to the nave.

While the long chancel remained as such throughout the Middle Ages, by the end of the fourteenth century its enclosed character was disappearing as it first became aisled and found itself absorbed into the wide spaces of the 'hall' church (Fig. 19), with the chancel arch finally abolished and only lines of screenwork remaining, as in the choirs of the great churches, to indicate its sanctity.

A feature of the English parish church plan hitherto ignored by historians is the concern of its builders to provide as great a width as possible immediately at the entrance to the chancel, by means of lateral transepts, suggesting the possibility that more of the parish service was being conducted at the entrance to the chancel than, as today, at the altar itself.

When trying to discover the development of the church plan

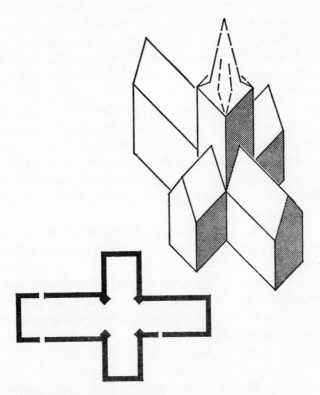

Fig. 11 *Early medieval cruciform plan*
   A thirteenth-century plan having affinities with the early
   turriform church but architecturally probably an attempt to
   emulate the form of the smaller monastic church. The transepts
   sometimes have small eastern transepts.

there are two methods to employ. The best clue is to note in what
style an entirely new church was being planned and in what fashion
it differs from its predecessors. The other method of approach is
to note in what fashion existing churches were being altered at the
time and thus discover what new features were considered desirable to bring old churches up to date.

   One type of church aimed at by the designers of the thirteenth
century is quite clearly discoverable. This is the cruciform plan

with a long chancel and a bell-tower above the crossing between a pair of proper transepts. Such churches sometimes have wide naves roofed in one span without aisles. The whole arrangement seems to aim at producing an architectural effect similar to that of the church of a minor monastic house. (Plate 11, Fig. 11.)

When considering this possibility it must be remembered that there were at the time scores of such buildings now virtually entirely disappeared, to serve as models for enterprising builders of parish churches. It is to be noted that many of these churches have chapels contrived in the east walls of their transepts, as at Amesbury in Wiltshire and Uffington in Berkshire (Plate 11), and that such chapels form a usual feature of the monastic transept, which needed a good supply of side altars whereas the parish church did not.

A not uncommon practice during the thirteenth century was to utilize existing wings as a basis for conversion to a cruciform plan. Sometimes a central tower was built up inside the east end of the nave—a reversal of the process by which the pseudo-cruciform plan had been developed. But a more common arrangement, where the nave was aisle-less and the wing arches remained, was to retain these for the lateral arches and throw transverse arches across the building to complete the crossing. (See Fig. 12*a*.)

To increase the accommodation of an existing small church three methods could be employed. A simple method was to throw out one or two wings at the east end of an aisle-less nave. Alternatively arcades could be cut through the whole of a side wall, or both of these, and an aisle or aisles built.

But the most effective way was to remove the existing chancel and build on a complete new east end with a crossing supporting a central tower, commodious transepts, and one of the new long chancels. (Fig. 12*b*. Plate 12.)

Naves were sometimes lengthened westward, but such extensions were uncommon, possibly because development of the accommodation away from the altar would not have been popular, and also because there might be a belfry of some sort existing at this point. Widening was clearly the device aimed at during enlargement.

A widening of early narrow aisles presented a problem in that this would probably require a reconstruction of the whole roof of the nave. If a roofing material such as lead, which only requires a flat pitch, could be used on the aisle roofs a major re-roofing might have been avoided, but normally the walls of the nave would

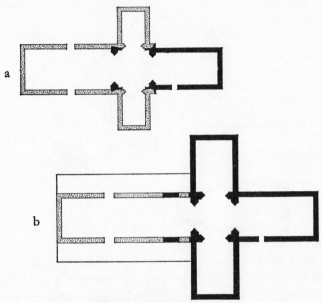

Fig. 12 *Thirteenth-century improvements*
    Showing attempts to convert the pseudo-cruciform plan
    to true cruciform. (a) shows a tower constructed between
    the original 'wings' by throwing two transverse arches
    across the nave on either side of these. (b) shows the
    wings abandoned and a complete new east end added
    with a central tower set between large transepts. The
    long thirteenth-century chancel is shown.

have had to be raised to take up the extra height of the widened aisle roof. As a widening of the aisles meant thrusting the natural lighting of the nave farther away from it, the 'lantern' system of lighting was introduced by the formation of a row of windows above the lateral roofs, a device known as the 'clearstory' which by the middle of the Gothic period was to become a standard feature of all the aisled structures. (Fig. 14, Plate 17.)

The 'Celtic' plan of nave with small chancel attached to it went out of fashion during the thirteenth century. Thenceforth the really small parish church is set out in the same fashion as the chapel of a palace or castle. This is a simple rectangle incorporating

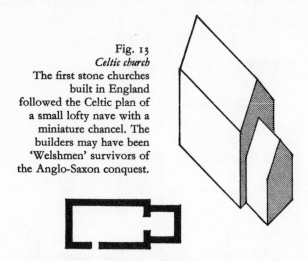

Fig. 13
Celtic church
The first stone churches built in England followed the Celtic plan of a small lofty nave with a miniature chancel. The builders may have been 'Welshmen' survivors of the Anglo-Saxon conquest.

nave and chancel under one roof. The internal division, if one existed originally, would have been achieved by some kind of timber partition. None of these, however, have survived, having been replaced at some later period by an ordinary rood-screen. Comparatively few of these small and humble parish churches would have survived into the era of the High Gothic.

At this time very many of the old parish churches of the country had become too small for their congregations, notwithstanding constant accretions which had muddled their original plans to a degree unworthy of a monumental building. Thus by the end of the fourteenth century the country was swept by a rebuilding programme which removed great numbers of old parish churches and replaced them by others of what had become a standard pattern.

The large parish church in the wool-rich market town would continue to vie with its monastic rival by adopting a complete cruciform plan with a fine central bell-tower. Village churches already planned cruciform would have been loth to abandon their towers but it is on record that some preferred to clear them away as obstructions and build anew at the west end, in what had become the accepted position for the bell-tower.

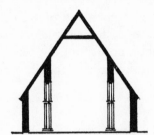 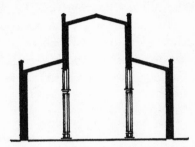

Fig. 14. *Development of aisles*
> Early aisles were narrow so that the nave roof could be extended to cover them. With the reduction of roof-pitch following the introduction of lead, the aisles became wider, and were covered with lean-to roofs abutting against a nave raised to accommodate a tier of clearstory windows on either side.

Rebuilt from the ground up, the standard parish church plan of the late-medieval period can be found in possibly half the parish churches in England. In the West it is ubiquitous. The nave is clearstoried and has wide aisles. Four bays is the common arrangement but five sometimes occur, possibly a relic of some eastern arrangement of transeptal nature existing in the old church and retained for convenience in the rebuilding, which would presumably have been carried out piecemeal so that the church could remain in use throughout. The eastern end of each aisle is almost invariably widened out in pseudo-transeptal form. In the second bay from the west a two-storied porch projects to indicate the southern entrance. The chancel is probably three bays long and lit by large windows; the arch leading into it is now as wide as possible. At the west end of the nave a tall arch leads into the lower part of the bell-tower and the 'processional' doorway in its west wall. Such was the fully-developed parish church plan which served until the end of the medieval period. (Fig. 15.)

These were of course the fully developed churches. The smaller parish church was in effect a perpetuation of the 'Celtic' plan with a broad aisle-less nave and a chancel of medium length, compromising between the long thirteenth-century type and the short twelfth-century form. But all these churches would have been provided with a western bell-tower costing as much as the rest of the building put together. (Fig. 17a.)

In the absence of documentation, the chronology of parish church architecture is of necessity vague. While the major churches can be assigned to the thirteenth, fourteenth and fifteenth centuries, Gothic parish churches really fall into two categories, the first of

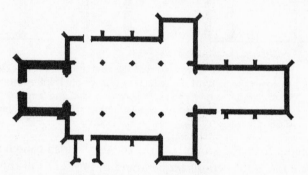

Fig. 15 *Plan of typical fifteenth-century parish church*
Note the nave, four bays and the vestigial
'wings' at the eastern ends of the wide aisles.
The long chancel is retained from early medieval
times. The western bell-tower has become
obligatory.

which, the early medieval, finds its designers aiming at emulating the form of the smaller monastic church.

The problem of the structural maintenance of the medieval parish church is one which must not be overlooked. The twelfth and early thirteenth centuries covered the initial period of development. Thereafter, the parochial establishment having been completed and accommodated in good buildings, a century seemed to have elapsed during which these were allowed to deteriorate without provision for maintenance while the greater churches continued to absorb most of the country's building potential. Contemporary reports on parish churches during the first half of

1. The old wooden church at Stock in Essex

2. A little wooden church at West Hanningfield in Essex

3. The stone tower-nave of Barton-on-Humber church in Lincolnshire

4. The turriform church at Breamore in Hampshire

5. The east end of the nave of Worth church in Sussex

6. The south wing and apsidal chancel of Worth church in Sussex

7. A small church of primitive type at Heath in Shropshire

8. A church with an 'axial' tower at Iffley in Oxfordshire

9. The twelfth-century nave of Whaplode church in Lincolnshire

10. A richly-ornamented arcade of the twelfth century
at Stapleford in Wiltshire

11. The thirteenth-century cruciform church at Uffington in Berkshire

12. A thirteenth-century crossing at Amesbury in Wiltshire

13. A richly moulded arcade of the early-mediaeval period
at Stoke Golding in Leicestershire

14. A fully-developed High Gothic church at Lowick in Northamptonshire

15. The High Gothic chancel at Walpole St. Peter in Norfolk

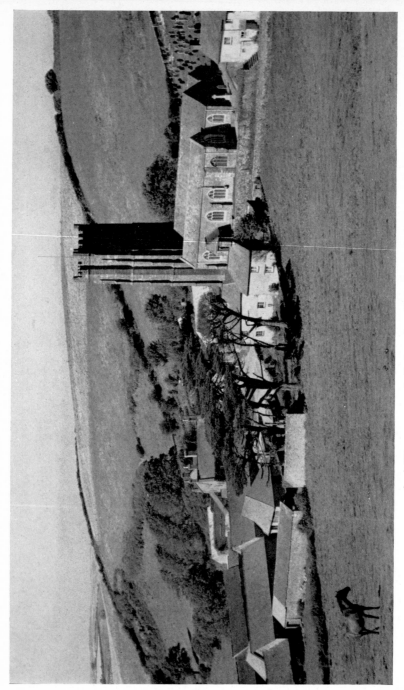

16. A West-country hall-church at Chivelstone in Devon

the fourteenth century often indicate an almost incredible amount of dilapidation, such as major churches lacking a chancel roof. It was not until the improvement in the country's finances with the coming of the wool boom that the parish churches were taken in hand, by which time very many may well have been past economic repair. This may have been the main reason for the nation-wide rebuilding programme which inaugurated the era of the High Gothic with its host of magnificent parish churches entirely replacing ancient predecessors.

The era of the High Gothic covers the fourteenth and fifteenth centuries, but only in respect of the greater churches. What was happening to parish churches during the first half of the fourteenth century is not clear, but it may be assumed that the Black Death put an end to whatever it was until the last quarter of the century. By this time the parish church in its final form was being developed, reaching its full flood of rebuilding during the next century. It is thus simpler to refer to this class of church as being of fifteenth-century type, even though it may in fact belong to the latter part of the previous century. As the architectural period continues up to the collapse of the Medieval Church towards the middle of the sixteenth century some of the buildings referred to as being of fifteenth-century type may well be in fact sixteenth-century foundations.

In each period of its history the church plan becomes stabilized to an agreed standard in regard to its essentials. It then goes on to expand in various directions to provide for contingencies associated with changes in fashion.

Possibly one reason for the vast size of the English monastic churches was their popularity as places for the burial of important personages. While their choirs were usually reserved for prelates, naves, aisles and transepts became filled with the country's squires and nobility. The tombs themselves, some of which were raised biers with arcaded sides and surmounted by a portrait effigy, were becoming notable architectural embellishments in the great buildings.

With the burial place was often associated a chapel in which prayers might be said in perpetuity for the soul of the deceased.

The chantry chapel too became a lovely architectural feature within the great church.

In default of interment within some minster, a rural nobleman might like to prepare a tomb for himself in the parish church he and his family attended. The ends of transepts are often provided with low arched recesses for such interments. Some of the altars now represented by their piscinae may have been employed for the use of the chantry priest.

But it would seem unlikely that a medieval squire would have been permitted to appropriate part of the accommodation of the church for use as a place of sepulture to be filled with family tombs. It would be necessary for him to provide an addition to the building for this purpose. An obvious site for this would be found beside the chancel, probably on its north side so as not to interfere with access to it. The walls of a chancel being comparatively low, the provision of an aisle to it would present a roofing problem. Either the roof of the aisle would have to be pitched very flat, or it would have to be provided with its own independent roof with a gutter between this and the chancel roof, both of which schemes would involve the use of lead.

The dignity of the east end of a parish church would have been greatly enhanced by the addition of aisles to its chancel. Within, the building would benefit from the more spacious eastern terminal probably furnished with fine tombs or even chantry chapels. But externally the aisle would have introduced a structural revolution by flanking one gable with another, an innovation only possible by the construction of a wide lead gutter to carry away melting snow. This discovery was to have wide-reaching results.

The use of lead having enabled roof-pitches to be reduced considerably, some of the old narrow-aisled naves had their arcades removed and a wide-span roof thrown across from one aisle wall to the other, thus increasing the accommodation and removing a number of obstructions with the one operation.

The fourteenth century was the period of nave-widening. Hitherto the nave had been as it were an ante-room to the chancel, but now it began to assume a greater importance resulting from an innovation in the form of the church service.

The change was due to the introduction of the Mendicant Orders into this country. These travelling friars specialized in the preaching of sermons. Their own churches were provided with exceptionally wide naves for the accommodation of large con-

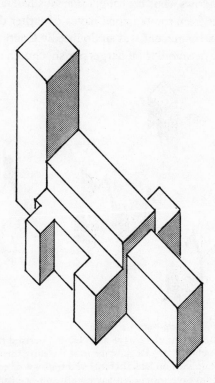

Fig. 16 *Sketch of typical fifteenth-century parish church*
See also Plate 14.

gregations gathered to listen. Unlike the older Orders, the friars contented themselves with eastern arms to their churches which were comparatively humble and in general form resembled large editions of the chancel of the parish church, the stalls being at the west end by the entrance arch. The excessive length of the old monastic nave was a disadvantage when listening to a sermon, and the friars built their naves short and as wide as possible. The old

clerestoried nave with its comparatively narrow aisles being un-
suitable, the wide 'auditoria' of the friars were constructed on the
'three-gable' principle with the side aisles as wide as the centre
nave itself and the whole magnificent structure lined with lofty
traceried windows, thus creating a spacious hall, airy and well-lit,
very different from the cramped naves of earlier days.

The new arrangement was undoubtedly Continental in origin.
At this time a number of large parish churches, especially in

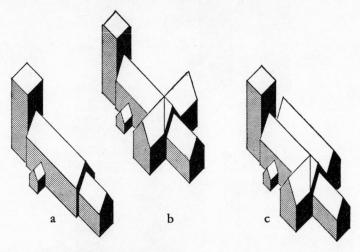

Fig. 17 *Types of fifteenth-century churches*
　　　　(a) Simple church of nave and chancel, derived from early
　　　　Celtic church. (b) Development of the early pseudo-cruciform
　　　　plan but with no lateral arches and transept of equal height to
　　　　nave. (c) Composite plan having aisle on one flank of nave and
　　　　a wing or transept on the other. Roofs are shown high-pitched
　　　　for covering with tiles. The western bell-tower is obligatory.

Germany and the Low Countries, were being designed on an
entirely different system from that obtaining in this country. The
buildings were set out as complete rectangles with a wide apse
embracing the whole width of the building with its aisles. The
arcades were very tall and the whole church was ceiled at the same
level, under a tall western roof. These churches are called by
Continental antiquaries 'hall churches' and this designation has
come to be applied to the triple-naved churches met everywhere

in the south-west of England and representing the final form of
the English Gothic parish church.

The planning arrangement of the hall church had been made
possible by the new device of roofing each portion of the plan with
its own pitched roof. (Fig. 18.) A development of this principle
was the reintroduction of the 'pseudo-cruciform' plan on an enlarged scale, with large transepts of the same width as the nave,
all three roofs being of the same height and thus easily joined
together without the intervention of a central tower. (Fig. 17*b*.)
The hall churches had of course no clearstory.

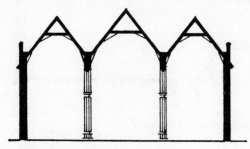

Fig. 18 *Section through 'hall' church*
    Nave and aisles of almost equal width and
    each covered with its own independent roof.
    The nave has no clearstory. See Plate 16.

The principle of building with independent roofs made it possible to plan churches unhampered by earlier formalities which had
regulated their lay-outs. A medium-sized church could now have
a single aisle to its nave, with perhaps a solitary 'wing' balancing
it on the other side. (Fig. 17*c*.) It is noticeable how the popularity
of the projecting 'wing' as an aesthetic feature of the elevation
continues (Plate 14.); thus such compromise plans seem to provide
for the aisle to be on the north and the wing on the south or
entrance front.

Planning with independent roofs, in 'hall church' style and
without clearstories, is most common with the late Gothic churches
of the south-west, with their pitched roofs, and less common with
the lead-roofed buildings, such as those of East Anglia. (Fig. 20.
Plate 16.)

Internally the English hall churches appear as plain rectangles with the chancel indicated by a screened enclosure, its western or 'rood' screen usually being carried for the whole width of the church so as to enable its loft to be reached by a stair formed in the aisle wall. There is no structural division between nave and chancel. (Fig. 19.)

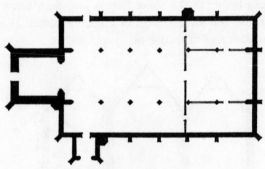

Fig. 19 *Plan of 'hall' church*
The building has become one single
rectangle, its chancel having been formed
by enclosing it within screens. The west tower
is sometimes absorbed within the rectangle
by carrying the aisles beside it.

This planning by means of screens, long the normal practice in the great churches where pillars and arches were structural features supporting the roofs and were not necessarily intended to be regarded as related to the accommodation, enabled the screen-makers of the monastic choirs to transfer their attention to the chancel of the parish church. The results were spectacular, with elaborate tracery maintaining vision through the screen and above it miniature vaulting systems carrying the overhead gallery or loft. (Plate 22.)

Most of the larger urban monasteries provided, usually to the north-west of the monastic church away from the cloister, a parish church for the use of the townspeople. The naves of the great churches themselves were open to the public except in the case of the Cistercian houses where they were used by the lay-brethren.

At the Dissolution, most of the great churches were swept away. Rarely, as at Christchurch in Hampshire, a monastic church was suffered to remain intact as a parish church. Nearly always, the choir at least was destroyed, that of Pershore Abbey, now a parish

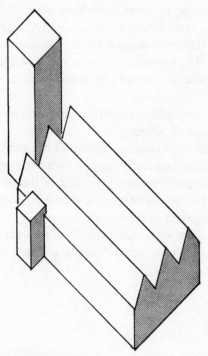

Fig. 20 *Sketch of 'hall' church*
This type of church is common
throughout the West Country.
See Plate 16.

church, being a notable exception. Sometimes a monastic nave, as at Dunstable in Bedfordshire or the towering fragment at Malmesbury in Wiltshire, was retained as a parish church. Or just an aisle, as at Little Dunmow in Essex, might remain in parochial use as a memorial of a great church of other days.

There were quite a number of small monastic houses which actually shared their churches with parishioners. The planning arrangement is uncertain and requires investigation. The monastic portions of such churches have of course for the most part been removed, leaving here and there a tantalizing arch or a wall-fragment to encourage speculation. The monastic choir would presumably have been at the east end, possibly beside the parish chancel. But a large transept may have been used for the purpose. Possibly only one of the two chancels may have been orientated. In any case the monastic portion of the church must have been accessible to the cloister or whatever comprised the living quarters of the community. So one may look for this on the customary south side of the church.

The 'professional' congregations of the monastic choirs, forced to long periods of worship by night as well as by day, had to be provided with fixed seating. The naves of parish churches had no seating but were bare halls about which the rustic congregations ebbed and flowed. Not until the end of the fourteenth century, when the introduction of the lengthy sermon changed the situation, did the parish churches turn towards the provision of fixed seating for their congregations, thus completely changing the appearance of parish church naves towards their present-day arrangement.

6

The Reformation

In 1539, when the work of obliterating the magnificent series of monastic churches was begun, the parish priests must have been concerned as to what the fate of their own churches was to be. Would their status be enhanced by the removal of such massive competition, or would the next step in the religious upheaval be the destruction of parish churches also? Contemporary writers have calculated that there were at the time some 46,000 parish churches in the countries forming the English realm. The Reformation was certain to affect them very considerably but in what fashion no one could be certain.

But the breach with Rome turned out to be a political rather than a religious revolution. The Dissolution of the Monasteries, establishments regarded both as enclaves of fifth-columnists and as parasitical to the economy of the country, had no counterpart in the parishes. The King made it clear that he had no wish to change religious practices, and demanded only that he be regarded thenceforth as the head of the English Church in place of the Italian Pope. The services in the parish churches continued as before in the care of their parish priests, still supervised, under the King, by the same diocesan bishops now increased in numbers to fill the huge gaps in the ecclesiastical hierarchy resulting from the monastic Dissolution.

In illustration of the continuance of the old order one may cite the existence of a beautiful screen erected at the entrance to the chancel of Washfield church in Devon. Although as late as 1624, nearly a century after the Reformation, this lovely feature is entirely in the medieval tradition except for the fact that instead of the 'Popish' Rood one finds the royal coat of arms.

The inevitable loss of prestige suffered by the whole of the English priesthood during the sixteenth century, however, was bound to exert a creeping effect upon the sanctity of the long medieval chancels which had for so long been its special preserves. So it comes about that the eastern end of the church, once its most important element, began to suffer the loss of the whole of its ancient dignity.

Almost simultaneously with the religious revolution carried out by Henry VIII, the reactionary anti-Reformation movement introduced by the Jesuits began to spread through the Continent from Italy outwards. This clever Order was too wise to ignore altogether the grievances underlying the now powerful forces opposing some of the more objectionable aspects of the medieval Church.

It seems probable that one of these objections may have been the existence of the long chancel which had carried the altar, and presumably the priest, much too far away from the congregation trying to take part in the service. Thus it is to the Jesuits we owe the abandoning of the long chancel altogether and the refashioning of the east ends of churches on the 'Baroque' plan with a short sanctuary and flanking transepts, a reversion, in fact, to the original Byzantine concept. This plan has been followed ever since in Roman Catholic churches.

Nothing of the sort was done, however, in this country. The Acts of Uniformity of 1549–52, though clearly envisaging the eventual abandoning of the chancel altogether, describe the altar as being set 'in the body of the church' *or* in the chancel, thus permitting retention of the latter if so desired. It is however clear that the trend was to omit the chancel from liturgical arrangements and reduce the church to the nave only. And as the spacious preaching nave had for more than a century become the primary concern of the church architects, the loss of the long chancel seems to have been readily accepted by most of them. Any new churches of the Elizabethan/Jacobean period are planned as simple rectangles with the altar against the east wall.

But with the rapidly expanding new class of lay magnates the parish churches were coming under fresh influences and developing a new significance as establishments the control of which had been removed from Holy Church and handed over to the King and his ruling class.

The monastic churches had sunk into piles of ruin burying in their fall the memorials of the emblazoned past. Thus the parish churches had become the only surviving places of sepulture for the new lords of the countryside.

Ample precedence already existed for using the eastern ends of parish churches for this purpose. And from the chancel aisles it was but a short step to encroachment upon the chancel itself, no longer protected from desecration by the power of Holy Church. The Elizabethan Age was one of great affluence displaying itself in wondrous raiment. The ponderous tombs of the period which began to clutter up the old chancels made full use of the space provided for sculptural extravagances.

The Dissolution of the huge monastic houses and the consequent cessation of all their activities released upon the country the whole of the monastic maintenance organization—which meant in fact a very large part of the building potential of the country—and diverted this to the provision of mansions and farmhouses for the new landowners. This transformation of the purpose of English architecture from the ecclesiastical to the domestic resulted in an architectural revolution as well as a religious one. This fact combined with the enormous stylistic revolution spreading through the Continent was to complicate the lives of the English architects for several generations.

The new architectural style entering the country from Europe bore no resemblance to the native Gothic which had for so long dominated English architecture. Gables, buttresses, pinnacles, traceried windows, battlements, carved grotesques—all these fripperies were being banished into history. The pointed arch gave place to the semicircular one and the detail attempted was based on the austere forms of the Italian Renaissance or as near to it as the isolated English architects could get. There was of necessity a 'Gothic overlap' which lasted into the middle of the seventeenth century and the churches of this period are interesting for their curious mixture of detail. But the plain rectangular buildings now being planned were best suited to the new architecture and by the latter part of the century the Gothic had disappeared altogether. The western bell-tower, however, a feature of the medieval plan, continued in use but with an elevation presented in Renaissance style.

With the approach of the eighteenth century the accommodation of the parish churches, the new ones painfully small by medieval standards, the medieval ones themselves drastically curtailed through the re-siting of the sanctuary at the east end of the nave, found their pew-space inadequate for their congregations. In order to increase the accommodation without building additions to the structure, the churches were provided with upper galleries in the manner of the contemporary theatre. These galleried churches are the 'auditoria' recommended by Wren for the rebuilding of the London parish churches after the Fire.

The plan of the post-Reformation sanctuary in the Anglican Church was very simple. The altar was set hard up against the east wall of the building with a small rectangular railed space before it from which the clergyman conducted the communion ceremony. Close by this was the pulpit, now an important part of the church furniture; pressing close upon it was the pewing. Galleries flanked the building, and with the introduction of the pipe-organ into the parish church during the eighteenth century to accompany the hymn-singing, these were accommodated in western galleries, often in the base of the tower. The organs were flanked by tiered seating for their choirs. In many small village churches the place of the organ was taken by a village orchestra of fiddle, flute and serpent.

Having suffered the closure or complete loss of their chancels, the naves of the medieval churches had now to undergo severe transformations to bring them into line with contemporary planning. Worst of the accretions were the galleries, their supporting beams cutting into the ancient stonework of pillars and being driven across the delicate tracery of windows.

When one deplores the drastic 'restorations' of the mid-nineteenth century one must pause to consider what the old churches must have looked like immediately after the galleries had been taken down and the scars and mutilations revealed in all their shame. The devoted church restorer of today, archaeologically-minded, would have done his utmost to preserve every vestige of antiquity. But in those days the equally conscientious architect would have been driven by horror at the mutilations to clear everything away and rebuild it tidily in his best Gothic.

As the eighteenth century turned into the nineteenth the rise of Nonconformity began to fill the villages with small and cheap editions of the Protestant auditoria. The over-all similarity between the churches of the two cults was sooner or later bound to create a demand for revision of the Anglican design in order to create a decent distinction. Anti-industrialism allied with neo-medievalism produced a remarkably speedy reaction towards the restoration of the church plan of the Middle Ages with the long chancel restored to favour, to serve as an immediate distinction that the building was a church and not a chapel.

The new or restored chancels, however, in no way resembled their medieval predecessors. There was no return to the old mystique, to the dim cavern of the past. The new chancels were cheerful apartments lined with seating, simulating the old monastic choirs, for the accommodation of the singing men and boys lately stimulating the efforts of the congregation from the elevation of a gallery at the west end of the nave.

Regrettable in the extreme as spoiling the lines and fenestration of many a fine old chancel was the custom of affixing to it 'vestries' in which the Protestant clergyman and his choir could don their laundered surplices. Worse still was the addition of a large and lofty 'organ chamber' to accommodate—and stifle—the instrument removed from the gallery.

It was a sad period for the old churches. Many which had come to be regarded as hopelessly de-medievalized were ruthlessly swept away and rebuilt, as were many humble village churches the architecture of which was regarded as substandard. And so many were restored not simply by removing unsightly accretions but by the removal of all post-Reformation features, many of them probably charmingly executed, and replacing them with bogus medieval substitutes designed by architects having but a superficial acquaintance with the style they were trying to imitate.

As with all revivals, design was based upon illustrated textbooks. For the English Gothic there were the publications of Parker and his imitators. Stylization was divided rigidly into the three accepted periods—Early English, Decorated and Perpendicular. Stylistic architecture had come to be regarded as so individualistic that each was regarded as an entirely separate style with an ordinance, and even sculptured detail, assigned to it for acceptance without question by the architect. Clients fancying a particular period would expect the architects to give them what they wanted. All this resulted in an utterly non-medieval rigidity of expression which banished sensitivity and has resulted in the bad reputation suffered by Victorian Gothic at the present time.

With the present century, during the first quarter of which there were a number of church architects who had outgrown the brashness of the Victorian period and were designing attractive churches which owed nothing to 'style' but were sympathetically English medieval in feeling, church architecture seemed to be likely to enjoy a revival. But many factors, the invention of the motor car amongst others, were drawing the old congregations away from their parish churches towards a lighter-hearted Sunday away from home.

With congregations declining in numbers and the clergy finding it difficult to fill their chancels with choristers, some church architects, notably the late Randoll Blacking, sought to reintroduce the Baroque plan by reserving the chancel as a morning chapel and bringing the parish altar west of the rood screen. In churches thus replanned one can once more appreciate the aesthetic, as well as the practical, value of the broad effect created by a long transverse wall forming an extended back-cloth to the altar instead of tucking it away at the end of a long chancel. And over the screen or reredos a distant view of the old east window still preserves something of an atmosphere of mystery.

From the point of view of the ritualist the arrangement has much to commend it. The traditional Elizabethan nave of the Reformed Church, with its altar at the east end, is pleasantly recalled. There is some resemblance to the monastic arrangement of high altar and nave altar. And in essence it is a return to the Orthodox plan of a nave shared by priest and congregation for the 'family' service but with a chancel reserved for actual Communion.

With architecture today in a state of chaos and all innovation equated automatically with improvement, the demand for change at any price was bound to affect the Christian Church. The Roman Catholics have decided to improve still further on the Baroque plan by abandoning that orientation which has throughout history been a basic factor of the plan of the religious building, or for that matter even of the theatre. In future the altar is to be brought into the centre of the building, from the perimeter of which the congregation can observe, as in a circus tent, the new liturgical performance. The Anglican Church, no longer, alas, willing to preserve its independence of thought, is following suit.

It is not only in respect of its planning that the English parish church is losing its ancient position as a building of architectural note. The waywardness of so much of modern church design will do irretrievable damage to the history of ecclesiastical architecture. The plea that modern trends represent reaction from revivalism is valid. That they represent 'contemporary' architecture, however, is specious.

For there is no such thing today as 'contemporary' architecture. At any historical period, and in any country, 'contemporary' architectural style is displayed in the form of variations upon a basic ordinance, framed by the leaders of the craft and accepted by all its practitioners. Only in variations of interpretation, as by detailing, may the architect display his individuality. For without the acceptance of a basic ordinance, any architecture will dissolve into chaos, history will come to a halt, and development cease for lack of an organization relying upon continuity.

7

The Masons

Architecture is primarily building. Thus it helps one to study architecture if one can appreciate the methods of building and the structural problems involved.

The medieval builder was not the head of a building firm as today. He was a craftsman, sometimes a carpenter or 'wright', more often a mason, who relied upon sawyers for his timber or quarrymen for his stone. From time to time he had to find specialists such as smiths, plumbers, or glaziers to add their particular contribution to the building.

During the Middle Ages only the more affluent could afford to pay a builder. The Church and the nobles built minsters and castles. The poor man had to raise his house himself 'of poles and thatch at every lane end'.

There were no architects. The greater structures had men of exceptional genius to design them. Small buildings were set out and detailed in contemporary local fashion.

The Anglo-Saxon building tradition was a timber one. The only word in their vocabulary to indicate building of any description was 'to timber'. The builders were thus the 'wrights', later known as carpenters from the Latin, but in truth the highly-skilled craftsmen we know today as 'joiners'.

Building in timber is an affair of posts set at intervals and joined at their tops by beams. In order to set out the plan of a building in an orderly fashion it was necessary to employ a system of measurement. The unit used was the rod or pole—later called the perch—of sixteen feet, still used by countrymen today when discussing their gardens.

The length of the village pole was arrived at by stopping sixteen grown men as they entered the church porch on a Sunday and making them place their right feet one behind the other. A pole cut to this length became the standard unit for the village. A cord of pole length folded twice became the yard. Firewood is still cut in lengths of four feet and called 'cordwood'.

Later on, variations of the yard—the ell and cloth-yard—came into use. When the yard became shortened to three feet the pole became sixteen and a half feet or five and a half yards. From this revised yard the furlong, mile and acre are derived.

Another ancient measure, long employed by mariners and miners, was the fathom, during the Middle Ages also used for the measurement of buildings.

By twice folding a cord of four feet the foot could be reproduced. Below this were inches, but what these were in early medieval times is now a mystery. The writer has often examined the courses of stone in a building to try to discover from differences in height what units were marked on the iron squares of the masons, but has failed to solve the problem.

Building contracts were in use during medieval days. Their language passed from Latin to French during the fourteenth century, English taking over about 1400. Work was measured by the rod or perch, varying from sixteen to twenty-four feet through intermediate stages, demonstrating the lack of any co-ordination of units of length throughout the country in medieval times.

The early builders could not calculate. Illiteracy apart, it must be remembered that until the end of the sixteenth century when arabic numerals reached us through Spain, the simplest sum, even ordinary addition, could not have been resolved without using counters on a chequer-board. At the beginning of the last century this was still in use, to add up parish accounts still being kept in roman numerals.

Measurements had to be kept as simple as possible. It is doubtful whether planners were aware of the 3:4:5 proportion for setting out a right angle. So rectangles were probably corrected by matching diagonals.

It is noticeable that when the long chancels were added to old naves during the thirteenth century builders who blocked up the chancel arch before sighting the axis of the new chancel often went astray.

The pole and its derivatives can be discovered everywhere in medieval buildings. A twenty-foot main span with eight-foot aisles is common in early days. But the variations of the pole are legion. Lincoln Cathedral and the Tower of London were set out using a pole of eighteen feet.

The span of the roof governs all building down the ages. But the system of planning longitudinally in a series of bays is a legacy of building with timber posts. This practice continues to assert itself upon the whole of English medieval architecture, being constantly expressed on the faces of masonry walling in the form of shallow pilasters and, later, projecting buttresses, separating the bays in which the main windows are sited.

Sleeper foundations or sills are essential for the support of timber posts, to prevent their pushing down into the ground. This sleeper foundation was known as the 'tablement' from the Latin word for plank. The medieval builders knew nothing of the principle of spreading footings over the ground to reduce the pressure per square inch on the soil, nor did they sink their foundations below ground level to avoid frost damaging the soft lime mortar, yet only in rubble walls where the flat stones are not large enough to stand on their own do we find much trouble today.

It was unusual to attempt to level the site for a medieval building; the builders preferred to pack up the lower part of the walling until they reached a level 'tablement' which in stone building became the plinth.

The craft of stone buildings, as opposed to that of skilled masonry, has been followed since prehistoric times. It originated from clearing the stones lying about land to be ploughed and moving them to the edges of the field to be heaped there in some kind of rough wall.

The first step in clearing would be to remove the large boulders —called in the West Country 'moor-stone'. These could be roughly shaped by hammering and built up, first into field walls and eventually into the walling of buildings. This is the kind of walling which can be found in the little church at Bradford-on-Avon in Wiltshire considered to have been built by St. Aldhelm at the beginning of the eighth century. From this technique develops the type of walling known as 'random rubble' which, properly faced-up and with the individual stones reduced from their original 'Cyclopean' scale, is frequently met with in pre-medieval days.

In most of the limestone regions—the Cotswolds, for example —the good freestone is overlaid by shallow strata, pieces of which break away and lie about on the surface as 'field-stone'. This may be seen everywhere used for field walls. When laid 'dry', without mortar, the proper system to employ is that known as 'herring-bone'. The stones are laid in rough courses eight inches or so in height, not flat on their bed but diagonally, each alternate course sloping in the opposite direction so that the whole locks together. This style of walling may be found in many ancient churches. A more sophisticated method of using this type of stone is to hammer it into shapes which can be laid in normal courses as 'coursed rubble', but this needs mortar to keep the stones from falling out of the wall.

All this kind of walling is known as rubble walling and is not masonry. Much of the walling of our parish churches is of this kind, worked not by freemasons but by wallers or 'nobblers' using hammers.

As long as mortar is available for bedding the stones a perfectly good wall can be made of the various kinds of rubble stones. But the limitations of such a wall would soon be found. Apart from the properly 'dressed' stone needed for lining openings, unless similar stones could be found for stiffening any angles of the building these would soon weaken and fall away. Where the building site was close to the remains of a Roman building bricks from this could be salvaged and used to strengthen the angles of rubble walling. Stones squared by the Romans may also have been dug up and used.

Thus good 'quoins' or angle stones are essential to the stability of a wall. In rural areas it was probably the desperate need for procuring these which first encouraged local builders to learn how to cut stone instead of just hammering it into shape. And from such beginnings they may have learned the principles governing the construction of a masonry wall.

Any wall is set out with two faces; the space between these is filled with a 'core' of 'spalls' or chips left over from the shaping. In a rubble wall there is little difference between the three portions. Towards the middle of the medieval period the core was of stones so carefully laid that the thicknesses of walls could be considerably reduced. In masonry the theory is to lay the stone so that it will take up a position in the wall similar to that which it occupied in the quarry. Thus it is hoped it will stay there for ever.

Each stone has a 'face' to show to the world. It has two 'beds', to lie on and to carry the stone above it. The face of the stone is squared-up on either side to meet its neighbours. The rest of the stone, its 'tail', is buried in the wall.

True 'freestone' is limestone. Its best quarries lie along a line sweeping round from Northamptonshire through Somerset into Devon. Lincolnshire also has fine freestone. There are also some lovely local stones such as those of Ham Hill in Somerset and those of Horsham in Sussex which are no longer used. Colour in a stone is due to impurities and affects its durability, but faint tints such as are found in Chilmark stone in Wiltshire add greatly to its interest, each stone varying slightly from its neighbours and the whole constantly changing between damp and drying out. The most perfect stone, Portland, is constant in colour and apt to be rather grim in consequence.

While true freestone is always a limestone, there are other building stones which are geologically speaking sandstones, or as the medieval builders called them, 'gritstones'. They are usually highly coloured and have comparatively poor wearing qualities compared with the freestones, but can be very attractive to look at. Derbyshire and the West Midlands are sandstone areas, also Devonshire.

The presence of stone quarries played a major part in the development of English medieval architecture. Wherever they happened to be founded, the great monastic houses were usually able to assure themselves of a plentiful supply of freestone and assemble a team of craftsmen to work upon it. As time went on and their maintenance teams became established in their lodges, these became a source of inspiration to the whole district and were able to no small extent to influence its architectural development.

Extensive quarry areas such as existed along the limestone belt could also provide their own sources of masonry mystique as masons and quarrymen came and went between lodge and quarry. In this connection it is sad to note that while a mason can be taught his craft in a school, the lore of the quarrymen is bound to the soil and can only be passed on from father to apprentice— if not to son—*at the quarry face*. Once closed, a quarry can never be reopened.

The combination of a rich monastic house with a stone-producing area such as the Benedictine Abbey of Gloucester hard up against the Cotswold oölite, could produce something in the nature of an Architectural School. Glastonbury in Somerset, similarly favoured, must have done the same in its region and may well have provided the inspiration and designing skill which produced the lovely series of parish church towers in that county.

Even the rural Cistercians, breaking away from their early austerity to the extent of raising gracious churches in the valleys of Yorkshire, were able to make their early Gothic architecture a style of great beauty which continued into the era of the High Gothic as a notable School creating a series of fine parish churches.

In the absence of adequate supplies of local stone, however, the great monasteries seem to have been less able to affect local architecture. Thus the enormously rich abbey of St. Edmundsbury in Suffolk played a small part in improving the local style until the very end of the medieval period when it may have helped with the design of the late Gothic churches of East Anglia. Even these are notable for the spectacular carpentry of the roofs rather than the excellence of their masonry.

It must have been difficult in medieval days to transport stone to a stoneless region. So monasteries, with their huge building complexes to maintain, may have been somewhat greedy for free-stone and unwilling to spare enough for the parish churches. It may well be that it is not until the building and maintenance programmes of the monasteries were slowing down that we find parish church architecture really coming into its own.

Certainly it is not in the surviving great churches—with the possible exception of the last of all, Bath Abbey—that we find the latest phase of the High Gothic at its most perfect, but in the parish church, often serving quite a small village yet possessing a large and beautifully-designed building complete with soaring bell-tower.

Vanished now into history are nearly all the quarries of England whence grew her lovely medieval architecture. For every one still open there are a hundred represented by an acre or two of tumbled turf or a thicket of brambles. The great quarries of Barnack in Lincolnshire which gave birth to the greatest buildings of the Age are known today as the 'Hills and Holes'.

The freestone was hacked out of the quarry in huge lumps and broken down into manageable sizes. It was then put on a heavy block of stone called a 'banker' for the mason to work on it. The Classical tool for working stone is the two-handed axe, double-headed for balance and very thick and heavy. Until the end of the twelfth century it was the only tool available for dressing stone and the uneven diagonal slashes it left on the faces of the small stones of the period are easily recognized today. (Plate 32a.)

The carvers who ornamented the timber buildings, however, used chisels for carving their motifs. These tools, which were struck with a wooden mallet or 'mell', were probably little more than a quarter of an inch wide, as are their successors today. Towards the end of the twelfth century a new type of chisel came into use. It had a blade about three inches or so wide and after about 1180 comes into use for dressing the face of a stone after it had left the axe. During the thirteenth century the 'bolster', as it was called, was used with great care. The stones had now become about twice as long as their height and the tooling was run absolutely vertical and so neatly that each stroke joined exactly with that below it. (Plate 32b.)

After the end of the century, however, the masons speeded their work up, holding the bolster diagonally and dressing the faces of the now much larger stones as quickly as possible without the refinement enjoyed by their predecessors. (Plate 32c.)

The mason at his banker was protected from the weather by a lean-to roof set against a wall. This was his 'lodge'. He cut his stones true with the aid of an L-shaped iron called a 'square', on which his inches were marked. To strike the curves of mouldings or tracery he had his 'compass'—which we should call today 'dividers'. A feature of many old buildings is the series of geometrical figures 'doodled' on old walls by jokers who got hold of the mason's compasses during his absence from his lodge.

Each mason had his own sign-manual or 'mark' to indicate the stones prepared by him. Such marks were not intended to show on the wall-face and are usually found on a bed.

With the change in roof design brought about by the use of lead, the whole 'eaves' system which since the beginning had formed the traditional way of bringing a roof out over the wall it was protecting underwent a complete change. Lead was unsuited to eaves construction, so these were abandoned and the foot of the roof concealed behind a parapet (Fig. 22) behind which was a lead gutter discharging through spouts or 'gargoyles'. The thin parapet walls needed special stones having no 'tail' but squared-up on both faces. This kind of stone is known as 'ashlar'. When both faces are neatly dressed as for a parapet it was known as 'perpeyn' ashlar.

By the end of the fourteenth century a new use was found for ashlar. It could be used for facing walls built of rubble, much in the same way as one uses concrete blocks today. One can always tell ashlar by the regularity of the stones—in the mid-fifteenth century eighteen inches by a foot high was a standard size—and by the absence of proper quoins, for the edges of the blocks, six inches or so thick, can be seen at each angle.

From this period, masonry began to deteriorate in favour of applied ashlar until masonry walling began to disappear altogether and mason-work is seen only at quoins to rubble or brick walling. At the time of the reaction against brick-faced buildings which is found at the end of the eighteenth century, a new vogue for ashlar facing appears in all good buildings.

The Masons

In medieval days the majority of the stones cut by the masons were facing stones or quoins. When an opening was reached, however, its lining stones had to be worked into the coursing, and the wedge-shaped 'voussoirs' cut to turn its head. Among other special stones needed were the 'serches' cut with extra-wide tails for lining the wells of newel stairs. The 'jambs' and arched head of an opening could either be simply-cut stones or could be ornamented with lines of mouldings carried round the lining and greatly adding to the mason's problems as each stone had to fit exactly with its neighbours without a break in the profile of the moulding.

The stone bracket or 'corbel' is an ubiquitous feature of medieval architecture. It is provided as a projection from the wall-face to carry anything from the end of a timber beam to the end of a heavy arcade. During the fourteenth century small openings were spanned by a flat stone lintel having its ends supported by a pair of opposed corbels. This is called by antiquaries the 'Edwardian' or 'Caernarvon' arch as it may be seen in a number of door-heads in that castle. Small timber-framed openings are sometimes lined with a similar feature, their jambs curving inwards and then cut back vertically to meet the lintel. The fronts of Gothic porches frequently display this timber version of the Edwardian arch.

The advantage of the lintel is that it needs no centering. Its disadvantage is that unless it is very deep a very slight movement of the building may crack it, for stone has no tensile strength. It was the experience of the Byzantine builders in the earthquake-ridden regions of Anatolia and Syria which taught them to use lintels in conjunction with arches over them. Thus if the lintel cracked the arch would keep the wall over it safe. During the twelfth century the system, probably noted during Crusading expeditions, was used to great effect in the doorway of the English parish church. The lintel made it easier to fit the door, for round-headed doors are liable to jam against the inner side of the arch unless it should be raised or made segmental as was done in some cases to prevent this. The semicircular 'tympanum' between lintel and arch became a site for sculptural decoration. (Plate 29.)

As experts in arcuated construction the medieval builders were always loth to trust stone lintels and made full use of the principle of the 'relieving arch'. Most flat-topped windows, such as are found during the High Gothic era, have these arches built into the wall over them.

Even mason-builders seem never to have lost sight of the timber origins of the English building trade. The curious lines of long stones ornamenting some of the stone tower-naves, held in position by short stones here and there set deep into the wall, recall timber construction in a remarkably emphatic form, translated with not inconsiderable difficulty into a crude stone technique.

The stone plank or 'table', from the Latin word meaning plank, is found everywhere in medieval masonry. Most buildings had the lower part of their walling built up to a common level and marked with a 'tablement' with its edge bevelled off to produce a plinth above which the wall was reduced slightly in thickness. All building heights were measured above the tablement.

Tablements—called today 'water-tables'—were set in projecting lines immediately above the junction of a roof with a wall so as to keep stormwater from running down the wall-face straight into the building. 'Table-stones' were used to form the internal sills of windows. 'Bench table-stones' provided the lines of stone benches sometimes found lining the sides of a medieval church The 'string-course' used for horizontal punctuation is formed of the same stone 'planks' and was known in the Middle Ages as a tablement.

Students of Classical architecture will recall that the Doric frieze of the Parthenon is formed of a series of 'metopes', carved in relief and separated by vertical 'triglyphs' which are reproductions in stone of the ends of the rafters. Above this frieze is seen the spreading cornice representing the eaves in architectural form. The eaves of the early buildings in this country had no such enrichment. Below them, however, is frequently seen a tablement projecting from the wall and carried by a series of corbels often carved into grotesques. In such 'corbel-tables' the corbels may represent the ends of the rafters converted, like the Doric triglyphs, to architectural use. (Fig. 22.)

The corbel-table was obviously a popular architectural expression and continued in use even after eaves had been abolished in favour of gutters concealed behind parapets. As it was an advantage to bring the parapet as far forward as possible to allow for a wide gutter, so the corbel-table was retained to carry the projection. During the early-medieval period the tablement was replaced by a miniature arcade of trefoiled arches springing from corbel to corbel.

From early parapets with their coping-stones is developed the battlement imitating the military device with its embrasures or 'vents' separated in the ornamental form by 'merlons', 'crests' or 'cops'.

Stone-carving was probably executed on the scaffolding, to avoid damage to it while it was being set in position. The mason would leave a rough lump called a 'boasting' as a basis for the intended carving.

As architect to the building, the mason would be responsible for explaining to the client by means of models the nature of certain complicated features. He might, for his own instruction, make small-scale models in stone of part of the building where the modelling became complicated. The writer has seen a Maltese mason make a model of a complete pier with the springing of its arches, with all the mouldings worked in, all to about one-twentieth full-size.

Such mouldings would be designed by the mason and cut out of a piece of lead sheet or board to form a 'template' or profile capable of being applied to each stone so that the moulding would pass round the opening without any awkward joints. It is believed that Gothic architecture was carried about the country by journey-men masons 'borrowing' such templates or even models.

All architectural detail such as window tracery would be set out by the mason on boards. Everything would have to be drawn full-size and each stone laid on it and worked to fit its part in the design before being sent up to the walling mason or 'setter' for fixing it in its assigned place.

As nowadays, prefabrication was not uncommon, quarries having their own lodges capable of supplying ready-made such simple features as doorways and even traceried windows of moderate size. Great Continental quarries such as those of Caen continued to supply such features right through the medieval period.

Window tracery was set into an opening the frame of which was lined with dressed stonework often embellished with mouldings of the period. The stones of the lining were each carefully bonded in with the walling material and were in fact laid together with this. Thus an inserted feature may at once be detected by breaks in the coursing between wall and lining. The tracery of windows was made separately and fixed into the lining without being bonded into it.

The opening though the wall, the 'reveal', usually splayed internally to increase the light, was also lined with masonry. In the inner face of the wall was the 'scoinson' arch, also formed in dressed stone. The inner edge of the scoinson arch was sometimes softened with a roll moulding passing round it. Sometimes this internal arch was converted into a feature in its own right, as at Bampton in Oxfordshire, by throwing out cusps and making its silhouette foliated.

At first windows were set in line with the outer wall face with a wide 'rere-arch' to carry the core of the wall. But during the High Gothic period the windows were set into the thickness of the wall where they helped to carry the core over. This reduced the inner splay and enabled the masons to elaborate the external elevation of the window with more moulding. The principal feature of the outer splay was a wide shallow hollow known as a 'casement 'moulding.

The elaborate Gothic mouldings which at first seem so complicated are in reality composed of a series of profiles which are individually quite simply cut. There are two basic forms, the roll formed by flanking an edge or 'arris' with grooves or 'quirks', and the plain chamfer. If the original arris is left on the stone instead of rounding it into a roll it becomes a 'bowtell'. Hollows are produced simply by deepening quirks and scooping them out between the rolls, multiplied to enrich the series. (Fig. 24.) The front of a roll can be varied by having a small flat 'fillet' left on it, with the sides of the roll worked up to it in a double curve or 'ogee'.

The above are the basic mouldings which produce the rich profiles of the early-medieval period. During the High Gothic era, when the carpenter was beginning to vie with the mason in his contribution to architecture, the forms of moulding based on the chamfer came into use. These are much broader in effect and lack the richly undercut rolls of the thirteenth century. The chamfers are either flat, hollowed like a shallow casement moulding, or wavy. In pillars the attached shaft is used to cover the flat portions between the chamfers. (Fig. 25.)

The turning of large columns was an operation playing no part in Gothic architecture, circular pillars being built up in 'drums' as in Classical days. The same principle was followed when forming slender shafts or colonettes by working a section of each with each course of stone. But in order to turn the Purbeck marble and other detached shafts of the thirteenth century it was necessary to construct a stone-lathe.

The writer, when advising upon the rebuilding of the buildings of Valetta after the last war, had a stone-lathe built for him by his master mason, Montebello. Its principle feature was a huge stone fly-wheel some four feet in diameter and having a hub, rim, and spokes all cut out of the solid and resembling an early wheel window. This heavy piece of machinery was mounted upon a sturdy wooden frame and turned upon an iron rod cranked at either end to form a handle.

The long square stone to be turned was held between two L-shaped spikes fixed into two masses of stone called 'logs'. A rope was twisted round the stone, taken to the wheel, and tightened into a groove cut in its rim.

The operation of a stone-lathe is sheer drama. First the master mason and his assistant had to apply themselves to the cranks and get the great wheel spinning faster and faster until it was whizzing round at an incredible rate. With the assistant standing well clear, the master mason took up a heavy chisel set in a long wooden handle nearly a yard long and approached the spinning stone. At the outset the bombardment of flying spalls appeared dangerous to a degree but by persistence he wore the stone down to a roughly circular form after which he was able to apply himself deftly to the delicate task of completing the column without making a mistake which would have wrecked an expensive piece of stone some five feet long and a foot in diameter.

The Maltese stone-lathe was probably constructed in a tradition handed down from Byzantine, if not from Imperial Roman, times. Its form indicates the kind of machinery which the combined efforts of the carpenter and smith were able to bring to the assistance of the masons.

The mason could not turn an arch without the help of the carpenter who had to construct the timber 'centering' for him. When extending a building, however, the cutting of an opening in a wall was simplified for the medieval builder by his rigid attention to the principle of 'bonding' which requires that in each course of masonry a vertical joint shall be as close as possible to the centre of the stones above and below. If this principle is followed, a hole cut through a wall will only let the walling above collapse until the bonding takes over and the top of the opening becomes triangular. The smaller the length of stone used in comparison with the height of the courses, the steeper will be the sides of the triangle and the stronger the resulting support.

It is possible that in early medieval days, when arches were acutely pointed, openings may have simply been knocked out in this way and subsequently lined with dressed masonry picking up the wall over. The change to long shallow stones would however have made this rather a dangerous practice, so one can imagine instead the slotting of the wall to accommodate the new respond or pillar and the subsequent turning of the arch stone by stone, working up to the apex and using the remains of the old wall as the centering. Building an arch in 'orders' would have been very helpful as such arches only need centering for their lowermost order.

Cutting openings in a rough wall of random or even coursed rubble with its bonding rather sketchily arranged, must have been a difficult operation and would have needed the introduction of short lengths of timber known as 'needles' thrust through the wall and supported at either end by vertical 'shores'. The better the walling, the fewer the needles required to hold up the structure while the opening below was being cut and lined.

Some parts of England, notably East Anglia, have as their field-stone flint, lying in great nodules capable of being broken in halves to provide two faces and a long tail which can be built into a wall. An ingenious system of using flint is to lay ordinary masoned wall-stones at intervals with flints between them, each course set out so that its opposite faces alternate the treatment. The next course is laid to be exactly the opposite of that below. The result is a chequer-board of flint and freestone. This is a useful method of using second-hand stone and is found everywhere after the Dissolution of the monastic houses and their subsequent wrecking.

The wool-rich parishes of East Anglia, too far removed from quarry areas to be able to build their large churches in masonry, imported small quantities of good quality freestone and worked this into fretted patterns similar to that used for the pierced parapets of the period. With this fretwork they built their wall-faces, backing them with flint rubble and filling in the interstices of the tracery with neatly squared flintwork. This is called 'flushwork'.

If one pauses to consider the large number of Gothic churches still remaining, adds to this a possible equivalent amount of material destroyed at the Dissolution, and then reflects upon the extremely elaborate nature of Gothic design, one may well wonder where all the skilled designers came from. The answer is probably that there was a great deal of copying of major elements and all individuality was left to the detailing introduced by the mason after his own special taste. One can imagine the medieval 'client' pointing out some feature which took his fancy and asking for something like it, with variations as in some other building, and so on. Contracts are in existence to indicate that the copying of the towers of parish churches, for example, was a not uncommon practice.

The general running-down of the magnificent medieval mason-craft following the decline of the great monasteries towards the sunset of the Middle Ages must have had the result of putting masons out of employment and reducing the intake to the lodges. Such innovations as the introduction of the 'ashlar' principle of *facing*, instead of building, with stone, point to the decline of interest in the great medieval craft, emphasized by the general coarsening of ornament and the retreat from the Gothic arch. Carpentry was achieving marvels in the roofs of parish churches, but the only contribution to the mason-craft of the Gothic twilight was the glorious fan-vaulting which could only be afforded by the most affluent communities. (Plate 30.)

Building in general was becoming less of an art. Speed of construction was being taken into consideration. A standardized form of building material, easy to make, transport and lay, and enabling building to be executed without the services of the highly-skilled and expensive freemason, was becoming popular. So into the sphere of building enters the 'red mason' with his pile of bricks.

The craft of brick-making was well understood by the Romans and most of their building in this country was carried out in this material. Even when building in rubble, bricks were used for quoins, for lining openings, and in the lacing courses, several bricks in depth, which were built into rubble walls to strengthen them. Salvaged Roman bricks, an inch and a half or so in thickness, were greatly sought after by the Anglo-Saxon builders for quoins and dressings.

From the early-medieval period onwards, bricks from the stoneless Low Countries were imported into East Anglia which was equally ill-provided. During the fourteenth century a region having good building stone but lacking stone suitable for paving slabs, might import such bricks—known as 'Flanders' or 'Holland' tiles—for flooring its churches.

The actual 'wall-tile' for building, about two inches thick, was being made in this country where suitable clay existed by the second quarter of the fifteenth century, but had been imported for use in East Anglian walls at least a century before this. By the end of the fifteenth century brick had come to be regarded as a suitable material for use in the best class of building, and was already being shown as a facing and not merely used for the core of the wall. Such bricks are known today as 'Tudor' bricks. They are encountered everywhere during the sixteenth century, especially during the Elizabethan Age.

During the seventeenth century when brick was becoming the universal English building material, about two and a half inches was the standard thickness, and by the eighteenth century it had settled down to the standard two and five-eighths of the present day. Peculiar to the Georgian era is the use of over-burnt 'headers' or 'chuffs' arranged in diaper patterns in the brick bonding. During the nineteenth century one sometimes finds three-inch bricks, especially in the industrial Midlands.

It took a long time for the bricklayers to discover how to bond their brickwork. At first they used them just as coursed rubble, maintaining the bonding principle as far as possible but employing no bonding plan. During the Tudor period, it is obvious, they were afraid that their 'stretcher' bricks would fall out, so they employed plenty of 'headers' to tie them in. The core of the wall was laid anyhow.

With the seventeenth century brickwork became so thoroughly studied that a proper system of bonding came into use. This was the 'English' bond which employed alternate courses of headers and stretchers neatly laid and properly interlocking in their courses and presenting an orderly appearance on the wall face. By the next century, however, the Dutch had taught us the proper way to lay bricks and introduced us to the 'Flemish' bond in which each course alternated headers with stretchers and changed step with those on either side of it. This is the established bond for this country which has been employed ever since.

No walling, whether of stone or brick, can be laid securely without beds of mortar. The manufacture of this requires lime, produced by burning the waste of limestone quarries. The quick-lime mixed with sand forms mortar, which is not only essential for bedding the face stones of a masonry wall but desirable for consolidating the core of rough pieces of stone often thrown in anyhow where no one could see them. Buckets or cauldrons were needed to bring the mortar to the building course.

Transport of stone to the site could be by pony-back or by sled. It is interesting to watch stone sizes increasing as transport becomes more efficient with the passage of the centuries.

Scaffolding was essential for access to building work. The holes for the 'putlogs', the timbers carrying the scaffold planks and passing from wall to pole, can be seen everywhere in medieval buildings, generally as neat little square holes filled after the scaffolding had been struck. The pulley-wheel was used to lift materials to the scaffold, where the 'setters' laid the stones sent up to them by the banker mason working below.

8

Carpenters and Others

═══

As one travels through the western counties, especially Devon or Cornwall, one cannot but remark upon the paucity of really old buildings. Church after church displays the soaring western bell-tower and the spacious fenestration of the High Gothic. It is true that freestone is almost entirely lacking in those regions west of the Exe, but so it is from East Anglia. And field-stone for walling is to be had for the taking and the local 'nobblers' and even the stonemasons seem to have had little difficulty in working even the grim granite to their requirements.

The deficiency may have been in that regular forest timber which since Anglo-Saxon times has been the basic building material, if not for walling, then for roofing. The heart of England provided an inexhaustible supply of this until a greedy iron industry began to denude it for fuel. But in the West, hammered by winds for so much of the year, timber trees seem to have been harder to come by and carpentry a trade far less common than that of granite-hewer. Thus it may simply have been the difficulty of roofing large buildings which delayed the development of medieval architecture in the West.

Oak, and by the fourteenth century elm, were the principal building timbers. For several centuries now we have employed imported softwoods for the purpose and even such hardwood as we may use for special purposes is brought to us from far countries. Thus our native woodland industry has long passed into history and it would be difficult to discover anything about it today. There must have been many hundreds of saw-pits in and about the great forests of the Middle Ages, each with its heavy bench and pair of sawyers, 'top-dog' and 'under-dog'—the latter always smothered in sawdust—hauling the heavy saws to and fro along the great trees. But the sawyer, like his colleague the quarry-man, has been forgotten while the memories of inspired masons and carpenters linger down the centuries among the stones and beams of the great buildings they raised.

Like the contemporary mason, the early 'house-wright' exe-cuted his work with what today would be considered very clumsy tools. After the felling axe had dropped, topped and lopped the tree, and the sawyer had squared-up the logs into beams, these were not taken into a 'shop' and put on to a bench but worked on the ground as they lay with swinging strokes of the axe.

Where a sawpit was not available the wright squared-up his logs by standing on them and attacking them with an all-purpose tool called a 'twybill', a double-headed axe having one side turned to serve as an adze. Fashioned in coarser mould, the West-Country 'toobell' is still in use as a kind of mattock for working amongst roots and boulders.

One of the interesting features of medieval carpentry is the way in which the tapering nature of a tree is accepted as fundamental to the design. No attempt was made to keep an even width of timber throughout the length of a rafter, though exposed beams were usually kept even for aesthetic reasons.

A common size for rafters was six by five inches tapering to five by four. They were of course always laid flat until the end of the seventeenth century.

Posts were set upside down so that the thick root-end could be mortised to provide seatings for the several beams the posts had to carry. These posts were known as 'teazle-posts' from some resemblance to the plant.

Only the heart of the wood was used, the sap-wood being axed away, possibly so as to discourage boring insects. It is the 'chamfering-off' of the edges of the beam to remove the last vestiges of sap-wood which is so typical of medieval carpentry and which forms one of the origins of the Gothic moulding.

The light, long-bladed axe was deftly wielded when cutting the mortices and tenons, and the augur or 'wimble'—from which 'gimlet'—bored the holes for the pegs holding the joints together.

Planks were massive timbers eighteen inches wide and six inches thick. They were used in belfry floors to stop the clappers of bells from hurtling down upon the heads of the ringers. Boards were of the same width as planks but about one and a half inches thick. During the fifteenth century when elaborate screenwork was being produced in large quantities, imported oak called 'Eastland' or 'ostrich' boards were used for this, Continental timber being apparently better seasoned than ours was.

The early timber buildings of this country were founded upon posts set in rows opposing each other in pairs at bay intervals, the space between the rows representing the span of the roof. Two lines of sleepers formed the foundations. In the tall churches these were beams about two feet square, but in normal buildings they were planks laid flat on a low wall of rubble stone. The timber foundation was called a 'tablement' from the Latin word for plank. The rubble underneath it allowed it to be levelled-up and at the same time kept it dry. In a stone building, the tablement became a stone plinth with its edge bevelled back so that the wall could be given an aesthetic foundation as well as a structural one.

From the sleeper foundation rose the posts, stepped upon it as masts on a keel, joined together as they rose by systems of curved struts and braces, the sweeping curves softening the aesthetic rigidity of the lines and enabling use to be made of curved pieces of timber. (Fig. 6.)

Ubiquitous are the curved 'saltires' which sweep across from post to post, their form probably deriving from the shape of the wooden packsaddles which carried most of the loads of the day. The double curve of the ogee, perpetuated in stone beneath the central tower of Wells Cathedral, must have developed from the graceful profiles of the timber prototypes.

After the hardwood logs had been sawn into squared timbers at the saw-pit, the round-faced boards resulting from this operation were adzed down at their ends and fitted into horizontal sills and heads to form partitions or 'bratticing' for the external walling.

The church at Greensted in Essex is still walled with bratticing of this description.

After the age of timber-building had given place to that of building in stone, the carpenter's primary task became to provide a roof. The principle of early roof construction was very simple, each roof consisting of a series of 'couples', pairs of rafters 'halved' and pinned together at the apex and set close together along the line of the building. There was no ridge piece. In order to give some sense of triangulation to each couple and prevent its collapse when the roof-covering was applied, a short horizontal timber called a 'collar' joined the rafters rather more than half-way up.

At the top of the wall, a heavy timber called the 'wall-plate' was laid flat on the masonry, in the manner of a tablement, to carry the rafter-feet. The plate was solidly bedded-down on the wall-top so that it would not slide off and imperil the stability of the roof. But often the outward thrust of the roof was so powerful that it could actually begin to topple the walls and force them to lean outwards. To check this the carpenters set massive beams called 'tie-beams' across from side to side to tie the opposing plates together and thus complete the triangulation of the roof.

But the tie-beam was aesthetically an unattractive feature as it cut across the building and spoilt its internal form. The great halls of the Anglo-Saxons were formed of lines of wide timber arches called 'crucks', each arch being constructed in the same way as a roofing 'couple' but the rafters being massive curved timbers rising direct from the ground without any walling. The interior effect of such a building is that of a long pointed tunnel. This is very probably the effect sought after in all English roofs even after they had been raised upon walls. It is in essence the form of the Gothic interior.

Tie-beams passing across this tunnel-like space would undoubtedly have ruined the effect. So the carpenters, the nature of whose material would have made them much more familiar with the principles governing statics than the more pedestrian mason, discovered ways of making the roof more stable without resource to the primitive tie. They had from early times discovered the principle of triangulation and during the early-medieval period were developing it in their roofs by adding extra braces from the collar down towards the rafter-feet to stiffen each couple and reduce the risk of its spreading. This began to introduce a curved outline into the roof which by the selection of curved timbers for the strutting could be smoothed down into the desired tunnel-like effect. In this way the medieval 'cradle-roof' came into being.

It is noticeable that while in the well-timbered parts of England the cradle roofs gave way to the magnificent low-pitched roofs of the High Gothic, in the West, where large timbers to construct the great trusses were difficult to obtain, and slate could be used for covering instead of lead, cradle roofs formed out of the curved western timber continued to the end of the Middle Ages. (Plate 21.)

But it was the gradual development upon the tie-beam which led to the introduction of the carpenters' finest contribution to English medieval architecture, the elaborate roofs of the fifteenth century which attained their finest form in East Anglia.

Although the tie-beam began as a device for tying the sides of the roof together, by the High Gothic era it had come to be accepted that it could be used as a base for actually propping up the roof in the centre. From this time the tie-beam became the basic feature of a device called a 'truss', set across the span at bay or half-bay intervals and used to prop up the roof by means of a series of timbers set, for the first time, longitudinally from one end of the building to the other. The uppermost of these timbers was the ridge against which the rafters leaned, no longer joined in 'couples' but each one an independent timber. Between ridge and plate were 'purlins' passing from truss to truss and carrying the rafters in the centre of their span. (Plate 19.)

The development of the High Gothic roof is expressed by the variations in the design of the roof-truss. These variations are innumerable both in respect of the systems of timbering used and the forms of decoration subsequently applied. The lowering of the roof pitch and the pressure of the lead covered on the flat-laid rafters made it necessary to increase the amount of timber needed to carry its covering.

Anyone who visits the churches in a region such as East Anglia one cannot but be impressed by the versatility and independence

Carpenters and Others

of thought displayed by the carpenters as each worked out his own system of roof truss independently of his neighbours. A number of devices can be seen, each used in a slightly different manner and augmented by the introduction of non-structural timbers, finally completed by magnificent carving.

Basic to the simple roof truss are the central 'king-post' and the pair of 'queen-posts', carrying the large 'principal rafters' between which pass the purlins. Sometimes a wide timber arch fills the truss instead of a system of vertical members. And as the ends of the tie-beam are often stiffened by timber brackets passing down the wall, the tie-beam carrying an arch sometimes has its middle portion omitted and only its bracket-supported ends retained. Such curtailed beams are called 'hammer-beams'.

Until the very end of the medieval period, when the pitched roof had vanished and been replaced by the lead flat, the tie-beam was never a readily acceptable feature of the church interior. The arched truss carried by a pair of hammer-beams began to open up the roof once again. Eventually the two hammer-beams were provided with another pair above them and the width of the arched truss reduced. In its final form the hammer-beam truss came to be built up in its entirety with these curious devices. (Plate 20.)

It is a curious fact that the excellent joinery technique and superb craftsmanship of the carved screenwork of the South-West is nowhere matched in its roofs. The roof-truss is almost unknown in that region; the old system of 'close-coupled' rafters continues in use to the end of the medieval period. But the 'cradle-roofs' of the West cover wide spans, over aisles as well as nave, and contributed in no small part to the development of the 'hall' church. (Plate 21.) Longitudinal timbers resembling purlins were used to strap each couple to its neighbour, carved bosses being provided to mask junctions between members.

The timber architecture of a country is bound to be affected by the nature of its material. England's timber is hardwood, capable of producing curved as well as straight members. The fact that the Gothic arch, constructed in stone, is less liable to spread and collapse than the Classical semicircular form, was probably discovered during the adventurous days of the twelfth century; but the Anglo-Saxon 'cruck' of two curved timbers, depicted on the Bayeux Tapestry and still to be met with in our villages today, is a Gothic arch and may have had a good deal more to do with the development of medieval English architecture than can nowadays be determined.

The earliest crucks were pairs of curved timbers used so as to form walls and roof in one piece without facing the problems resulting from trying to balance rafters on the tops of walls. At first the crucks were set close together to be used as rafters but during the later Middle Ages they were set at bay distance to form trusses and carry purlins. Originally the crucks were formed of bowed timbers but at the end of the medieval period bent timbers, giving more headroom, took the place of the old curved profiles. From an association of the angled truss and the wall was developed an open type of roof displaying the truss in its least obstructive silhouette. The cruck principle, used to the full in the Midlands but seldom seen in the West, appears to have given birth to an interesting form of open roof, its trusses formed of specially selected angled timbers, in a number of High Gothic roofs to be seen in East Anglia.

The 'saltire' or diagonal cross formed of two struts crossing, was nearly always formed of two serpentine timbers, so that these met in a silhouette of 'ogee' form finishing in a sharp point. It is interesting to note that the French equivalent of 'Gothic' is 'Ogival', thus giving recognition to a feature which is certainly not of masonry origin as representing the most magnificent masonry style the world has ever seen.

In order to support the centre of the purlins midway between the trusses, and at the same time brace the roof longitudinally against wind pressure on the gable ends, systems of 'wind-braces' were introduced along the sides of the roof. These were formed out of arched or serpentine timbers. They add greatly to the elaboration of the High Gothic roof, and in a simple form are met with everywhere in the roofs of the mid-sixteenth century, being retained at the ends of roofs for a century after this.

The roof of the High Gothic era began as a soaring piece of carpentry determined to uphold the Gothic tradition. But the demands of a lead covering, difficult to stop from creeping down a steep pitch, forced the eventual abandoning of the traditional form.

As the roof-pitch sank towards the flat, dignity was restored by raising walls and increasing the size of the fenestration. The truss disappeared and was replaced by a massive tie-beam having just enough rise in the middle to retain a small degree of pitch in the roof. Thus in its final form the roof became a fine timber ceiling (Plate 18.), a panelling of tie-beams and purlins, often elaborately ornamented and with long brackets carried from the ends of the tie-beams down the lofty walls of the nave or its clear-story. (Plate 20.) Such coverings could not compete in magnificence with the trussed and hammer-beamed roofs of recent years, but the effect of the whole interior, albeit reduced to an austerity of detail, continued to appear spacious and dignified by virtue of its impressive proportions.

At the end of the medieval period the parish church had become an edifice of simple proportions, lofty in the Gothic tradition, and covered by a flat roof which showed beneath as an attractively carpentered timber ceiling. One might have supposed that the Dissolution of the monasteries would have released material and enabled the parish churches to launch out into even finer archi-tectural adventures. What happened, however, was that the whole of the building industry went over to building great halls for lay magnates and ignored church building as belonging to an obsolete social order. It also happened, however, that some parish churches were able to expand here and there by salvaging some fine timber roof from a monastic house in course of demolition. Such may still be discovered today.

Parishes needing lead for roofing repairs might find that the enormous tonnage salvaged from the monasteries had all been assigned to lay people for their new mansions. Thenceforth the tendency is to go back to high-pitched roofs which could be covered with the clay tiles now coming into more general use.

The church roofs of Elizabethan and Jacobean days are often quite interesting. A great many exist which have not been re-placed by sham-Gothic cradle roofs during nineteenth-century restorations. They are all built on the truss principle. Both kinds of pitch may be found, the high for tiles, the low for lead. The trusses carrying the former still display, in simplified form, the old devices of wide arches and even hammer-beams. The low-pitch trusses have king-posts and queen-posts, often indicating their post-medieval date by employing shapes for these suggestive of the Renaissance baluster. Nearly all the roofs of this period make full use of the strange 'square-onion' drops, usually pierced, possibly a pathetic attempt to recapture something of the lovely pendants of fifteenth-century fan-vaulting which the plasterers of the period had already introduced into their domestic ceilings.

The roofs of our parish churches have suffered far more seriously than the walls supporting them. During the comfort-loving eighteenth century many medieval roofs lacking in any particular aesthetic charm were ceiled-in with lath and plaster.

While we are fortunate in that so many of our magnificent High Gothic church roofs still survive notwithstanding the encouragement given to the spread of the death-watch beetle by the change-over from oil lamps to electric lighting, still more of the lesser roofs, deemed not so worthy of retention, were swept away during the age of restorations. Most of the roofs which replaced them have gone back to the early-medieval pitches indicated on tower walls by the remains of water-tables. The type of roof most favoured by the nineteenth-century restorer was the open cradle form.

The plaster ceiling was not a feature of medieval architecture, though boarded 'wainscot' was often provided over the altar to keep dirt from the roof from falling upon it. The final elimination of the roof-truss under the lead-covered roofs of the fifteenth century had created the situation that the underside of the roof, like that of the 'solar' floor, had become a ceiling. The very great skill of the contemporary carpenters enabled them to make the late-Gothic ceiling a thing of outstanding merit. (Plate 18.)

The original incitement of the medieval carpenter towards aesthetic achievement was the conversion of the structural roof into an object of beauty in its own right. Centuries were to elapse before even a start could be made. Meanwhile the jumble of rough 'couples' formed but a rustic heaven when viewed from below. Thus the early architects were trying where possible to conceal it behind some kind of ceiling.

In the Age of the Mason the ceiling was a stone one. It first consisted of a system of stone tunnels running along the building with lateral ones crossing this at each bay. The amount of timber centering required to turn these vaults was very considerable. A scaffolding had to be erected and each stone held up by its individual prop until its particular ring of 'voussoirs' had been completed and the whole arch would stand.

By the twelfth century the principle of building arches in 'orders' had been extended to cover vault construction. Each 'groin' where the various tunnels intersected was set out as an arched rib built up on the usual timber centering. Between the skeleton thus provided each section of the vault could be turned independently and with greater ease than before. During the High Gothic era the number of ribs increased and the masons began to devise patterns to be set out in a reticulation of tracery sometimes even foliated like that of windows.

Vaulting, however, really belongs to the architecture of the great churches. A very expensive item, it is seldom found in parish churches except in some chancels and under the wooden floors of towers and the muniment rooms over porches, the 'stone solars' of the medieval builder.

The latest development of vaulting, in which it becomes a richly panelled ceiling springing in cones from each point of support and displaying the most enterprising pendants suspended in space between its sweeping spans, is only occasionally met with in unexpectedly beautiful side chapels contributed by some wool magnate of the fifteenth or sixteenth century. (Plate 30.)

Whether of boarded wainscot or stone vaulting, the ceiling of churches prior to their being covered with lead must have been a valuable asset. Early churches would have undoubtedly been covered with thatch of marsh-reed—the straw of those days would probably have been too short for the purpose. There are still some thatched churches remaining in East Anglia suggesting that all the original churches of the region may have been so covered.

The best buildings of pre-medieval England were covered with shingles. Salisbury Cathedral was designed to be so roofed and remained so until the middle of the thirteenth century. Shingles were narrow boards, today about two feet long, and probably then of oak. The bottom edge of each was rounded so as to direct storm-water passing down it away from the joint beneath. This produced a curious fish-scale appearance to the buildings which may clearly be seen in the Bayeux Tapestry. The original roof of the twelfth-century church of Kilmersdon in Somerset was carried on an exceptionally fine corbel-table supported on large and elaborately-carved corbels, between which the roof covering was repeated in stone to form a frieze passing round the building. The shingles depicted are four inches wide and laid to a gauge of six inches.

We do not know whether the shingles were fixed to battens as they are today. It seems possible that the roof was first boarded over to provide a ceiling below. The Bayeux Tapestry makes it clear that the 'bratticed' sides of timber buildings had the boarding hung with shingles.

The use of certain types of stone which could be saturated with water and left to a frost to split into tiles was known in Roman Britain. Many of these may have been salvaged from the ruins by the Anglo-Saxons. And the technique of manufacture must have been passed on to the medieval builder, for stone tiles were in use in many parts of England right through the Middle Ages and indeed right up to the present day.

Clay roofing tiles were being made in England as early as the thirteenth century and were being used in some districts for covering the high-pitched medieval roofs with something more durable than shingles. The manufacture of such tiles was however limited to such areas as could find suitable clay. The supply seems never to have been anywhere near up to the demand.

In addition to the frost-riven tiles of fissile stone there are the ancient slates of Westmorland and Cornwall, true slate-stones which make the finest roofing materials and moreover display lovely colours. At the end of the eighteenth century the grim grey slates of North Wales began to spread over the country. Their weatherproofing qualities make them the most watertight of this type of covering and they will last as long as their nailing can be kept from rusting. And their appearance, not so far removed in colour from the grey of lead, made them acceptable to the church architects of the Victorian era.

The builders of the High Gothic were particularly fortunate in that this country produced most of Europe's lead. The effect of this on our architecture is very noticeable. Continental architects continued to build the tall Gothic roofs to the very end of the medieval era, maintaining to the end of the Middle Ages the soaring effect of their buildings. In England, however, the use of lead brought the roof-pitch down towards the flat, and with it the form of the late-Gothic arch. A parallel example of the effect of materials upon architectural aesthetics may be found in Spain, where the low-pitch roof of interlocking 'Roman' tiles enabled the architects to build with depressed arches as in England. During the early sixteenth century we can detect a curious sypmathy between the two countries in respect of their architectural affinities—in England the four-centred arch, in Spain the three-centred.

Although we do not hear anything of the medieval plumber, as we do of his more expressive colleagues the mason and carpenter, his craft has always been a highly-skilled one and his contribution to our medieval architecture, albeit from what might be called the industrial angle, of the utmost significance to its development. Medieval lead was very heavy and had to be melted down in great cauldrons, probably on the building site, and there cast into sheets in wooden trays made up by the carpenter and covered with sand. The writer has employed such a plumber who worked in this fashion, stripping the old lead from a roof, melting it down, re-casting it, and re-laying it on the roof, all without leaving the churchyard.

The actual laying of the sheets is a skilled operation. The sheets are lapped horizontally like tiles but their edges have to be cunningly folded together after a fashion known only to the plumber.

Everything connected with the laying of lead is a specialized operation, for lead should not be nailed or it will tear. Its coefficient of expansion is so high that it is always on the move creeping to and fro. The replacement of the early projecting eaves with lead gutters set behind a parapet forced the plumbers to develop their special skill in laying their remarkable material until they had reached a degree of efficiency almost forgotten today.

The lead 'flashing' used today to cover the junction of leadwork with a wall was not used in medieval times, the practice being to divert the stormwater running down the wall-face with a projecting stone 'water-table'. The sites of these now cut back to the wall-face give the clue to many a vanished roof.

England has always been fortunate in the possession of good supplies of metallic ores which could easily be extracted by open-cast mining. Much of the lead used in the Roman Empire came from Mendip; the lead mines of medieval Derbyshire supplied much of Europe. The Forest of Dean and the Sussex Weald provided England with all the iron it needed.

In the days before the Factory Age most villages had a black-smith. The amount of ironwork used in the medieval village was minute by modern standards, but everything there was had to be his concern. And with the spirit of the age of craftsmanship affecting all tradesmen, the smith would if desired mould his practical rods and bars into interesting shapes for the greater glory of his craft. Thus magnificent church ironwork, especially in the orna-mentation of the church door, may be found from Anglo-Saxon days, in addition to the humble 'hooks and bands' upon which every door had to be hung. The smith had to fashion the 'ferra-menti' of stanchions and saddle-bars to which the leaded glazing of the windows was secured. And every nail used in the construction had to be hand-wrought by him.

A great deal of the ornamental ironwork of the medieval period is still in existence unaffected by the rust of possibly as much as a thousand years. This seems incredible having regard to our climate. It may be due to the fact that the medieval iron was smelted with charcoal instead of mined coal.

In a climate such as that of England the weakest point in the design of any building is the potential leakage to rain and wind represented by its windows. Thus all early windows were kept as small as possible. For quite apart from the areas presented by large windows to the elements, anything closing the opening would have

to be made of perishable materials. Thus where the quarries permitted, a common form of window used in belfries is formed of
thin stone slabs pierced with foliated openings.

Primitive windows, if they were closed at any time, used
wooden shutters for the purpose. They were not hinged but were
wedged into a rebate cut into the outer edge of the window such
as can still be seen in many a pre-medieval window. During the
last stand of the Saxon army at Hastings their shield wall was made
of hastily collected shutters.

Oiled linen fixed into a wooden frame was employed as 'glazing'
in small windows well into the medieval period, even in churches.

The glass of medieval days was made with great difficulty from
the outer portions of blown sheets and set as a mosaic of diamond-
shaped 'quarries' fixed together with a network of delicate grooved
strips hand-tooled by patient plumbers and known as 'calms'—
pronounced 'cames'. The painting and firing of pictorial glass
came into the province of the glazier whose methods may have
shared something of the experience of the contemporary potter.

During the twelfth century painted glass was reserved for the
great churches. It does not appear in the parish church until the
High Gothic era. In early days, heraldry provided the most popular
form of expression.

'Wide windows y-wrought . . .
Shining with shapen shields . . .'

The floors of humble churches may have been of beaten earth,
sealed, perhaps, with the blood of oxen. For only in certain parts
of England can one find stone suitable for splitting into the comparatively thin slabs required for paving. In the West, huge slabs
of slate were available, but it is only in the stone regions of Somerset
and Yorkshire that true paving stones could be discovered. Many
churches may have been floored with water-worn cobbles from
stream beds or old alluvial areas of geological days.

Since the ninth century the ecclesiastical authorities had insisted
upon the kneeling position for confronting the more sacred phases
of the Mass. Hence many church floors may have been carpeted
with rushes. There was of course no fixed seating until the fifteenth

century. Prior to this the congregation had stood or moved slowly about the building when not actually kneeling.

The altar would have always been raised upon a 'foot-pace' similar to the dais raising the high-table above the rush-strewn 'marsh' of the contemporary great hall.

Special tiles were being made for this purpose by the thirteenth century. They were usually yellowish in tone and were decorated with the tri-lobate 'stiff-leaf' motif of the period, later with beasts and heraldic shields. Highly glazed to preserve their surface, they are today known as 'encaustic' tiles, but in medieval days simply as 'painted' tiles. They were often set out in groups of four; borders too were manufactured. A number of monastic houses, notably Chertsey Abbey in Surrey, had factories for making these tiles. During the nineteenth century vast quantities of them, known as 'Minton' tiles, were made in the interest of church restoration. Thousands of grave-slabs were levered up from the floors of medieval chancels and replaced with Minton tiles.

For the paving of the main body of the church imported bricks could be used. 'Flanders tiles' and 'Holland tiles' had come into use by the fourteenth century, probably brought back as ballast in ships carrying wool to the Low Countries from the great East Anglian ports now vanished beneath the waves.

It should be remembered that the interiors of churches were places of sepulture for local notabilities. This must have caused frequent disturbances to the church paving which must in consequence have seldom presented a level appearance. When fixed seating came in during the fifteenth century interment would presumably have been thereafter restricted as far as possible to the open spaces between the blocks of seats.

As early as the twelfth century the walls of churches were being decorated with paint. By the end of the medieval period much of the wall-painting is of a high order; but nothing is known of the artists who contributed it as well as probably a still greater amount of painted pictures once ornamenting the walls of the great churches now vanished for ever. Much 'superstitious' painting must have been obliterated during the seventeenth century when the white-washing of church interiors was in vogue.

9

Pre-Medieval Architecture

To the Anglo-Saxon, building was an incomprehensible trade. There was no word for it. All construction was known as 'timbering'. Boat-building they understood, and the stepping of a mast on its keel. When raising a tall building they first laid sleepers on the ground and then erected posts on the foundation thus assured. Such a rapid system of building, far quicker than the raising of a wall by placing stone upon stone, was ideally suited to the erection of a church which needed at all costs to achieve the monumental element of height. Raise four tall posts and a tower was well under way.

As workers in wood the Anglo-Saxons were familiar with the principles of joinery technique and thus could provide their timber towers with the struts and braces necessary to assure their rigidity. (Fig. 6.) For covering they had two methods of using the by-products of their timbering. Oak shingles could be used as in later tile-hanging to provide a waterproof sheathing. Or a sturdy wall standing up in its own right could be formed with the rounded planks sawn in the pits from the squaring of the great posts and beams, framed into horizontal timbers at sill and head.

A few of their timber churches of late date have been preserved to serve as bell-towers at the west end of later stone naves (Plate 1), connection with which has resulted in the loss of their eastern aisles and their chancels. In addition to these almost perfect tower-churches, the remains of many more are probably to be found enclosed within the western ends of later stone naves, having been retained to carry bells. Hundreds must have disappeared without trace, burnt by Danes or in later conflagrations, or simply pulled down for shame at their rusticity. They have however their memorials in stone towers such as those of Barton-upon-Humber (Plate 3) in Lincolnshire or Barnack and Earls Barton in Northamptonshire. The so-called 'long-and-short' work at the angles of early stone churches is clearly intended to represent timber posts, each separate vertical stone having, however, to be held in position by a horizontal one 'bonded' into the wall.

An early stone tower such as that of Earls Barton is of the greatest interest as it indicates the elaboration of the contemporary wooden structure. Cross-bracing or 'saltires' are shown, and even timber arches—recalling the wooden 'stave-churches' at Urnes and Borgund in Norway. Short stone 'headers' are built in here and there as required to tie in the long stone 'timbers'. The system is of course purely decorative. It may be partly nostalgic, partly in the nature of an apology for a lack of proper architecture with which to embellish a building of such importance.

When one recalls that early Anglo-Saxon England built entirely in timber and that perhaps from the eighth century onwards they were actually constructing churches in that material, it is indeed tragic that the whole of that early timber architecture has been lost to us. During the following century the forays of the Danes across England resulted in church-burning on an extensive scale and much of the original work must have vanished at that time. But following the pacification of the invaders at the end of the ninth century church building would presumably have recommenced on an extensive scale. Thus we might have hoped that at least a few tenth-century examples of Anglo-Saxon timber architecture could have been preserved.

Such buildings as remain, however, are probably two centuries later. Complete ones—save for their chancels—form a group in Essex. They are timber parish churches on the 'four-poster' plan. The great church at Blackmore, however, is believed to be of monastic origin. Its nave is two bays in length, on the Byzantine 'duplex' plan. (Fig. 5.) Above this reaches an impressive network of timbering crossing and criss-crossing on its way towards the belfry stage high over the centre of the church. It was aisled about, but the eastern aisle was removed when a twelfth-century stone nave was added. This great timber church is possibly itself of mid-twelfth century date, but only by subjecting its timber to the modern radiological test could one obtain a closer dating and even then the factor of error could cover more than a century.

It was not until recent years that the true nature of these remarkable turriform churches, Anglo-Saxondom's tribute to Byzantine architecture, came to be realized. For some reason they were regarded as bell-towers added during the fifteenth century to the stone naves. But scientific investigation of the timbers of Navestock church in Essex, carried out by Mr. C. A. Hewett, confirmed the writer's view as to the real date of the structures by indicating the year 1193 with an allowance for error of sixty years each way. The preservation of the Essex group of churches is undoubtedly due to the difficulty of obtaining stone for bell-towers in this part of the country. Others, however, may be discovered elsewhere, absorbed by the stone walling of a thirteenth-century nave.

One can learn a great deal from a study of these remarkable buildings. One is struck most forcibly by the pure Gothic of their elevational form due to the use of the wooden 'cruck' or timber arch everywhere in the design. We know that the pointed arch had entered into Eastern Byzantine architecture as early as the seventh century and must have often been encountered by Crusading travellers; and it is clear that the Gothic arch is far more stable structurally than the primitive form. That Gothic as a *timber* style was in existence as early as the eleventh century is indicated by the illustration in the Bayeux Tapestry of the Confessor's hall at Westminster.

Passing from Anglo-Saxon timberwork to their efforts as builders in stone we find the picture shrinks considerably, for their work is primitive and appears to lack any stylistic influence at the level of the parish church. One may even wonder whether the ordinary Anglo-Saxon builder ever really learned to build in stone at all until a date well after his conversion to Christianity.

It must surely now be accepted that Anglo-Saxon England was not in fact destroyed at the Norman Conquest. And recent ethnographical research has suggested that the Anglo-Saxon settlement itself did not automatically eject the indigenous inhabitants and that for a long time to come the 'Welshmen', as they were called, continued to play a large part in the social life of the country. It is even suggested today that cranial measurements and so forth indicate the average Englishman is far more Celt than Teuton.

So the possibility exists that the men who raised the early stone churches for the first Anglo-Saxons who were received into the Celtic Church of their day were in fact themselves Celts, building in the same primitive rubble style as was employed in contemporary Ireland.

The churches they would have built would have been of the utmost simplicity, having but a nave and a chancel. (Fig. 13.) This type of plan survived in hundreds of small parish churches right through the glorious days of the twelfth century and indeed right through the Middle Ages, always recalling the Celtic, not the Byzantine, origins of the English Church. (Plate 7.)

While for ritual purposes the Celtic plan of nave and chancel was all that was actually required architecturally such structures must have been very unsatisfying. The great minsters were showing what could be done to raise a church towards the clouds by means of towers. And when one realizes that every tower had to be roofed in steeple-fashion it at once becomes apparent that the architectural brilliance of those days has gone without recall.

Four types of towers were to be found. There were original turriform structures of Western Byzantine form, some of them still serving their original purpose and others attached to the western ends of expanding churches. In the minsters were those central lantern towers, lightly-constructed upward projections of the walling providing a tier of windows lighting the choirs below. A number of stone turriform tower-naves of the Barnack type must have been in existence as well as scores of timber towers such as was to be seen later at Blackmore. In addition to all these structures there were the slender Byzantine bell-towers which we can see today all along the eastern side of England from Durham through the East Riding to Lincolnshire and East Anglia. These towers look impressive enough under their medieval lead flats.

What must the countryside have looked like when every tower was steeple-crowned?

Although the bell-tower at the west end of the nave is in by far the majority of cases an addition of the fourteenth or fifteenth century it would seem very likely that the England of the eleventh twelfth and thirteenth centuries was a many-steepled land and this not only by reason of the great host of monastic houses whose countless towers have toppled into the dust.

It may be that the continued existence of such an apparently inexplicable structure as the axially-planned church of the twelfth century with its central tower but no transepts is simply due to the need for incorporating a tower into the design. And while a bell-tower of the Anglian type can carry a bell but is no use for accommodating a congregation, a central tower can serve both purposes.

It is also possible that the type of church-plan represented by the remains at Barton-upon-Humber in Lincolnshire which has a chancel and west nave but no wings (see Fig. 7b) may have been quite common in eleventh-century England and that the axial church is thus simply its twelfth-century successor.

Returning to the early stone churches of England and their possibly very primitive character there can be no doubt that although timber was the national building material at the time, there was ample field-stone available for the raising of a simple stone-walled structure such as a primitive 'Celtic' church. If lime could not be obtained for making mortar—and one can imagine that the monasteries were very probably monopolizing supplies of this expensively-produced substance—the stones could be laid 'herringbone' and and thus prevented from falling out of the wall.

In this or any other form of stone building the real problem was how to secure the angles of the building. Here the ruins of Roman towns may have provided the solution. One can imagine the search for cut stones and salvaged bricks to be used for the essential 'quoins' of the structure.

Apart from primitive doors and windows only one important architectural feature was needed, the doorway leading from the nave into the chancel. The building style being basically arcuated, the opening would have to have an arched head. During the development of church-building in stone one can follow the gradual widening of the chancel arch from the first narrow openings lined with massive stones to the more spacious features more daintily formed in architectural style with properly masoned stonework.

The next most important feature architecturally was the entrance door. The uncertainty with which the early builders tackled arch construction is indicated by the way in which they would avoid it by using a triangular door-head formed of two lintels leaning against each other. (See Plate 3.) Yet even by the eleventh century the influence of Byzantine architectural contacts led them to adopt the combined arch-and-lintel construction with the semicircular 'tympanum' for spanning narrow openings.

To the early builder in stone the turning of an arch upon its wooden centering must have been a considerable feat. And as he attempted wider spans, his ignorance of the principles of abutment would have constantly led him into situations when his new arch began to let him down. Many a chancel arch of the twelfth century —and later—looks alarmingly unstable today, having been steadily collapsing until some late medieval-builder at last saved the situation by adding a buttress.

During the eleventh century the principle of centering an arch in expanding 'orders' saved some of the centering and lightened the appearance of the finished arch. Finally the introduction of ornament in the way of roll-mouldings to soften the edges of the orders began to pave the way for the richly-moulded arches of the Gothic era.

The 'imposts' from which an arch sprang were important to the design. Early imposts, like the soffits of the arches they carried, were plain stone faces. But with the ordered arch came the half-shaft passing up the centre of the impost to carry the lowermost order (see background in Plate 9.)—a Byzantine device used in connection with the 'duplex' system of employing small arches carried on columns within the span of great arches supported by heavy piers. Sometimes there was a pair of such shafts set side by side. All have caps of some description, either the formal 'cubical' type or crudely-carved where the architecture was unsophisticated and the carvers enterprising.

In those early days, carving was an alternative to a sophisticated architectural ordinance. The latter is clearly illustrated by plain arches rising from square imposts with embellishment restricted to neat rolls worked on the edges. When carved caps appear one knows that local enthusiasm has replaced architectural supervision.

This is in fact the key to that fascinating period in the history of architecture, the twelfth century in England. For the great monastic houses not only monopolized the building trade but the architectural 'profession' as well. The minsters were set out and detailed in accordance with an accepted ordinance. The parish churches 'did it themselves' making up for lack of sophisticated knowledge by taking full advantage of the versatility and enthusiasm of the amateur. It is to this charming quality of the vernacular in Anglo-Saxon church building that we owe the wonderful riches of the 'Norman' doorway with its limitless range of motifs. No other western historical style can equal this for exuberance.

It was during the twelfth century that the style reached its zenith. Beginning with the two doorways, the entrance doorway and that leading into the chancel, the riot of sculpture spread over arcades and even wall-faces, in almost oriental profusion. The church of Elkstone in Gloucestershire is an example of one of the liveliest of these sculptors' playgrounds.

None of this detail is architectural. For such is usually restricted to the great churches. The Byzantine wall-arcade is an example of this staider form of ornament, which may however still be seized upon by the sculptors for embellishment according to their peculiar taste.

A great deal of architectural embellishment is of the form known as 'aedicular'—the repetition of a structural feature in miniature for ornamental purposes. The 'blind arcade' is an example frequently met with in all periods of medieval architecture, formed in or in front of a plain wall-face and often providing a framing for a range of small windows. The miniature arcade occurs everywhere as a wall-decoration, either as a dado or imitating one of the upper galleries found in Eastern Byzantine churches. Another aedicular device is the flanking of windows with tiny reproductions of columns with cap and base. (Plate 8.)

The beginnings of architecture in England were the result of the colonization of the country by Benedictine monks from the Continent. Eastern Mercia was the original Benedictine sphere of operations, and the Barnack quarries in Northamptonshire its first source of building stone. In this connection it is of interest to note that three of the most elaborate stone tower-naves surviving today, Barnack, Earls Barton, and Barton-upon-Humber (Plate 3), are grouped together at this north-eastern end of the freestone belt.

It is tempting to suggest that the stone tower-nave may have originated there and spread south-westwards along the stone areas. The writer has noticed them at North Leigh in Oxfordshire, Netheravon in Wiltshire, and Hemyock in Devon.

The western arch at Netheravon is a very elaborate one. Hemyock has lateral arches only, which is of interest as the planner of the church at North Elmham in Norfolk actually regarded the north-south axis as the more important and his nave runs across the building, which in this case, however, has no central feature. The church at Breamore in Hampshire (Plate 4) with its large turriform nave is quite close to the stone belt.

The 'Anglian' architectural style which developed with the original Benedictine areas in eastern Mercia is almost pure Byzantine and used the massive square pier with angle rolls or shafts as its characteristic supporting member for aisle arcades. This might be called the 'Doric' of Anglo-Saxon architecture—indeed the cubical cap it employs upon its shafting is actually a derivative of the Greek Doric capital.

At one time there must have been a great many parish churches lined with arcades founded upon the heavy Anglian piers. (Plate 9.) The obstructive nature of the supports, however, resulted in nearly all these arcades being subsequently remodelled with lighter pillars in the Gothic style. In many churches though, the old Anglian responds remain as mementos of the original design.

The Anglian style spread throughout the eastern parts of the country and into Wessex. But at the close of the eleventh century a new monastic immigration began to take root in Western Mercia beside the heart of the stone belt where it formed the Cotswolds. It was the Burgundian Cluniacs, a wealthy Order which aimed at rivalling the Benedictines with their building programmes. With them the Cluniacs brought the first sophisticated architectural style.

It will be recalled that the principal feature of Classical architecture was the circular column, first drum-built then turned on a lathe, and always provided with a sculptured capital. It was these columns which had lined the original basilicas of Rome, and in Latin eyes must have represented the only supporting features acceptable in a Christian church, the massive piers of the Byzantines being regarded as crude and barbarous.

At the close of the eleventh century, the Cluniac monks began to set about the introduction of the circular pillar as a rival intended to oust the Anglian pier. While the turning of a column required the construction of a stone lathe, circular pillars could be built up in masonry or even in drums if the pillar was small in diameter. Thus during the twelfth century a Western type of circular pillar —perhaps the only true 'Romanesque' feature in English architecture—came into general use in the parish churches of the period. (Plate 10.)

The finest of the Byzantine churches were provided with upper stories set between the great piers, the floors of these galleries being carried upon small columns. This association of pier and column—the last in Western Byzantine architecture represented by a circular pillar—resulted in the 'duplex' bay system in which pier and pillar alternate, an effect which may sometimes be detected in the aisle arcades of twelfth-century parish churches.

The Anglo-Saxons employed only the simplest forms of architectural embellishment. The most common form is the edge-roll, used both to soften the edges of arch orders and the angles of the piers supporting them.

In vertical situations the edge-roll becomes virtually a slender colonette and as such needed a cap and a base.

Here the Classical Orders came under review for the purpose. The spreading Doric capitals known to students of such temples as the Parthenon were unsuited for use in confined situations such as the head of an edge-roll or a 'nook-shaft'. If on the other hand one should find a Doric capital with one angle broken off and should be tempted to break off the other three to adjust the balance, the residue would have very little projection beyond the shaft and would thus be quite suitable in a confined situation. Finished at the top with a suitable moulded strip these 'cubical' caps were adopted for completing the fully-developed shafts passing up the angles and filling the recesses of the ordered Byzantine piers. Immature moulded bases finished the shafts off at the bottom. The piers, like all walling of the period, rose from a simple chamfered plinth.

Such simple treatments completed the interior ordinance of the Anglian church of the eleventh century. But the new 'Romanesque' elements beginning to filter into the westerly districts required a different treatment.

The secondary columns which had supported the galleries of the major Byzantine churches had required spreading capitals which would provide a sound seating for the wide soffits of the arches springing from them. The architects, stronger here on the constructional side than on the aesthetic, produced a curious travesty of the Doric capital which is known as the 'cushion' capital and resembles nothing so much as one of these domestic objects split in half.

It was some form of the cushion capital which crowned the circular pillars of the Western style in England. As the twelfth century wore on it developed its own regional peculiarities. By association with the equally curious cubical capital it developed the system of convexities forming the 'coniferous' capital, while the Corinthian inspired the concave variation known as the 'scalloped'. Under the influence of the Crusades this began to sprout odd-looking 'volutes' at its angles until it eventually began to take upon itself some of the attributes of the Corinthian capital itself, the most beautiful architectural feature the world has ever seen and which could hardly have failed to enchant anyone who had ventured into Hellenistic lands.

A device which penetrated down from the great churches was that of vaulting. This was only used in parish churches where the walling was low and the building lacked aisles. Chancels were the part of the twelfth-century church most frequently vaulted. Ribbed vaulting was used, the heavy ribs being carried down upon imposts similar to those supporting main arches. The ribs themselves often lent themselves to the same elaborate ornamentation as the other arched members of the system.

While according full admiration to the building achievements of the twelfth century, it is necessary to recall that these were the result of a prodigal use of materials employed with an almost complete absence of the most elementary knowledge of static engineering. Simple stresses in buildings were beyond the comprehension of those who made them. As experienced timber-workers they were familiar with the spread of roofs and the effect of this on any walling upon which a roof might be raised. They could secure the timbers with braces, but the use of abutment to prevent the overturning of a wall was beyond their comprehension. They could strut up a timber wall, but never discovered how to turn a wooden strut into a stone buttress.

The arch was a mystery to them. They knew it had to be turned on a timber centering but had not the remotest idea of the forces waiting to destroy the arch as soon as the centering was struck. With supreme faith they performed immense labours in raising the huge crossing piers of their minsters. Again and again these collapsed under pressure from the surrounding arcades. But the builders never understood why. Even as late as 1225 they had not discovered where the fault lay, as the distorted crossing piers of Salisbury Cathedral demonstrate to this day.

The low arcades of the parish churches carried little load and have survived without misfortune. But as chancel arches widened and absorbed more and more of their abutment the weight of the gable over began to squash the arch and spread the imposts until many collapsed. And the buttress—as an *abutment*—does not in fact reach the parish churches until the era of the High Gothic.

So the buttress in its familiar Gothic form was not a feature of the pre-medieval church. Yet they were not by any means lacking in external punctuation.

The Anglo-Saxon builders—and that includes those of the trade who continued operations after the Norman Conquest—would have had their architectural approach to any building coloured by hereditary familiarity with timber techniques, in particular the basic ordinance of bay design as represented by the row of posts forming the long side of a building. As a stone building has no posts, the temptation would be to indicate the bays by some masonry feature externally. Internally, of course, pillars supporting an aisle arcade would automatically establish a masonry bay ordinance. The early masons recorded this on the external wall-faces by applying vertical stone projections or pilasters as it were recalling the posts of a timber building.

These pilasters played an important part in the elevation of the twelfth-century church. Often they had their angles softened by the edge-rolls of the period. Sometimes the slender shafts thus produced had their own small cubical caps and primitive bases.

At the angles of the building the pilasters might be paired, with perhaps an extra nook-shaft between them. But the most common arrangement was a square projection known as a 'clasping pilaster'. (Plate 8.)

The ordinance which became established at this period for the exterior of the parish church is of the utmost simplicity. The bays are indicated by the pilasters, but these reach neither the ground nor the eaves, being set on the plinth and merging into the 'corbel-table' above, all three features having the same projection from the wall-face to facilitate the union. In the centre of each bay is a window.

While some churches had quite large windows filled with glazing, the windows of the pre-medieval parish church were generally very small and had their interiors widely splayed so as to diffuse as much light as possible. They are always set high up in the walling, probably so as to collect as little stormwater as possible. And as the walls of early naves were usually extravagantly high in themselves in order to emphasize the dignity of the building, they seem to us today to be very high indeed.

One may often find traces of small round-headed arches showing above a Gothic nave arcade. These are not, as might have been supposed, the remains of an earlier clearstory, but simply vestigia of the original windows of a pre-medieval nave.

The window most typical of Byzantine architecture is the *bifora* with its two small arched heads divided by a squat colonette carrying a rectangular slab set at right angles to the wall-face. It was incapable of being glazed and is met with for the most part in belfries. (Plate 3, also 6.)

Punctuation is an important factor in all elevational architecture. It tidies up the elevation by establishing an ordinance, without which the building may appear as an ill-considered assortment of odd features. Vertical punctuation disciplines an elevation by sorting it out into orderly compartments and replacing confusion with a pleasant rhythm. (Plate 6.) This is the function of the bay as used not for constructional purposes but as an aesthetic device. Vertical punctuation is of course achieved by the pilasters, later becoming buttresses.

Horizontal punctuation is primarily concerned with maintaining a sense of stability. The tablement or plinth is of course a primary example of this. The impressive ordinance of the corbel-table performs the same function for the upper part of the building by disciplining the eaves of what might be a somewhat rustic roof. The other function of horizontal punctuation is the linking together of what might otherwise be isolated features, especially windows. Horizontal lines joining the sills of windows stabilize an elevation.

Any arcuated style is apt to produce a restless effect through the constant rise and fall of the series of arches covering it. The value of horizontal punctuation here is its use to join together the arches at their springing lines, a device which at the same time stabilizes the individual arches themselves. (See Plate 11.)

The complete medieval window usually incorporates a projecting moulding called a 'drip-stone' which passes round the arch and throws off stormwater coming down the wall-face above which might continue down the glazing. These moulded drip-stones play a significant part in medieval architecture aesthetically as well as practically, as they are frequently carried across from window to window as 'string-courses' and thus form an important item in the horizontal punctuation of an elevation.

The string-course is of the utmost value internally for it plays a number of parts. As a drip-stone passing round the arcades it prevents condensation from dropping on the heads of the congregation. (Plate 10.) But its most important function is to serve as an 'impost moulding' marking the top of a pier or impost and indicating the springing line of its arch. As it does this it may be extended along the wall, as it was externally, to link one springing line with another. When joining the sills of windows together it provides horizontal punctuation to the interior of a building.

All these 'tablements' or moulded stone planks which may seem so insignificant compared with the major architectural features of a building play in fact a very important part in Gothic design. In each period their mouldings are more or less standard; thus they can give important clues to the dating of a building. The pre-medieval profile was square at the top but had its underside chamfered away. (Fig. 27*a*.)

The principal architectural feature of the pre-medieval parish church was its doorways. Of these the most important was the entrance to the chancel. At first this was simply an arched opening, but the extraordinary development of vernacular carving during the twelfth century completely transformed this most significant feature into a portal of barbaric splendour unparalleled in any other historical architectural period.

The doorway into the church was a miniature of the chancel arch and probably served as the original model for the greater feature. The 'arch-and-lintel' combination developed in earthquake ridden Syria and brought over at the time of the Crusades introduces the semicircular 'tympanum' as a site for pictorial carving. (Plate 29.)

The development of the elaborate arches grows out of their construction in a series of expanding orders. The imposts of the chancel arches and the jambs of the entrance doors are similarly ordered to match those of the arch. Sometimes the sides of the openings are carved with the same abandon as the arches, but more often the shaft with its cap and base is used instead.

One of the aesthetic delights of the study of architecture is the investigation of the aesthetic expressions common in each individual generation. While today the architect seems determined to be different from his colleagues and painfully striving to devise new methods of expression, his predecessor during the great days of English architecture worked with the national team, accepted the general lines of any particular type of treatment, and within these limitations demonstrated his skill and inventiveness.

Each period has had its own sign-manual in respect of running ornament. The ancient Greek fret is an example, and so too are the lovely sweeping vine-scrolls of the heyday of the Hellenistic which architects could not bear to allow to disappear but carried along with the centuries through the Byzantines and into Anglo-Saxon England.

Our own pre-medieval sign-manual is the ubiquitous zigzag or 'chevron'. Clearly of wood-carving origin, it must have been developed from taking two opposing swings of an axe at the edge of the timber to remove what woodsmen call a 'kerf' and then continuing all along the edge of the timber until the whole edge had become serrated. It is less a carver's device than a lumberman's. During the twelfth century the zigzag develops every conceivable kind of variation and begins to achieve the systems of rolls and deep hollows associated with the Gothic mouldings of the next century. It becomes altogether lively and not without charm. (Plate 10.)

The heavy angle-rolls with which the early masons relieved the crudeness of their jambs and arch orders began to expand into moulding systems which for the most part consisted of convex members. Occasionally broad shallow hollows appear, but nothing approaching the deep channels of the early-medieval period. And should a hollow appear, the carvers seem to have been constrained to fill it in at intervals with punctuation in the form of little pyramids or 'nail-heads'.

Part of the charm of Anglo-Saxon carving lies in its irresponsibility. This is particularly noticeable in connection with the voussoirs of which an arch is composed. No attempt was made to keep each stone equal in size. Thus the angles of the zigzag were all different, though set out to the same template so that they would meet at the joints. This casualness presumably originated with the grotesque schools of carving which produced beak-heads and similar motifs needing no system of continuity. (Plate 29.)

It is strange that any art historian could ever have regarded an architectural style which makes such a feature of the grotesque as 'Romanesque'. Surely the writhing dragon is a product of North-Western Europe and can have no counterpart in the folk-lore of Italy.

How welcome are the Anglo-Saxon dragons into the architecture of our land! And how homely seems the vigorous human element displayed by the caricatures ranged along a corbel-table! Childish, perhaps, but after all they represent the childhood of our architecture.

10

Early Medieval Architecture

═══════

For many decades past, architectural historians have been concerned to divide their subject into stylistic periods. They encounter the difficulty that such divisions are anything but clearly delineated. For styles not only merge into each other but change and interchange amongst periods and between regions. The early antiquaries employed a simple yardstick for separating the 'Saxon' and the 'Gothic' in the change of the shape of the arch from semicircular to pointed. They still, however, had to try to explain such anomalies as the appearance of zigzag ornament along a pointed arch, or a semicircular arch which unaccountably rose above graceful Gothic shafting. So they set aside the tremendous twelfth century as a period of 'Transition'.

Actually the change of the arch silhouette, though due to structural reasons, was of less architectural significance than the changes in the church plan and the abandoning of the old pseudo-Classical forms of the capitals which marked the end of the so-called 'Transitional' period and indicated the end of Byzantinism and the beginnings of a national English style later to develop into magnificent architecture and produce buildings of superlative beauty.

The troubled reign of King John, with its tale of quarrelling armies straggling from siege to siege of antiquated fortresses, may be said to mark, approximately, the end of the early or Byzantine period of English architecture.

The long reign of Henry III was ahead. The previous century had experienced the Anarchy, followed by the turbulent reign of

Henry II during which barons and bishops had been building sturdily and had left their sign-manual on glorious minster as well as massive donjon. It had seen the Crusades, and many an English journey to Outremer and the cradle lands of the East. And thus contact with its origins must have done much to help perfect the architecture of the great Anglo-Saxon churches and their humbler brethren in the parishes.

But the Crusades had at the same time brought about a complete reorientation of England's Continental associations. Until the end of the eleventh century the link had been with the Teutonic lands, the Benedictines, and Byzantium. But colonization by Burgundian Cluny had fostered the Latin influence and started a centripetal swing focused on Rome which the Crusades had greatly strengthened. During the twelfth century England's long association with Teutonic, Byzantine, Germany was to weaken to extinction, to be replaced by a strong cultural contact with 'Romanesque' France, even to its language taking the place of English as the speech of the intelligentsia as well as of the new nobility.

With the coming of the thirteenth century refinement came to English architecture. The replacement of the axe as a finishing tool by the driven bolster revolutionized masonry technique and paved the way for an elaboration of architectural ornament worked on the banker and not left to the enterprise of the enthusiastic but undisciplined sculptor. Stones were better cut and walling more carefully laid with proper attention being paid to the strength of the core, so that walling could be less massive and openings more generous. The tooling marks were neatly aligned over the faces of the stones, and the whole presentation was clearly intended as a rejection of earlier barbarous effects.

The change from the Classical form of arch to the form which was later designated by the derisory adjective 'Gothic' is one of the most dramatic incidents in architectural history. That the latter is structurally more reliable is indisputable, and from this point of view alone it must have been more than acceptable to the illiterate successors of the great empires. Initially it was undoubtedly regarded as aesthetically barbarous. One might almost imagine that the Renaissance movement was started as a holy war for its extermination. Yet for a few generations it formed the basic element in what is probably the most beautiful architectural style the world has ever seen.

A great many students of architecture have been speculating upon the origins of Gothic architecture, as represented by the distribution of the pointed arch.

Once a more liberal and experimental type of architecture had superseded the established ordinance governing Imperial Roman architecture, the more reliable type of arch was bound to replace the simpler form. By the middle of the first millennium, the eastern parts of the Byzantine Empire which had absorbed the great Hellenistic culture had adopted it. The Omayyids, Moslem heirs to the Byzantines, took it up, and the lands of Outremer in which the Crusaders operated had changed to it well before their day.

Gothic architecture is in reality an abstract sensation—an urge to build, not vastly as in the days of the great empires, but as close as possible to the clouds. Its greatest achievements are triumphs of faith over ignorance. It employed the pointed arch because it had 'arrived'—that it happens to suit a vertical style is possibly quite fortuitous.

Its forms are not derived from masonry. For this produces massiveness. The lightness of Gothic architecture seems to indicate a structural system based upon carpentry. But its aesthetic spirit seems to link it with the forest glades of Western Europe, glories the Ancient World had never known.

The architectural style used by the designers of the great churches of the Anglo-Saxons had been a degenerate form of a noble style developed far away in a great empire. And it is difficult to appreciate today that the huge minsters raised by the Anglo-Saxons were actually the greatest buildings of their age. And their architecture died with them. It was not possible to bring them into line with the architecture of medieval England. They had either to remain as they were or be pulled down and rebuilt from the ground up.

The English Gothic marched more or less in step with that of the Ile de France. But magnificent though our efforts might be, they fell hopelessly behind the Continental achievements. Lincoln Minster is a beautiful thing, but Beauvais or Le Mans can look down upon it. In magnitude, England's supremacy had been surrendered.

But for beauty of style the English Gothic can hold its own. Not only at Lincoln and in a host of glorious churches now vanished except for forlorn fragments, but in the humble arcades of many a village church, allowing its rustic congregation a glimpse of surpassing loveliness. (Plate 13.)

The underlying difference between the early-medieval building and its predecessor is due to the excellence of its masonry work which enabled it to attempt a lightness of form which was the antithesis of the massiveness that marked the Byzantine. This light-handedness is all the more remarkable in view of the ignorance of structural engineering which plagued the builders. It seems essential to credit them with a perfect faith in their efforts to build to the greater glory of God. And when one realizes that the whole of the building potential of the age was absorbed in this work to the exclusion of improvements to living conditions, one can begin to realize a little of the inspiration behind medieval Christendom.

The ancient Greeks, the Romans, and the Byzantines, were mathematicians, and the two last civilizations produced capable engineers. Yet their buildings were massive and employed a wide factor of safety to achieve moderate heights. The English builder of the Middle Ages, lacking the slightest knowledge of engineering, would raise a lantern tower on tall piers which he had watched as they leaned inwards, watched again as they leaned outwards. When the tower began to break up he would pull it down and build it higher, finishing it off with a spire of stone until he had taken it over four hundred feet into the air. He could have had no idea whatever of the load per square inch he was placing on the bases of the piers. Did the masons as they piled stone upon stone ever consider for a moment that each one might be the last they would ever lay? Had they done so, would Gothic architecture have ever been?

Gothic architecture owes its effect to two factors, the grace of

its construction and the richness of its ornament. As in all architectural styles this is of two kinds. One is the carved ornament
applied to completed stonework and woodwork by artists. This
has no structural function. The other is the true architectural
detail by which structural features are moulded aesthetically to
disguise their purely structural application. This is the higher
function of the mason.

Peculiar to Gothic architecture is the running moulding, the
origins and development of which will be discussed in Chapter 15.
With the plainly ordered arch of Classical times submerged for
good beneath this Gothic richness, any such Classical remnants as
circular pillars or Corinthian capitals must have seemed anachro-
nisms. An early modification of the circular pillar was the addition
to it of four slender shafts, which helped it to equate more easily
with the moulded arch above. At first these shafts were detached,
turned on a lathe and secured to the pillar by built-in collars. But
the cruciform plan soon became homogeneous, with the four shafts
formed together with the stones of the pillar. This in various guises
became the standard parish church pillar for the remainder of the
medieval period. With the development of mouldings those of the
arch and pillar sometimes matched each other. In the richest
examples the springing line was indicated by small caps breaking
the lines of the more salient members passing up the column.

As the old capitals disappeared, and the mouldings of arches
and the pillars supporting them became closer in outline, two
methods of marking the springing line are found. One is the
presence of the small caps referred to above. The other is the
introduction of an impost moulding, sometimes quite elaborately
carved, passing round the whole perimeter of the pillar. The
versatility of the medieval builder is, however, also indicated by
the frequent use of a continuous treatment passing along pillar
and arch with a complete disregard for indicating the change
between the two.

We have noted that the pre-medieval string-course was a
crudely-shaped member having a square top surface and a chamfered lower edge. The early medieval was always a round 'bull-
nose' or 'torus'. In the richest work it was deeply undercut. A

narrow version used in both pre- and early-medieval architecture and continuing throughout the medieval period below the bells of caps is the 'astragal' retained from Classical times to mark the junction of capital and shaft. A Gothic impost moulding often consists of an upper 'torus', a carved bell, and an astragal below to contain this.

The carvings on capitals, though possibly derived from those on the Classical imposts, were soon to be completely Anglicized, the acanthus which formed the basic motif of those early days being replaced by other leaves presumably of English origin. The trilobate 'stiff-leaf' clover possibly represented the Trinity. Found everywhere during the thirteenth century, it later becomes replaced by less rigid, more naturalistic foliage.

Pillar bases were restricted to the simple chamfered plinth, except where colonettes or other special members called for individual bases to complete them. The model for the pre-medieval and early-medieval base was the Classical form having two torus mouldings separated by a concavity. Pre-medieval bases were shyly moulded, but with the moulding development which characterized the thirteenth century the Classical form was revived with a vengeance, the intermediate 'cavetto' becoming a channel so deep that it is called a 'water-holding' base.

While the buttress, as such, had still not become a part of the exterior ordinance of the medieval church, the pre-medieval pilaster had grown outwards from the wall until it had begun to resemble one. The aisles of Salisbury Cathedral were vaulted and there must have been a considerable strain upon the light walls. The buttresses, however, although part of the aesthetic design, were not built with the walls but added afterwards as ornament.

This introduction of a buttress-like feature is, however, an architectural event of the greatest significance. Byzantine architects, in common with those of all previous building styles, had limited their elevational treatments to a display of flat surfaces only broken by features of quite small projection. The presentation of anything of a protuberant nature was a development new to elevational architecture.

The significance was twofold. Firstly by emphasizing the bay it established the general lines of the architectural style to come. Above all it gave an assurance that Gothic architecture was to become a style which concentrated upon the vertical element in its punctuation and developed this as the very essence of its aesthetic appeal.

Forgetting for the moment that these features were eventually to project at right angles from the wall and become Gothic buttresses, and accepting them for the moment merely as punctuation devices with breadth and projection about equal, we can see that their appearance began to transform the whole of the exterior ordinance of the parish church. The determination with which the rhythm of the bay was maintained is indicated by the presence of a 'buttress' in the centre of the west wall of the thirteenth-century nave, having a window on either side of it instead of a central west window such as one would have found during the next century when the High Gothic style had become fully established and sophisticated designing was replacing primitive empiricism.

The west doorway is Byzantine in origin and is common during the twelfth century where it carries on the tradition of central feature to an entrance façade. It disappears during the thirteenth century as attention becomes drawn to its unsuitability in the English climate. The High Gothic restores it to its original status, regardless of whether or not a bell-tower is acting as a kind of porch for it.

Continuing the normal practice followed in bay design, windows were set in the middle of these. Few church naves or their aisles can still show windows of the thirteenth century as these were still very small, only differing from the pre-medieval window in that they had become slightly taller and had a pointed head. Thus most of these windows have since their introduction been replaced by more spacious ones displaying the tracery of the High Gothic era.

Development progressed, however, to the extent that windows became grouped in pairs. This is of importance as it was by closer grouping and reducing the amount of stonework separating the pair that the mullion was eventually discovered, a device which was to transform fenestration and pave the way to the traceried glories which play such a large part in Gothic architecture.

The place where early-medieval windows may usually be found today is lining the long chancels of the thirteenth century. Possibly the dim lighting they produced was helpful to the atmosphere required of a medieval chancel. The east wall was almost invariably lit by a triple group of lancet windows with the centre light higher than its fellows. These have nearly all been removed and replaced by larger windows. (Often, however, they may be found reinstated in a new position, in an aisle or the east wall of a transept.)

The cross-section of the early-medieval nave differed little from that of its predecessor where aisles were included in the design either originally or by enlargement. The aisles themselves were still quite narrow so that they could be gathered in within the compass of one wide roof. The clearstory does not really descend from the great church to the parish church until the era of the High Gothic when such features became common to all. (See Fig. 14.)

Between the twelfth and thirteenth centuries there came about a considerable change in carved ornament. All the earlier woodcarving crudities disappeared and were replaced by an attempted stylization which was tentative and unenterprising. This is possibly due to the monopolization of the more able artists by the monasteries which at the time were absorbing practically every craft concerned in building. Here and there, however, we find a parish church displaying really beautiful carving on capitals in an arcade. But generally speaking there is nothing in the early-medieval period to approach even remotely the enrichment of doorways and chancel arches one finds in the humblest churches during the twelfth century. (Plate 29.)

Something wonderful had been lost, leaving a void. That something was the glorious swan-song of a vigorous art become, alas, in contemporary eyes barbaric.

What happened to them all, that race of natural artists from whose skimming chisels grew the breath-taking chancel arch of Rutland's Tickencote? Did they really apply themselves to a study of other models until they could produce such entirely different forms as one finds during the thirteenth century? What one fears is that this carving emanates from schools founded and instructed by the monastic Orders, and that the feeble carving one finds in contemporary parish churches represents attempts by the remnant of the grand old carvers of Anglo-Saxondom to try to copy the new forms that were quite beyond their comprehension.

So passed the era of English Byzantine which in its day had given the world its greatest buildings. By the end of the thirteenth century the mason-craft of England had achieved establishment. From Barnack to Beer the quarrymen of the freestone belt had assured the country of its supply of walling material. Spreading forests were still there for the roofing.

Cistercian colonization of the wilder regions of the North and West had done for them what the Benedictines had done for Mercia a century or two earlier. The South was keeping going with chalk and flint and imported materials, still far behind Yorkshire and the Midlands in everything connected with architecture, its Continental links quite unable to help it to overcome the basic shortage of essential materials.

England was riding on the sheep's back. The parishes were flourishing. The country was ready, under the aegis of Holy Church, for two centuries of High Gothic.

II

High Gothic

=====

The era of High Gothic reaches from the last quarter of the thirteenth century across the first half of the sixteenth, the whole a period of the noblest architecture. Its complexity is only now beginning to be understood. It comprises those periods called by Rickman 'Decorated' and 'Perpendicular'. But this devoted architect, together with most of his successors, was working solely on stylistic grounds and failed to appreciate the difference between aesthetic style and historical period. In point of fact both of his styles, marked as they are by curvilinear and rectilinear window tracery, interlock throughout the period in accordance with local taste and structural requirements.

It is nevertheless possible to detect two divisions of the High Gothic period, which one might call Middle and Late Medieval, separated by the Black Death at the middle of the fourteenth century which destroyed half the population and must have brought an end to architecture on the grand scale for a generation. Prior to this catastrophe one finds exuberance, after it a loss of charm and a kind of hardening into austerity. Yet even the four-centred arch, assumed to represent the sign-manual of the fifteenth century, may be found associated with the normal Gothic arch, representing not period, but current taste.

The first or Mid-Gothic period was one of church-building on the monumental scale, mainly under monastic patronage. Its second half was the era of the parish church, funds for which were becoming diverted from the monasteries towards the expanding finances of the wool trade.

Thus for a start we have building on two scales, one emanating from the highly organized workshops of the great monastic houses, the other recruited locally in the parishes from journeymen and what might be called 'local builders'. Hitherto these men had been tradesmen of indifferent skill, not even the leavings of first-class establishments. But now church-building had become the province of properly trained and experienced men. Once it had only been possible to employ such craftsmen for important features such as arches, doorways and windows. Now the whole church was being built by professionals.

Nevertheless such 'local builders' lacked the contacts available to the large monastic workshops. Thus local style is much more noticeable in the parishes than it would be among the great church buildings.

It is this regionalism in parish church architecture which is still confusing students and making it virtually impossible to detach one period from another. A century and a half ago, Rickman was able to detect the difference between what he called 'Decorated' and the more austere 'Perpendicular'. Styles they certainly were, but as periods they cannot be so clearly established. Broadly speaking the graceful tracery of the 'Decorated' window preceded the panelled ordinance of the 'Perpendicular' but in actual fact both appear in important buildings at the very beginning of the High Gothic era and features of both styles may be found inextricably mixed together in parish churches of the fourteenth century. Thus it becomes hopeless to try to dogmatize about dates on stylistic grounds only.

Nevertheless both these manifestations have come to be accepted as *styles* for a century and a half; thus it is possible for them to be kept separate up to a point. But it must always be remembered that, unlike the pre-medieval and the early Gothic, they more than just overlapped, they actually intermingled, not for half a century, but for two.

The principal element which differentiates the early medieval from its succeeding periods is the use of lead for roofs. Most of Europe's supply of this material came from England, so that even the parish church could make use of it.

The true English roof, built of timbers and designed for a hard climate, was very steeply pitched to reduce the danger of its spreading or even collapsing under a load of snow. Originally thatched or sheathed with shingles, it was adequately watertight and could protect the timber buildings from deterioration. But such roofs, one of the basic elements from which Gothic architecture was created, suffered from lack of permanency.

Lead began to appear on the great churches during the late thirteenth century. Its introduction brought about a revolution in English architectural style. On a steep pitch it gives endless trouble as its weight causes it to slip down; its high coefficient of expansion makes it subject to continual 'creep'. Properly laid, however, it has the great advantage of needing hardly any pitch at all to keep out the weather and gives far less trouble from the two properties noted above.

Thus the High Gothic is based not on high roofs but on high walls carrying roofs which may at times be barely visible. The bottom of the roof suffered at the same time vital changes, for the high-pitched roof is carried out in wide eaves over which the stormwater falls clear of the walls and windows, while the lead roof is finished at the bottom with a lead gutter set behind a parapet and discharging through long spoutings. In this way the parapet came to be an integral feature of the High Gothic building, concealing behind it even more of the once all-important roof. (Fig. 22.)

The great church of the Ile de France had replaced the lofty Byzantine nucleus with a building raised as high as possible above the ground throughout its whole length, thus setting the pace for future Gothic buildings throughout Europe. The English church was far from aiming at anything of like scale. Bearing in mind that the village home of the period was a hovel owing nothing to the builder, it was very easy to raise the parish church to a height sufficient to enable it to soar above such pathetic structures. Thus stylistic factors changing the elevational form of the great contemporary abbey or cathedral have no bearing on that of the parish church.

The towering nave of a great church could double the width of its bays and still span them with a tall Gothic arch. But if a parish church were to do the same with, say, its chancel arch this would look ridiculous with a tall arch on comparatively stumpy columns. So with the increased spans coming into use the arches themselves came to pe pitched lower, a modification conveniently conforming with the lowering of the roof, now lead covered.

The early parish churches had been, each in its parish, of a magnificence most spectacular when compared with its architectural surroundings, though as nothing when compared with the great churches of the monks. For its particular purpose, however, it may well have been much too small and cluttered-up to accommodate all its parishioners. So the aim of the parish church builders of the High Gothic era must have been to provide more spacious buildings, still far removed in point of scale from the greater churches but still displaying a vertical element proportionate to their plans so that every aspect of dignity could be maintained. And for a crowning feature there would be the soaring bell-tower at the west end.

Internally, much of the archaic atmosphere of mystery had been banished from the chancel by the widening of its entrance arch. Privacy however was soon to be partly restored by the provision of a chancel screen.

The most noticeable improvement in the parish church was the enlargement of its windows. The development of the mullion which followed the coupling of windows during the thirteenth century had resulted in a multiplicity of lights and the consequent need for devising some system of carrying the glazing into the arched head of the window. It was in the course of solving this problem that the masons devised the technique of tracery, the innumerable variations in which bestow such glamour upon the churches of the High Gothic. The development of tracery design is undoubtedly due to the masons' experiments with the 'compasses'—which we should call today 'dividers'—on pieces of board available in the lodges. The stonework of medieval buildings is covered with examples of 'doodling', especially in geometric designs and rosettes, scratched into the stone.

The lines of mullions could be carried up into sub-arches concentric with the main arch. Or their direction could be changed every so often so as to form a reticulation. Each change of direction produced an 'ogee' form, the shape which provides French architects with their name for Gothic architecture. It may have been the French who invented the 'foliations' in which the lobes or 'foils' are separated from each other by projecting teeth or 'cusps'. One type of foliation displays a rounded foil attached to a long tail, called a 'flamme'. The popularity of this feature during a certain period in France gave a name to the style known as 'Flamboyant'.

One of the delights of Gothic is the silhouette which gives the whole style its French designation of 'Ogival'. Probably derived in part at least from the wavy cross-braces of timber architecture and encountered everywhere when following the flowing lines of tracery, the lively ogee is peculiar to the Gothic and creates one of the most opulent silhouettes in architectural history. In aedicular form, as for example when used above niches and completed with a crocketed finial, it provides a notable crowning motif unparalleled in any other architectural style.

Improvements in the natural lighting of parish churches during the High Gothic era were almost universal and resulted in the replacement of many of the earlier pre- and early-medieval windows. Sometimes, however, such improvements were restricted to the provision of new large windows at the most important point in the church, the neighbourhood of the chancel arch. Such windows may be seen at the east end of the nave or, where this is aisled, at the west end of the chancel. If there is a solitary window it will be on the south side.

The French builders who since the thirteenth century had been raising their towering churches, must have acquired a much wider experience of building statics and the means of combating them than was known to us here. Calculation was of course impossible, but the general nature of the forces involved in the destruction of an arch, and the means of opposing this, must have been appreciated by them. By the fourteenth century the device of the flying buttress was being employed by English builders. But it was still only just being realized that the principle of top-loading a buttress to provide a counterpoise against a lateral thrust could add greatly to the defence against the arch. It was this discovery which not only encouraged them to raise their central towers but also enabled them to check the creeping collapse which had for so long been threatening the early crossings and the lanterns above them.

In parish churches the buttress comes into its own during the fourteenth century. At the angles of buildings it henceforth adopts a diagonal stance so as to appear to be checking any possibility of the angle coming away through the loosening of its quoin-stones. In masonry of any quality whatsoever the risk was very small. But the diagonal buttress becomes a standard item of ordinance for the remainder of the medieval period. (See, however, Chapter 8.)

With the buttress was associated the pinnacle which provided its top-load and also served as an ornamental finial. And with the

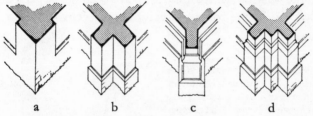

a   b   c   d

Fig. 21 *Buttresses*
(a) The 'clasping pilaster' seen at the angles of twelfth-century buildings. (b) The thirteenth-century arrangement. (c) The 'French buttress' found throughout the High Gothic period. (d) A fifteenth-century arrangement.

pinnacle is also associated the parapet, the crowning feature of the wall which had superseded the eaves of earlier days. The early-medieval parapet retained the corbel-table and employed it to bring the parapet forward and allow for a wider gutter behind it. The later parapet replaced the corbel-table with a string-course which was usually of a cornice-like form and enabled the parapet to be advanced as before if required.

By perhaps the year 1400 the elevational appearance of the well-masoned Gothic parish church had settled down to a recognized ordinance, based, of course, on the bay. This seems to have varied from twelve to sixteen feet in width, indicated by buttresses passing up the elevation, divided in two or three places by receding set-offs, and either dying into the string-course below the parapet or carried up through it to end in a pinnacle.

The lower part of the wall is given a standardized plinth treatment. The lowest member of this is the 'tablement' forming the base of the building and may be simply a plain chamfered plinth. After a couple of feet or so of plain stonework the main plinth moulding appears. This is a curious ogee-shaped projection hanging down in a not very attractive fashion. It seems difficult to equate this with the 'pedestal' ordinance found in Classical ordinance but there seems to be no other possible origin for this curious triple arrangement. The Classical form of pedestal is crowned by a cornice—a clumsy projection upon which even the ugly Gothic ogee is an improvement.

At the wall-top, where this changes to become the parapet, there is always a string-course, usually a wide 'cove', which is the

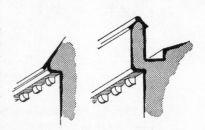

Fig. 22
Eaves and Parapet
The original function of the 'corbel-table' was to fill in under the eaves of a high-pitched roof. It was retained beneath the parapet of a low-pitched lead roof to bring the parapet forward and increase the width of the lead gutter behind.

Gothic equivalent of the Classical cornice. This is an important feature as it indicates the level of the vital gutter which collects the stormwater from the roof. The spoutings or gargoyles are set out along the line of this string-course.

The parapet may be flush with the wall or may take advantage of the coved string-course to project slightly. In humbler work the parapet may have a straight 'saddle-back' coping, but the most common arrangement is the battlement, often supported aesthetically by the pinnacles separating the bays.

Within the area enclosed between the buttresses, the heavy plinth, and the parapet is the large traceried window of the High Gothic era. This usually has a 'drip-stone' passing round the arch to prevent stormwater running down the wall-face above from continuing down the glazing. Sometimes these drip-stones rise from carved 'stops' at the springing line, but often this line is carried across between the buttresses in the form of a string-course.

Even the smallest parish church endeavoured to build for itself a bell-tower, almost invariably at the west end. It might be very plain, with no angle buttresses—indicating that such were regarded as ornamental but not essential. By the High Gothic period it would be parapeted and very probably have pinnacles at the angles. The most important element in the tower was its belfry stage, now carrying a ring of bells, perhaps as many as eight. The belfry windows would be treated as architectural features. Below the belfry was usually a ringing-floor, lit by a small window on each face.

The lower part of the tower formed part of the accommodation of the church with which it was connected by a tall arch. At the base of the tower there was usually a west door, not intended to be a normal entrance to the church but for the re-entry into the building of the Palm Sunday procession. The west doorway was usually treated architecturally so as to give an effect of a façade. Normal doorways were seldom so treated, but during the High Gothic era the front of the south porch was nearly always embellished to form a frontispiece.

The effect of the west tower of the English parish church relies upon the fact that it may be seen to rise from the ground. It is axiomatic in architectural design that every tower must do this if it is to achieve its full status. Imagine the effect of Canterbury's Angel Tower standing in magnificent isolation instead of rising above a clutter of roofs which absorb half its height!

The appeal of the central tower—seen in so many of the thirteenth-century parish churches—is partly that it carries on the old Byzantine tradition of providing a crowning feature to a great building, and partly due to its being the 'status-symbol' expected of a great church. And there can be no wonder at the appearance during the High Gothic era of such glorious parish churches as Yorkshire's Hedon or Patrington. But such were enormously expensive productions and are exceptional. The average village church could produce something equally impressive in height by building a western tower, a fact which is demonstrated by so many villages in Devon and Somerset.

The tradition of the timber 'broach' is continued with the High Gothic spire of timber or stone but the feature is surrounded by a parapet, often ornamental and sometimes provided with angle treatments based on tall pinnacles and perhaps flying buttresses. Some of the more elaborate tower-tops were adjusted to form elaborate stone 'lanterns'. (Plates 14 and 28.)

Records tell us that there were once many more parish spires than we see today. They were expensive items to raise, and once the elements had brought about such injury to a spire that it had become unsafe, a change in the fortunes of the parish might have made its replacement impossible. The same can be said of our cathedrals, a number of which have lost their spires. Add to these the spires of vanished abbeys and one can imagine the English landscape of the fourteenth and fifteenth centuries alive with Gothic steeples. (This subject is elaborated in Chapter 14.)

The great enemy of a spire is lightning. The lightning conductor is a modern invention. Even in these days the writer has seen more than one stone spire riven by a strike. A timber broach would have speedily been transformed into a beacon. Should this have happened after the thirteenth century the broach would almost certainly have been replaced by a simple flat lead roof.

While externally the churches of the High Gothic era had become architecturally excellent due to the accumulated skill of centuries of mason-craft, their interiors, although not very much more spacious and lofty, had lost much of the charm of earlier days and as time went on began to approach austerity. The semi-barbaric mouldings which had rioted with such enthusiasm over the arches had been pruned down to basic forms which now appeared coarse. Most of the sculptural ornament which graced the fourteenth century had vanished by the next. But the coldness of the masonry was being used as a foil to the splendid efforts of the carpentry.

It has been explained earlier how the interior of the roof had become an architectural feature of the highest quality and how the roof itself had been in some cases so much reduced in pitch that its almost flat underside now formed a magnificent panelled ceiling. (Plate 18.)

The carpentry of the ancient 'wrights' had relied for aesthetic embellishment upon the use of curved timbers. The new carpentry was what we call today 'joinery' which relies basically upon the framing together of straight timbers to form various types of panelling. This class of Gothic 'carpentry' may be seen on the grand scale in the ceilings of the period.

But the introduction of the 'parclose' screen as a system of partitioning enclosing the chancel and its chapels, brought the carpenters in touch with a highly refined branch of their craft. During the fourteenth century many stone screens were erected having tracery similar to that seen in the windows. But such had very wide openings and failed to provide the privacy needed. Hence the introduction of church woodwork on a furniture scale. (Plate 22.)

All such work relies basically upon a system of panelling. Whatever refinements in the way of mouldings and carving may be added subsequently, screenwork is framed together in panels. The rectangular panel was a form foreign to Gothic aesthetics, but under pressure from the carpenters it had to be accepted. The masons introduced it as a wall-ornament. And of course it found its way everywhere into the tracery of the window-head. The foliations were still as prominent as ever, but the window-lights had their arched heads flattened considerably to suit both the panelling and the current form of the main arches of the building.

A feature of the High Gothic era is the square-headed window. These were not large, but, appearing as they did as early as the fourteenth century, seemed to indicate the eventual fate of Gothic architecture and its sweeping arches. The arch developed from the necessity of spanning large openings with small stones, but the development of window tracery enabled the masons to carry a series of stones laid flat across the heads of the mullions. It will be noticed that in doing so they were greatly helped by the use of the ogee arch. The drip-stone covering the top of the window was of course flat at the top, the first appearance of the 'label-mould' which was soon to be employed everywhere in domestic architecture and continues in use in the masonry regions until the end of the seventeenth century.

The flat-topped opening, and the rectangular frame to which it led, become an important feature in the masonry work of the High Gothic. In doorways especially, the frame is found enclosing the arched opening. The triangular areas or 'spandrels' between the haunches of the arch and the frame become sites for carving, either foliated panels or heraldic shields.

Within these High Gothic frames one can watch the arch changing. In the majority of cases it retains the 'equilateral' form of the Gothic arch, but it is often four-centred or, in some of the more opulent examples, the three-centred 'Spanish' arch.

The Gothic was not a style which appreciated the façade. Even the west fronts of the great churches were designed with little understanding of the principles governing the creation of a 'frontispiece'. There were two towers, and between them a west window with a gable over it. Most of the English west fronts look unbalanced and top-heavy, that of Wells cathedral being the exception. In the parish churches the architectural façade is met with only at entrance doors, where some attempt is often made to achieve co-operation between the west window and the doorway below it. The most determined effects are usually those achieved by the large south porches with their chambers over them. Churches and great halls were probably at this time pooling their design experiences.

Gothic architecture, based as it was upon individualism and never properly organized, never succeeded in attaining perfection as an architectural style. Its creations remained assemblages of features—ranges of buildings with here and there a tower—gathered together with none of the architect's regard for composition as a whole. Gothic design never really developed beyond the bay, perfection in itself but only an architectural sample, incomplete and incapable of being assembled with others to form a considered entity. Plans were never adjusted, as in highly developed architecture, to enable an architect to build up a fine three-dimensional presentation. Gothic employed no textbooks: its success does indeed lie in its lack of such sophistry. It is thus essentially a primitive style, incapable of being assimilated into an advanced civilization—a product of an illiterate, ignorant culture sandwiched between the Ancient Wisdoms and their renaissance.

The lack of a means of communication between ourselves and the Middle Ages is quite profound. Even as late as the end of the medieval period we are still in the dark as to how the church services were organized. We know from the buildings themselves that the long chancel still remained, and that its obscurity, relieved for a time by the widening of the chancel arch, had now been restored behind the richly-carpentered rood-screen. The nave was basically still a great hall thronged with congregations attending upon the priest in his chancel.

What we do know is that the popularity of the parish sermon had introduced a new element into the service. It may be a result of this that fixed seating at last began to appear in the naves.

This was the biggest revolution the parish church had known. It is impossible to over-stress the importance of the change and its effect upon the architectural appearance of the interior of the building.

Hitherto the naves had been great empty halls. One might almost have called them architectural barns. But now they had become seated auditoria, in the style of a theatre—something quite new in architectural history.

The loss to the proportions of the building was catastrophic. One only has to enter a cathedral nave whence its chairs have been removed to appreciate this. And the lesser proportions of the parish church made the situation worse. The new screenwork became half-submerged in the sea of seating.

It may have been due to the introduction of church seating that we owe the raising of the pillars of the arcades on what amounts to the Gothic equivalent of a pedestal, a rather more refined version of the exterior plinth arrangement. It would be interesting to discover which of the two treatments was devised first.

The provision of fixed seating also had the result of finally obliterating any record in the church plan of the use of the nave by the congregation during the earlier seat-less days. With the seats in the transepts, however, facing inwards, it still seems difficult to appreciate what part the elongated medieval chancel played in the service if most of this was performed by the priest at the altar.

As we watch the Middle Ages drawing to their close we are forced to accept the fact that the whole era, with its many magnificent architectural creations, is unlikely ever to emerge with clarity from the native mists which still enshroud that curiously inarticulate period in our history. To attempt to understand it seems at times as difficult as to try to appreciate the mind behind Stonehenge. We can only reach a general impression of the approach towards an architectural ordinance, but with parish church architecture represented by a collection of individual items, each in itself utterly charming and each contributing to cheerful confusion, their tale is not easy to unravel. And when an ordinance at last begins to appear, it produces dignified external presentations behind which bleak interiors seem to mourn the livelier fantasies of the early days.

The Gothic fervour had evaporated. And the friendly dragons which had teased our Anglo-Saxon ancestors had long ago returned to their misty homes taking with them so much of the ancient splendour of barbarism.

12

Renaissance and After

The revolution of 1534 during which a stroke of the pen extinguished the main inspiration behind English architecture and brought about its virtual collapse, can have few parallels in architectural history. Parish church architecture of the period had reached a high degree of perfection by producing spacious well-lit buildings beautifully furnished and crowned by soaring bell-towers of superlative beauty. (Plate 28.) The last of these had been built.

With the disintegration of Holy Church in England, during the sixteenth century, the building trade shifted its allegiance towards the erection of mansions to house the heirs of the monastic lands. Few churches were built and fewer enlarged. A century and a half was to elapse before an interest in church building began to reappear, and that in a very restricted form. During the interregnum architecture in this country disintegrated into a state of chaos, suffering a series of influences which increased confusion rather than leading to a real revival in the art of church design.

These influences notwithstanding, the Gothic tradition continued in some strength. During what is known as the 'Gothic Overlap' which carried on throughout the seventeenth century, the main lines of buildings developed away from the medieval while details and ornament remained much as before but on a reduced scale owing to loss of patronage.

The broadening of plans continued, with a reduction in height away from Gothic extravagances. Main arches were Classically semicircular, but windows were more domestic in form and adopted the Renaissance square shape, the retention of mullions enabling the flat lintel-stones to be carried without fear of collapse. Gothic cusping, omitted from domestic windows by the middle of the sixteenth century, remained in churches for another hundred years.

At the end of Elizabeth's reign Renaissance motifs were appearing in parish church doorways, brought over in most ill-digested form via Spain and the Netherlands, the last sending over its quota of refugees from religious persecution. Curious distortions notwithstanding, one cannot fail to notice the arrival of small flanking pilasters with their Classical caps and bases, linked above the doorway by some attempt at the Classical 'entablature' of architrave, frieze and cornice. These doorways of the beginning of the seventeenth century are first found in mansions, whence they transfer themselves to parish churches, often getting themselves mixed up with debased forms of the Gothic arch in an attempt to become ecclesiastical.

It was sub-Renaissance features of this description which were being introduced into existing churches during the seventeenth century. The architecture of the period was basically domestic, and this fact makes itself clear. Even the transomed window, designed to enable the lower lights to be opened as casements, may be encountered in some places. For while no doubt a great many small medieval churches were abandoned as redundant during the seventeenth century, those which remained in use were still kept in good order and repair.

There was, of course, a great deal of mutilation, owing to a general architectural indifference. Windows, for example, might lose their tracery. Maintenance would have been limited to essentials, with neither money nor skill available for the fal-lals of 'Romish' architecture. While most of the work of this period was swept away during the restorations of the mid-nineteenth century, some of it still remains in poor and isolated parishes. It is perhaps a pity that we have lost with it what might have been some quite charming manifestations of Renaissance vernacular.

At the beginning of the seventeenth century the Italian Renaissance in its authoritative form was beginning to reach this country by way of printed textbooks. These were used first of all to help with the design of large houses, later with smaller ones. Not until the next century with its 'Georgian' architecture do we find such sophisticated features as windows designed on the aedicular principle, with surrounds and pedimented tops, appearing in the parish church. Even then, the style is either found in the towns or in parishes where the squire or parson had some special interest in architecture or could obtain the services of one of the few professional architects of the day.

The English parish church of the seventeenth century relied upon brick for its walling. Its windows were possibly as large as those of its High Gothic predecessor but, having no mullions, had to be covered with a semicircular arch. The only tribute to architectural style would be the springing lines marked by square impost blocks and the crown of the arch locked by a keystone.

The construction of a square-headed opening without support from mullions was a problem the Renaissance builder solved by devising the 'flat arch' which employs voussoirs but works them to a flat soffit. With the aid of this method of spanning a window opening, the Renaissance style was able to develop unimpeded by constructional problems.

It is surprising to discover how many old arcades, some of them pre-medieval, were rebuilt during the seventeenth century, the remains of the earlier responds giving the game away. Within the village church the pillars became rough imitations of the Classical form with very primitive copies of the Tuscan or Roman Doric capitals crowning them. Ordered arches came to an end with the medieval period; the soffits of the future were invariably flat.

Brick was the material commonly used for the village churches of the seventeenth century, even the openings being lined with this material. Stone was however often used for quoins. From the seventeenth century onwards most interiors of churches were plastered.

Most churches after the middle of the century were covered with roofs of low pitch, and their gable ends were often worked up with moulded cornices to form a triangular 'pediment'. Both methods of finishing the bottom of the roof were used. Eaves were supported underneath with some kind of large cornice, often a wide 'cove'. Parapets concealing lead gutters were quite plain with a flat coping instead of the medieval 'saddle back'. The Gothic cove was often succeeded by a small Classical cornice at the same level.

The sturdy bell-tower continued in favour. It was quite plain, its angles unbuttressed, and displayed a simple arched window in its belfry stage. The angles of its parapet were capped with urns or obelisks instead of pinnacles.

As North-Western Europe's contribution to Byzantine architecture had been the steeple, the same was its retort to the tower tops of the Baroque. As a country England seems always to have been addicted to the 'whispering spire'; even the Reformation seems to have been unable to break it of the habit. The Renaissance steeple was an interesting essay in architectural ingenuity, being in effect a diminishing pile of aedicules, every stage a little Classical temple, and crowned by an obelisk, the Renaissance retort to the Gothic pinnacle. During the eighteenth century even village churches produced such features, probably inspired by a squire with an interest in architecture.

The Georgian era, during which the part of patron of architecture, once the role of the medieval abbot, had been taken over by the farming squire, was the time for the full establishment of the English Renaissance style. It is necessary, if one is to make a study of post-Reformation parish churches, to familiarize oneself with the ordinance of the Italian Renaissance as devised and published by its great architects like Vignola.

The style was derived from that of Imperial Rome, building with arches but presenting its elevations in the only architectural style its engineers knew, that of the Hellenistic world. The basis of this was the Classical Orders, reduced in Roman architecture to a modified form of Doric for general use and the glorious Corinthian for special effects. Each Order had two main parts, the column—sometimes attached to a wall as a flat 'pilaster'—and the entablature which it carried. The column was divided into base, shaft and capital, the entablature into architrave, frieze, and cornice. Each Order had rigidly established proportions.

It was the ignorance of these which at first contributed to the charm of the post-Reformation parish churches. The style reached this country fourth-hand. From its source in Italy it flowed to Spain as the Baroque, whence it emigrated to the Low countries and became inextricably muddled and mixed with various Gothic elements until it became practically a style of its own. Thence through commercial contacts and the troubles of Protestant refugees it reached the English countryside.

Only by research into authoritative Renaissance publications and comparison of some element with its English variant can one begin to appreciate the parish church architecture of the seventeenth century. Even by the time of Wren, English Renaissance architecture was still a style of its own.

But by the eighteenth century, however, not only had the textbook triumphed, but under the Georgians English architects had developed a fine native style, so that the newly-built parish church of the period could be regarded as an unexceptionable contribution to the architecture of the Renaissance.

The most outstanding feature of post-medieval architecture is the cornice, unknown to the Gothic world which had substituted for it the corbel-table. This relic of Hellenistic days has three parts of which the most important is the square 'corona'; below this is the 'bed-mould' and above it another moulding called the 'cymatium'. Cornices may be found crowning the building itself and aedicular features such as the surrounds of doorways and windows.

Although the cornice should properly speaking be supported by a frieze and architrave to form a Classical 'entablature', one most frequently finds it in this country on its own. The Classical architrave, however, is frequently used as a *surround* to openings such as those of windows; again a feature having no counterpart in Gothic architecture.

A medieval feature, which although not forming a part of Renaissance ordinance had nevertheless to be used where required, was the buttress. Buttresses dating from post-medieval times can often be found attached to old parish churches, having been added to check the thrust of an arch or the toppling of a wall threatened by a spreading roof. They are generally of brickwork, the nature and bonding of which will often give the clue to their date.

Vertical punctuation was still being employed in post-medieval days, being effected by Classical pilasters having proper bases and capitals. In the richer churches the pilaster was used extensively for interior punctuation—a device unknown to the medieval designer except as applied to the whole of a wall surface—especially to help carry the heavy cornices which helped to transfer something of the exterior elevation into the treatment within the building.

The Renaissance architects reintroduced the apse, employing it as of old to be a setting for the altar. It was in this part of the church that the English reaction to the dreariness of the Reformation seems to be particularly emphasized, both by the architectural elaboration of the apse itself and the richness of the Baroque reredos which it often incorporated.

For its greater glory the Renaissance incorporated into its neo-Roman architecture the Byzantine dome, raising it upon a tall drum and setting it up to be not only the focus of the church plan but also the crowning glory of the building. Here and there the dome finds its way, under Georgian patronage, into the English parish church.

Every architectural period has its own peculiar feature acting as a kind of sign-manual to the period and appearing in no other. The Early Renaissance in England is marked by the baluster, the stumpy, vase-shaped colonette which is found everywhere in balustrades, lightening these in similar fashion to the pierced parapets of the High Gothic. Unknown in Classical or Gothic days, it is the Baroque contribution to the Renaissance, and first appears in quaint forms cut out of boards in the balustrading of Elizabethan times.

Finials have always been an important feature of architectural elevations, breaking into what might be a too-rigid skyline and adding a spice of gaiety to the silhouette. In Gothic days it was the pinnacle with its climbing crockets. The Renaissance architects employed the bare pyramid for the same purpose. Another feature encountered everywhere during the eighteenth century, not only on funerary monuments but as architectural finials, was the Classical urn, perhaps less suited, by reason of its rather top-heavy silhouette, than the tapering obelisk but clearly regarded as more refined than the obelisk and generally replacing it during the eighteenth century as an angle finial.

The changes in the interior of the English parish church between the medieval and the Renaissance are very marked. Architecture, originally intended to be employed on the exterior of the building for public display, began to be transferred to the interior of the building for the delectation of the congregation. In this connection it has to be remembered that a feature such as an aisle arcade, much though it may delight us today, was introduced as a structural necessity and ornamented only as an afterthought.

But the most noticeable change would have been the clear evidence that henceforth the congregation was aiming at attending communal worship in as much comfort as possible. With the introduction of fixed seating during the fifteenth century the first steps towards eliminating the primitive austerity of religious practices had been taken. Thenceforth the development of church seating makes a steady progress towards the cosy 'horse-boxes' of a hundred years ago which were to be swept away with such determination by the doubtless horrified 'restorers' of the middle of the nineteenth century.

Some way had to be found of excluding draughts descending from the open roofs of the unheated buildings. With this in mind the practice of what was until recently called 'under-drawing' was developed. Wall-plaster, which requires a prodigal use of expensive quicklime, was rarely used during the Middle Ages. But occasional lime-washing must have eventually produced a similar finish and certainly enabled the walls to be painted. Roofs were open to the underside of their covering, though boarding known as 'wainscot' was often fixed to the underside of the rafters in the bay over the altar to keep droppings away from it. Sometimes these boarded ceilings were treated architecturally with miniature vaulting ribs and carved bosses at intersections in the form of a canopy.

Contrary to general belief, plaster will not adhere to wood. It requires a system of thin laths round which it is 'keyed' by the skill of the plasterer who with a sweep of his trowel flicks the material between and behind the lathing. This is a highly skilled craft and does not appear in this country until the sixteenth century. Moulded plaster ceilings, however, developed rapidly and by the beginning of the next century had reached a very high degree of art which was deriving its motifs partly from the contemporary vernacular Renaissance and partly from the lovely forms seen in that fan vaulting which was the High Gothic's greatest achievement.

But such magnificence apart, the introduction of the plaster ceiling was an important innovation in all buildings including churches. (Plate 24.) During the eighteenth century in particular, a large number of the old open roofs were 'under-drawn', their plaster all having to be torn down and the roofs opened up again when the 'restorers' got at them. With the Classical Revival of the second quarter of the nineteenth century, when flat ceilings were the vogue, even ancient churches had flat ceilings thrown across them.

In parenthesis it should be noted that the open cradle roofs of Western churches, with their patterns of slender ribs meeting carved bosses at the intersections, are quite suitable for plastering and indeed probably have been so treated from pre-Reformation days.

We have seen how unpopular the brick elevation had been to the late eighteenth century-observer and the attempts which had been made to conceal it behind 'ashlar' stonework. Such treatment, however, was costly and could not have been employed by the custodians of the village churches.

Lime plaster used externally will not stand up to the weather. The nodules of 'Roman' cement, however, can be burnt to form a substance which mixed with an aggregate will produce a water-proof 'rendering'.

This form of rendering became acceptable as a decent covering for brickwork or old rubble walling. The aggregate used was collected from the sides of the water-bound 'macadam' turnpikes of the era, now, alas, no longer available to the architect restorer trying to patch old Roman cement renderings which have parted company with the walling behind them.

The writer cannot at this point forbear to comment upon the modern practice of covering church walls with Portland cement rendering. The colour is most unsightly and will never weather, as the old renderings could, by growing algae. Even the addition of 'pebble-dash' to improve the texture produces but a poor substitute for the fine old work. And cement can never be removed from stonework and will destroy its face *for ever*. It is greatly to be hoped that this practice, which in particular is ruining a number of ancient bell-towers, will be abandoned before our countryside becomes covered with cement church towers. The writer has enlarged upon this problem in Chapter 19.

Although it is preceded by the Late-Georgian reaction towards the medieval, the Classic Revival of the second decade of the nineteenth century is best considered in conjunction with the Renaissance, as it was based, in effect, upon a wish to reform the Baroque excesses of the High Renaissance and force it back into the austere rigidity of its original Classical derivatives.

Appearing about 1840, its influence may be detected by rather coarse Classical mouldings and an absence of ornament other than frets, keys and similar geometrical devices. The Greek Doric Order of the Parthenon appears in heavy porticos, a poor successor to the charming portals of Georgian days. Unlike the modified Roman of the Renaissance, the Greek Revival remained utterly pagan and was never absorbed into English church architecture.

The romantic revival of the Gothic style which came about in the latter part of the eighteenth century found a building trade utterly unable to cope with it. The Gothic mason had long since departed with his lodge into history. With most of his quarries weed-grown the art of the quarryman had been largely forgotten. Smoking brick-kilns provided the country's building material, a substance virtually unknown to the medieval church-builder.

But the 'carpenters', now 'joiners', were as good and better, than ever, and able to turn their hand to anything. So the first Gothic Revival was in part a Carpenters' Gothic. Then there was the new craft of the plasterer, with his armatures of 'stick and rag', to help with the detail. The old Gothic sturdiness, born of structural necessity, was not repeated. Only the beauty was retained, to be utilized as a stage architecture—the 'Romantick Gothick' of Strawberry Hill.

Is there a lesson still to be learned from the lovely 'Gothick' of the Regency which the visitor to an old parish church may some day be privileged to encounter? It seems impossible to deny that it was in essence retrogressive in that it represented an architectural style which had in process of time risen to a zenith and thence not so much to a final disappearance as to a submergence beneath a torrent which had set impassable obstacles in the path of its future progress. Had it not been thus, one must always wonder how our national architecture might have developed as it disembarrassed itself from lingering archaisms of medievalism and its obsolescent building practices.

Fearful was the blight of ugliness which drove the rediscovered Gothick from our pleasant land, to return again unrecognizable as revivalism in its most sterile form, unintelligent sophistry lacking the lightest touch of tenderness. For even in the original, the stateliness of the loveliest medieval building is something awe-inspiring—infinitely remote. The dainty playfulness of the Regency Gothick must surely go straight to the heart. Why did it pass, like the mayfly, in the span of a summer's day in the architecture of our land?

Some of the charm of the Georgian Gothic was even allowed to stray into the little Nonconformist chapels of the period, but soon after the beginning of the nineteenth century the majority of these had rejected such frivolities and settled down into an almost featureless form seeming to call attention to the miseries of the early industrial era. Such dreariness being inacceptable to the parish churchman, however, Gothic forms began more and more to represent the appropriate Anglican architecture.

This somewhat pathetic period in church architecture is not without interest in that one can detect the devotion underlying the work performed at the time. There were only a very few architects available to design Gothic churches. Even the best architects were still inexperienced in the style, and the churches built by the Ecclesiastical Commissioners were desperately lacking in charm. But it was 'Commissioners' Gothic' which set the pace for the

17. The stately East Anglian church of Lavenham in Suffolk

18. A spacious High Gothic aisle at Thaxted in Essex

19. An elaborate High Gothic roof at Somerton in Somerset

20. The hammer-beam roof of March church in Cambridgeshire

21. A West-country cradle-roof at St. Endellion in Cornwall

22. The rood-screen at Manaton church in Devon

23. A post-Reformation church at Wolverton in Hampshire

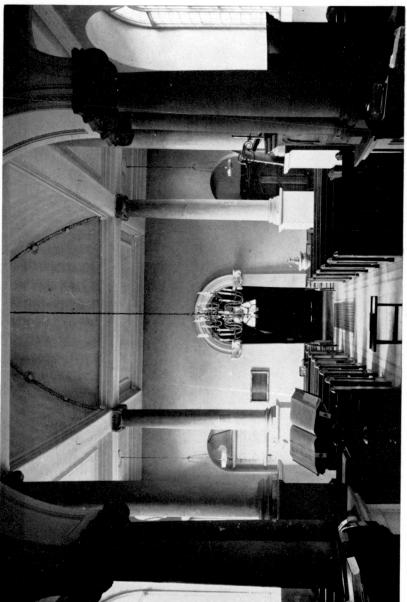

24. A post-Reformation interior at North Runcton church in Norfolk

25. A timber broach at Bury in Sussex

26. A stone broach at Slawston in Leicestershire

27. 'And little lost Down-churches praise The Lord who made the hills'
Southease, Sussex

28. 'Boston . . . Boston . . .
Thou hast naught to boast on . . .
But a great church, with a tall steeple . . .'

29. The art of the Anglo-Saxons enshrined for ever
at Kilpeck in Herefordshire

30. The dainty fan-vaulting of Cullompton church in Devon

31. (a)
Masonry of
the time of
the Conquest

31. (b)
Early Gothic
masonry

31. (c)
Late mediaeval
masonry

32. (*a*)
Pre-Gothic
axed
stonework

32. (*b*)
Stonework showing
early use of the
bolster

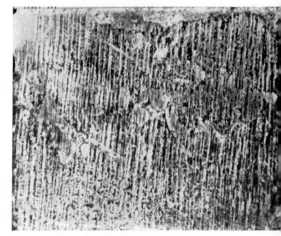

32. (*c*)
Late mediaeval
diagonal tooling

eventual Victorian Gothic Revival. And although its architects studied their 'styles' with devotion, few succeeded in breaking away from the grimness of its beginnings. Only such inspired men as Pearson or Gilbert Scott the younger, who could on occasion break through the bonds of copyism, succeeded in creating really fine churches capable of being compared with those of the past.

Much more interesting is the rustic 'do-it-yourself' style known as 'Churchwardens' Gothic'. This made no pretence of erudition and dispensed both with architects and skilled builders. What was however clearly displayed was a sympathy with the 'national' style and a determination to get back into it and away from the uglier manifestations of the brick Renaissance. The brick remained, but the arches went back again to Gothic forms. There was no stone available, nor were there masons to work it, but tracery there had to be, so this was indicated in joinery, generally simply by a pair of pine mullions. Rough and even ludicrous it might be—but it was Gothic.

The growing interest in the 'national style', which Thomas Rickman had committed to print, was making it clear to the architectural profession that Gothic was to be the only suitable form of architectural presentation for churches.

Unlike its light-hearted Georgian predecessor, Victorian Gothic was a serious affair, constructed in stone and with all its details properly studied and reproduced in unexceptionable form. Rickman's three divisions of the style were accepted without question, and no deviations from the published ordinances of each were countenanced. This is undoubtedly the principal reason for the dullness of the churches of the period, for the charm of the medieval parish church lies in its ever-changing moods as each generation laid a light hand upon it.

With the Gothic Revival came the Gothic Restorations. We shall never know what our losses during that period were. For our parish churches they probably equalled in aesthetic and archaeological damage the destruction of the monasteries. The interiors of churches were relentlessly stripped of everything accumulated during the past three centuries as the re-medievalizing process went on. What was perhaps worse was the way in which whole buildings lost their character beneath an overlay of flint and stone and even brickwork, making them look as though they had just been built. In this craze for a most un-medieval tidiness all external wall-faces disappeared—for ever . . .

. . . and with them vanished for ever the patina of the centuries.

13

Some Features of a Church

The essential parts of a church are its nave and chancel. To the enlargement of the congregational area are given the aisles and the wings or transepts. The bell-tower, central, western, flanking or detached, is an important, but not essential, part of the parish church.

The transept or, in its humbler form, the wing is an almost universal feature of all but the humblest churches (Plate 14) and is provided to increase the width of the building at a point immediately before the entrance to the chancel. These lateral projections may be prominent, with a pitched roof, or may be a short length of aisle with a lean-to roof. Sometimes they form the base of a bell-tower. During the early-medieval period transepts flanking a central tower were popular as giving the parish church something of the distinction of a minster. At this period they often have one or two shallow chapels projecting from their eastern walls to accommodate altars to some favourite saints. Though these chapels disappeared during the High Gothic era the eastern walls of transepts still had altars set against them here and there, their piscinae remaining to remind us.

A distinction should be drawn between the transept of the great church, which is a structure set athwart the main axis of the building at a 'crossing', and the 'wing' of the parish church which is an extrusion from the side of the nave in order to increase its width, the widening in every case occurring immediately west of the entrance to the chancel. The transept or wing continues in use to the very end of the medieval period, and is often found breaking out of the rectangle of the hall church. The greatest possible width at this point appears to have been the ultimate aim of the builders of parish churches at the time of the Reformation.

During the twelfth and thirteenth centuries the end walls of transepts were often used for the interment of important lay folk, broad low recesses being constructed in the walling for the display of effigies. After the Reformation the transepts of parish churches were often converted into family mausolea and, cut off from their naves by screenwork, no longer appear to add their projection to the width of the building.

The crossing, if one exists, is always an impressive part of any church. (Plate 12.) During the pre-medieval period the arches carrying the four walls were designed and built separately, with their responds projecting well into the building. But by the early-medieval period each corner of the crossing was being properly designed with a crossing pier built as an entity to carry the arches on either side of it, a much less obstructive arrangement.

Externally, the most impressive part of any church is its bell-tower. Attempting a rough survey of the distribution of medieval bell-towers in England, one can omit the very humble parish churches which clearly could never have afforded the cost of one. Churches of cruciform or 'axial' plan can also be omitted as these had towers which formed part of the building and were not provided to be purely bell-towers. The same can be said of all old tower-naves retained.

If one excepts all these special types of churches and concentrates upon the normal western tower typical of the English parish church, one finds very few that are earlier than the fourteenth or fifteenth century.

Of these normal examples, perhaps half are the result of a complete rebuilding of an early church which had thus entirely vanished (one would however have expected that such an expensive item as a bell-tower, had one existed, would have been retained).

The remaining towers have been added to existing churches by removing the west gable of the nave and building there a tower with a tall arch leading into the church.

Some Features of a Church

One wonders what arrangements for bell-hanging were available before the new tower was built. Some of these may have replaced early timber naves retained for the sake of their belfries. But from remaining examples it seems most probable that the belfry of the early-medieval church was a small construction of timber or stone attached to the west gable. Early-medieval roofs were insufficiently stable for them to take the load of a bell. One often sees at the west end of the nave of a small church a beam carried upon posts and stiffened by curved struts, to serve as a support for a timber bell-turret carried partly upon the beam and partly upon the west gable.

Many tower-less churches still have stone bell-cotes, some of them single, others double. Some are charming little turrets with pyramidal coverings. The central 'buttress' passing up the west gable of the thirteenth-century church would have helped to carry the turret. (See Plate 7.)

The examples one finds today are all on small churches, but one can conceive that similar turrets may well have served as belfries on quite large buildings until such time as the enormous cost of a proper tower, having a whole ring of bells, could be accumulated.

Similar turrets can be found on the east gable of the nave to carry the 'sanctus' bell rung during Mass at the Elevation of the Host.

Of great importance was the church porch, not only as a place for the doffing of headgear, but as a public meeting-place which played an important part in the social life of the medieval parish. The early porches were simply roofed areas before the church door, its protection to the interior of the building being, however, incomplete as it never had an outer door and thus did not act as a proper air-lock.

The church porch possibly owes its origin to a similar adjunct set before the great hall of the manor house to protect its occupants to some small degree from draughts every time the main door was opened. Architectural tradition requires that an entrance feature, which plays an important role in advertising the dignity of the building to which it gives access, should be accorded special treatment. (Plate 17.)

It may well be that the medieval porch developed along domestic rather than ecclesiastical lines. We can see, however, that it came to be given the monumental dimension of height, being raised to two stories, the upper serving traditionally as a depository for important records best kept, away from rising damp, on an upper floor.

In parish churches the 'solar' was either carried on timber joists wrought on their undersides to form an attractive ceiling, or else constructed as a 'stone solar' upon ribbed vaulting.

The church entrance thus developed into a fine two-storied frontispiece having an ornamental outer arch with often a good traceried window over it. The porch parapets were often carried up over the entrance to form a parapeted gable often with crenellations and pinnacles to match the rest of the building. The wide outer arch would, as abutment was now understood, require sturdy angle buttresses to support it, and these would be carried up towards pinnacles. Various types of panelled devices might be employed to cover areas of walling left between features.

Within, the porch might become an apartment of considerable charm. It might have seats flanking it for use during conferences, official or merely social. Corbels carrying ceiling beams or vaulting ribs might be attractively carved, the system extended to bosses marking the junctions of joists or vaulting ribs. At the back of this fine ante-room would be the entrance door of the church, probably itself a feature of architectural magnificence.

Probably few visitors to an ancient church pause to take note of the entrance door itself which may often be contemporary with the opening in which it hangs. Medieval doors are formed of two thicknesses of boarding, the outer vertical, the inner horizontal, the two thicknesses being clamped together with rows of heavy hand-made nails clenched on the inside. Hinges were straps fixed to the boarding and turned into loops swinging on hooks built into the stonework of the jambs.

During the pre- and early-medieval period the straps were elongated and carried across the boarding to give the door additional strength. They were wrought into strange shapes of writhing dragons, later into conventional scrolls with 'stiff-leaf' and similar forms of terminal. Those at Haddiscoe in Suffolk are notable examples of the medieval smith's artistic ability.

This kind of ironwork went out at the end of the early-medieval period, as the door of the High Gothic era had its outer boarding covered with strips of moulded wood applied in the form of tracery and matching the tracery in the church windows. Many of these doors remain today as fine examples of Gothic woodwork.

A lot of the door furniture of the village churches is of considerable antiquity. Many an old iron draw-handle remains today which is possibly as old as the original church, having been transferred from door to door as each wore out.

After the main buildings of the church, its next most prominent features are its buttresses. Originally non-structural, they developed from the pilasters affixed to pre-medieval walls to recall the posts of timber structures and provide vertical punctuation at these points. (Plates 6 and 7.)

These pilasters were gradually extended outwards from the wall and during the early-medieval period their projection about equalled their width. (Plate 11.)

In pre-medieval buildings the pilasters adjoining the angles of the building were either kept separate or were joined together solidly to form a 'clasping pilaster' embracing the angle. As pilasters were often embellished with slender shafts up either side, the angle of the clasping pilaster was frequently provided with this feature. (Plates 7 and 8.) During the twelfth century, buildings lacking pilaster treatment were frequently provided with angles reinforced by double quoins to give them added strength in view of the weakness of the mortar used.

With the development of the true buttress during the thirteenth century as a definite projection from the wall-face, the angles of the building were augmented by pairs of these which were in fact merely prolongations of the walls themselves. These buttresses set at right angles to each other are characteristic of the early-medieval period and—with a reservation to be noted later—disappear entirely thereafter. (See Fig. 21.)

The standard angle buttress of the High Gothic—comprising

the fourteenth and fifteenth centuries—is the diagonal one called by English builders the 'French buttress' and thus presumably an importation from the Continent. At the end of the Gothic period, however, there is a return to the early-medieval pair, modified, however, in that a portion of the angle of the building itself is left between them.

Thirteenth-century buttresses were finished off with gablets. Although the principle of applying top weight upon an abutment to counteract a side thrust was not appreciated in this country until the High Gothic era, one finds here and there buttresses capped with rough pyramids resembling embryo pinnacles. During the High Gothic era, the pinnacle in its most elaborate forms, covered with 'crockets' and finished with a finial, frequently tops the buttress of the period, joining with a pierced and crenellated parapet to form a coronary system round the top of the walling.

What would Gothic architecture be without the pinnacle? The spire and the pinnacle—the latter being the aedicular offspring of the former—are both peculiar to the Gothic style.

To recapitulate the theory behind the buttress and the essential factor in its design, it is easiest to recognize it as a portion of the wall set at right angles to the main wall-face to counteract a thrust upon the wall from some internal force. As this force lessens with the height, buttresses are reduced in projection, by means of 'set-offs' as they rise. Where not required to carry ornamental finials, or to support a counterpoise, they normally die out into the wall at the height of the string-course which indicates the top of the wall and the beginning of its parapet.

The flying buttress, a half-arch carrying a thrust from a wall over to an isolated buttress, is not often found in parish church architecture, but examples are seen serving an ornamental purpose at the angles of spires, pretending to support these from the angles of the tower. (Plate 14.) Flying buttresses always need a pinnacle as counterpoise.

The stone stair enclosed in an octagonal turret is a common feature in the medieval parish church. There was usually one leading to the ringing-floor of the tower, often carried right up the belfry and the leads. (Plate 16.) During the High Gothic era of elaborate rood-screens with 'lofts' over, all these had to be reached by stone stairs. Many of these were contrived in older walling and at times seriously weakened the abutments of the chancel arch. Where possible, new stairs were built attached to an outside wall, that of an aisle for example, leading to the end of an extended screen. Such stairs might be continued to the ringing-floor of a central tower. As the porch stair gave access to the southern leads one generally finds the rood stair on the north side of the church, carried up to the leads there.

Some parish churches were provided with a sacristy, usually on the north side of the chancel, the priest's door being on the south side. It is a small room, lit only by narrow windows, often vaulted over as its purpose was that of a strong-room. Sometimes there is a chamber over for the priest.

A crypt is rarely found in a parish church, but such were sometimes built at transept-end to provide a bone-hole. In towns and where the soil was hard for digging graves, these could be used several times over provided their contents were decently transferred to a consecrated building.

To be found in many churches is the so-called 'low side window'. It is a small window having its sill well below the normal level, always situated near the west end of the chancel and generally on its south side. The fact that the purpose of these windows has never been explained is a measure of the lack of research undertaken into the ecclesiological aspect of the English parish church. The writer has discussed the problem with Continental priests and has been told that it is a normal feature of old parish churches and is an opening originally provided for donations, in particular 'oil for the lamps'.

Among odd openings found within the medieval church are the 'squints', mostly obliquely pierced, beside the chancel arch, enabling persons who might find themselves crowded into a corner there to catch a glimpse of the altar.

An important feature of the sanctuary is its 'piscina', the stone sink, usually cut into the sill of a low niche, but sometimes carried clear of the wall on a short colonette, provided to accept the water with which the sacred vessels were washed after Mass. Piscinae may be found in other parts of a church, in a transept or the end of an aisle. They always indicate the site of a vanished altar and are usually on the south side of this.

Stone seats were sometimes provided at the sides of a church, along the aisle walls. No other permanent seating was provided except in the sanctuary, where one may often find elaborate stalls formed in the masonry, surrounded with carved ornament in the style of large niches. These are the 'sedilia' provided as seats for clerics. They are usually arranged in ascending stages towards the east. They generally form an elaborate architectural composition and often incorporate the piscina in its niche.

Another niche found in the sanctuary is the 'aumbry', a cupboard in which the sacred vessels are kept before Mass. The aumbry is usually on the north side of the altar.

On this side, too, may sometimes be found an elaborate niche designed as a tomb. This is the Easter Sepulchre, provided to accommodate the sacred elements during this period. Sometimes an actual tomb was set there and designed to incorporate a niche for use at Eastertide.

With intra-mural interment a normal practice, the chancel was the most favoured situation for sepulture. In the small parish chancel there was no room for the 'altar' tombs erected in the great churches; thus monuments had to take the form of features set in a wall. The southern wall being occupied by the sedilia and the chancel doorway itself, the least encumbered one was that opposite; thus the northern wall of the chancel, near its east end, was usually the site for the tomb of its builder.

A feature similar to the piscina but always found at the church door is the 'stoup' for holy water into which persons entering the building dip their fingers.

A 'chantry' is a prayer offered up for the soul of someone who has died. Bequests to finance such were common in many parishes. The proprietary 'chantry chapels' founded in the great churches for the chantry priests are found only in the large parish churches in the market towns. But there were many places in a village church—a chancel aisle or a transept-end—appropriated as mortuary areas for important families. Altars in such situations could be used for the offering-up of chantries.

There are no indications that the early-medieval church had a chancel-screen. The introduction of this was probably an attempt to restore to the chancel something of the seclusion it had enjoyed since Anglo-Saxon days and before chancel arches were widened during the early-medieval period. There are some stone chancel-screens of fourteenth-century date remaining in parish churches, some of which are in their original position while others have been removed into a transept arch to enclose a family chapel.

The elaborate wooden screens of the last Gothic period completely cut off the chancel from the nave with a partition having its upper part pierced for restricted vision but still of suffi-cient solidity to confer an atmosphere of privacy upon the most sacred part of the building. (Plate 22.) Chancels flanked by aisles also had the openings into these closed by screens, the whole arrangement being derived without doubt from that of the screened choirs of the monastic churches.

Chapels lying beside chancels were also screened at their west ends, usually in line with the chancel-screen itself, so that a con-tinuous line of elaborate timberwork might reach across the church at its old focus of interest, the line passing across the front of the chancel arch.

The chancel-screen itself was crowned by a crucifix or 'rood' and thus became the 'rood-screen'. As candles were lit before the rood and these required attention, the screen had to be capped with a narrow gallery or 'rood-loft' to provide access. (Plate 22.) The stairs formed in the wall to reach the rood-loft usually remain to this day even though screen and loft may have vanished long ago.

The rood-lofts of the fifteenth century are carried out over their screens on aedicular representations of stone vaulting, always richly laced with ribs and sometimes approaching the 'fan' variety. The whole feature was designed to form a frontispiece, similar to the Byzantine 'iconostasis' of long ago, displaying before the eyes of the congregation a vision of beauty denied them in their every-day lives and preparing them for the mysteries associated with the dimly-seen altar. The resemblance to the iconostasis is heightened by the dado of painted saints filling the lower parts of the chancel-screen.

During the fifteenth century, when the English parish church reached the zenith of its architectural excellence, the rood-screen with loft and access stairs seems to have been as obligatory a feature as the western bell-tower.

The roofs of parish churches were probably not always maintained to perfection. Thus one frequently finds the bay over the altar provided with a ceiling, often elaborately ornamented, to protect it from droppings. As the rood-screen came into general use, the same kind of ceiling was often provided in the half-bay immediately to the west of this so as to protect this magnificent architectural feature and the rood above it.

There are indications that in some parish churches the upper part of the chancel arch was blocked by a boarded 'tympanum', possibly painted, acting as a back-cloth to the rood and completing the seclusion of the chancel. Those tympana which exist are believed to be post-Reformation, but in view of the attitude to both the rood and the chancel itself at this period this seems most unlikely.

The carved stone 'reredos' which is set into the east wall of the chancel to act as a back-cloth to the altar is but seldom found in medieval parish churches, though a great number were added during the last century.

The particular feature introduced by the reforming element which attained its most significant form during the Commonwealth was the altar rail, a wooden balustrade of typical Renaissance design fencing off the altar and restoring to it something of the dignity lost to it with the rejection of the rood-screen. Some of these seventeenth-century altar rails, a great number of which have fortunately been retained to this day, afford excellent examples of the joinery of their period.

One of the great differences between the medieval churches and the 'Reformed' ones of today is the elimination of statuary from their interior architecture except that associated with their monuments. In the ancient parish church the tall niche is a frequent feature of the eastern walls of chancels, aisles and transepts. They were provided as settings for the statues of favourite saints, but most of their occupants were destroyed by the Puritans of the seventeenth century.

The niche is a Gothic example of that favourite architectural device, the aedicule, which is a miniature reproduction, for the purposes of ornament, of some larger feature actually forming part of the structure. The Gothic niche is usually flanked by little buttresses ending in pinnacles and over it is a charming composition suggesting an elaborate gable end complete with finial. Within this may be a dainty foliated arch partly concealing miniature vaulting covering the head of the niche. The whole feature is usually founded upon a small corbel that once carried the statue itself and the miniature architecture by which it was flanked.

Gothic Architecture was the product of the craftsman developing his own details upon a series of familiar elements accepted by his contemporaries as forming a basic ordinance. The only assemblage of such elements being the vertical bay, the elevational design of a major building remained nothing more than a row of these. By the sixteenth century, however, the south side of a parish church having had forced upon it the special dignity of displaying an entrance front, we find this joining with the contemporary great hall in utilizing such features as the two-storied porch, projecting wings, stair turrets and details such as buttresses, niches, and a battlemented parapet, to introduce for the first time in this country the elaborate architectural façade.

14

Towers

=====

The tower as such is not a part of the church plan for accommodating a priest and his congregation. It serves two functions, one
practical, the other psychological.

Christians are called to church by the ringing of a bell, a tower
being provided to raise this above surrounding obstructions, hills,
trees and houses, so that its sound can be carried about the parish.

Moslems are called to prayer by the voice of the muezzin. The
writer was once asked by the priest of a Byzantine Christian village
near Irbid in Jordan to design a church and was anxious to make
certain that nothing essential was omitted from the design. The
priest told him 'The Moslems hate bells—so we must have a tower
with a bell in it.'

The architectural significance of a tower, however, lies in that
it supplies its church with the element of monumentalism, the
dimension of which is height. Probably costing as much as the
rest of the church put together, it raises the building above everything else about it. To this day it overtops the village. How much
more must it have done so when the village homes were mere
hovels.

It is of interest to try to imagine what might have been the
architectural landscape of England during the twelfth century. The
principal edifices would have been the great monastic churches,
their elaborate steeples towering over all. After them would come
the sinister keep-towers of the castles, their pitched roofs barely
visible above protecting parapets. Above the humble roofs of each
village or township would rise the walls of its parish church, either

of stone or timber, crowned in each case by a bell-turret or the steepled roof of a tower. During the next century the central towers would be rising above the village churches, each capped by its lofty timber broach dominating still further the village beneath.

By the end of the fourteenth century most of the churches would be building a tall west tower, lead-covered and no longer needing a spire to emphasize its height, though in many cases the traditional monumental form might have been retained.

A large building is not necessarily monumental. For monumental architecture must display the element of height. The Byzantine church architects appreciated this. All their churches are lofty, their elevations leading up to the central dome. The early French cathedrals were of immense height so that the buildings themselves towered above the roofs of the city encompassing each. The Anglo-Saxon minsters were very large buildings but even as their architecture advanced they never attained the height of the great Continental churches of the thirteenth century. It is to this characteristic of the English great churches that we may owe the development of the church tower to the degree of splendour it achieved in this country.

The bell-tower has existed in this country since before the Norman Conquest. But at this time their scarcity was such that a landowner whose church possessed one was entitled to the rank of Thane.

The monastic developments of the ninth century began the expansion of the great churches along their axis to a new focal point where transepts joined the main structure. With the addition of aisles to all four arms, the lighting of the 'crossing' presented a problem. As the nave was lit by its clearstory, this was carried up over the transept roof to perform the same duty for the crossing. Thus in the heart of the building we find a low tower or 'lantern', similar in principle to the lighting arrangements under the Byzantine domes but having windows all round it which matched those in the adjoining clearstories. Contemporary illustrations suggest that some of the first timber steeples erected over these early crossings may have incorporated a ring of windows at the base.

The lantern tower is not however a bell-tower and was of too light a construction to have stood up to the swinging of bells. Those lantern towers which survived the destructive forces inherent to their construction were sometimes subsequently raised by a belfry story. But most churches with lantern towers had to build a separate bell-tower close by, as at Chichester or Salisbury.

Most of the early great churches had expanded eastwards from the original turriform nuclei and some of these may have remained, as they may be seen to do in the German cathedrals, as western adjuncts to the completed church. Such structures would have had belfries built into them and thus would continue to serve as bell-towers for the enlarged church. It is clear that well into the twelfth century the bell-tower of the great English church was at its west end. The cathedrals of Winchester and Old Sarum had them, flanked by their original transepts. The sole survivor, one of the world's most beautiful towers, may be seen at the west end of what is now the cathedral church of Ely.

The two types of church plan which had developed by the time of the Norman Conquest, the 'Celtic' type with nave and chancel (Fig. 13) and the Byzantine type with the turriform nave (Fig. 7), have been described in Chapter 4. The latter had a ready-made place in which to hang its bell, the other had no tower at all.

Only a very small tower is needed to carry a bell. The Byzantine campanile is a slender structure having no resemblance to the Gothic bell-tower of medieval England. We may find a series of such structures which have been added to early churches all down the Anglican littoral from Durham to the East Saxon border, each with the primitive Byzantine *bifora* in its belfry stage. North of the Wash they are square stone structures, typically Byzantine, southwards in East Anglia they are of flint, circular in plan for lack of stone for quoins. (See also Plate 27.)

Although the parish bell-tower hardly appears at all in permanent form until the fourteenth century, many old timber naves may have been retained to carry the bells. (Plate 1.) Some had stone naves built on to them, others incorporated the posted structure within the new stone walls. Some stone bell-towers have been built up inside the west and of an early nave, perhaps on the site of an early timber tower.

The twelfth and thirteenth centuries saw the foundation of a number of small monastic houses in the English countryside, each with its church of nave, transepts, choir and central tower. Practically all of them have disappeared today but when they were standing they must have produced a very strong influence on the church-builders of the locality. With such examples before them, it is no wonder that many designers of thirteenth-century parish churches adopted the cruciform plan with the central tower (Fig. 11 and Plate 11), as often as not with an aisle-less nave. The small church with the central tower but no transepts, common in the twelfth century, indicates the desire to introduce the feature wherever possible. (Fig. 10 and Plate 8.)

In addition to the church and minster towers which covered twelfth-century England there were scores of castle towers, massive fortified houses of a type never before known in architectural history. Limited to England and the Norman Empire, these massive structures, three stories in height, were covered with pitched roofs concealed behind high parapet walls to prevent their being shattered or burnt by artillery. Larger towers had two roofs side by side to reduce their height, a very early use of the internal lead gutter.

Architecturally their exterior ordinance was clearly defined by large clasping pilasters at each angle. Larger towers had one or more pilasters between these emphasizing the essential bay design. Some of the later towers reduced the wide Byzantine pilasters to a narrow form having greater projection, embryo buttresses of early-medieval type.

Neither the twelfth nor thirteenth century saw much building of bell-towers to parish churches. The tall Byzantine campanile seems never to have spread westward from the Anglian littoral into the rest of England. Here and there, however, one finds very large and massively-built towers at the ends of parochial naves, clearly intended to serve the dual purpose of extra accommodation and bell-tower, perhaps in the same way as the axial towers. These towers, which appear to be of early thirteenth-century date, all have the intermediate 'buttress' in the middle of the side walls in the style of the contemporary domestic tower.

When examining old churches it is of interest not only to discover what new types of church came to be introduced with each changing fashion, but also how existing churches were 'modernized' to bring them into line with the current fashion. For example at the close of the twelfth century a number of pseudo-cruciform churches had central towers built at the east end of the nave between the early wings so as to convert them to the fashionable cruciform type. (Fig. 12a.) It is usually easy to tell whether a central tower is part of the original design or not, for if it is not one cannot fail to notice the confusion which has been caused inside the church by trying to fit in a stair to the ringing floor. Had the tower been planned from the start access to this would have been incorporated into the design so as not to obstruct the church below.

On the other hand, there are indications—and records—that as time went on the central tower not only lost its popularity with the congregation but was actually pulled down so as to free the most important part of the nave from the obstructions created by the crossing piers. Apart from this, however, it is doubtful whether a stone tower, once erected, would have ever been pulled down and replaced. We may therefore consider the possibility that our losses of western towers of early date will have been negligible.

It is impossible to overstress the essential monumentalism of the bell-tower, costing possibly as much as the rest of the building put together and serving only to carry bells. The spirit that raised the towers of English churches is identical with that behind the great temples of dynastic Egypt: the erection of a monumental structure to advertise the glories of religion. The accommodation provided by the ground story of a west tower was of little value as it was so far away from the centre of interest at the opposite end of the building. It is for this reason that we find a not inconsiderable number of transeptal towers the ground stories of which added considerably to the accommodation just at the point where it was most needed. Another saving in cost was to set the tower over the porch to the nave door. This however gave the church a somewhat larger porch than it might have needed.

Detached bell-towers, in the fashion set by many of the great churches, are not uncommon in parish churches also. The beautiful thirteenth-century example at West Walton in Suffolk is well known.

Towers were not covered with flat lead roofs until the High Gothic era. Before that time there were several methods of roofing a tower.

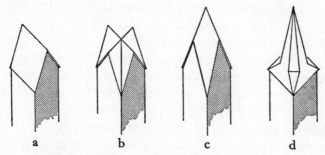

Fig. 23 *Early tower roofs*
> Some types of tower roofs which preceded the lead flats commonly seen today. (a) The saddle-back which is simply a pitched roof. (b) The cruciform roof which may be seen at Hinton Charterhouse in Somerset. (c) The Rhenish 'helm' roof of which the only surviving English example is at Sompting in Sussex. (d) The broach, of which many examples remain. Copied in stone it becomes the Northamptonshire type of spire and from it is derived all forms of this feature.

A simple but not very subtle method was to provide two opposing walls, usually the north and south, with gables and then roof it as any other building. (Fig. 23*a*.) Towers on a rectangular plan suggest a roof of this sort. A 'saddle-back' roof, as it was called, may be seen on Sarratt church in Hertfordshire.

The standard Rhenish tower-top was the 'helm' which was built up on four gables with timbers joining their summits to form a diagonal square carrying rafters meeting to form a spire-like roof having four diamond-shaped planes. (Fig. 23*c*.) There must at one time have been many helm-roofs in England, but their only survivor is at Sompting in Sussex.

It is doubtful whether it would have been possible to build an ordinary pyramidal roof at a period when ridge-pieces, and therefore in all probability hip-rafters, were unknown.

It seems most probable that the tower roof of early days was set up with rafters set at a very steep angle like the poles of an Indian tepee. And it is of interest to note that this kind of structure is favoured by timber builders, some of the early timber towers having their posts set sloping inwards at quite a considerable angle.

Subsequent developments indicate that the top of the tower was converted into an octagon by having beams set across its angles. Upon this base the rafters would have been set up at a steep angle to form a spire or 'broach'—meaning a spit—exerting no outward pressure and thus requiring no transverse ties.

Four triangular spaces were left at the angles of the tower and these were covered with low lean-to 'roofs'. The whole structure was covered with shingles and capped with a lead 'poll'. A number of these timber broaches remain to illustrate what must have been the commonest form of covering to the top of an early tower. (Plate 25.)

Contemporary illustrations of great English churches—on seals for example, or in the Bayeux Tapestry—suggest that the broach may sometimes have formed the central core of a steeple of considerable elaboration, with a surround of lean-to roofs raised upon timber wall-frames to provide tiers of windows for lighting the church below. During the thirteenth century the enormous central tower of St. Albans Abbey, even in those days as high as it is today, was crowned by an elaborate octagonal steeple. The staggeringly beautiful towers of Lincoln once had spires on them.

So it is not inconceivable that many of our pre-medieval parish churches may have been crowned by timber steeples displaying a degree of elaboration impossible nowadays to imagine. In this connection it is of interest that during the whole of the Middle Ages the word 'tower' was only used to designate the military structure. The church tower was always called the 'steeple', as though this feature had become inseparable from the form.

An indication of one type of feature may be found in most of the stone spires which replaced the timber ones. This is the dormer window. It is not a medieval type of window at all and does not appear serving this purpose until after the end of the Gothic era in England. The Renaissance dormer is much wider than the kind seen on the sides of the stone spires and is formed by cutting several rafters and 'trimming' them to form the opening. The prototypes of the spire-dormers must have been fitted in between the rafters; they are indeed very narrow with acute little gables. (Plate 26.)

The form of the base of the broach, like all other medieval roofing-forms, changed with the introduction of lead. The small roofs round the base were omitted and the space left at each angle covered with a lead flat. The corbel-table associated with all early eaves was often retained, but it would in future carry a parapet in the same way as elsewhere in the church.

In order to carry a dome upon a square tower it is necessary first to convert the square into an octagon. This can be done by throwing diagonal arches called 'squinches' across the angles. The device was well known throughout Byzantine architecture. The towers of the early Rhenish cathedrals were generally converted into octagons as soon as they had cleared the roofs, in readiness for the timber steeple.

By replacing their timber angle-beams with squinch arches the English masons could begin to copy the timber broach in stone. At first the stone forms imitated their predecessors, sometimes throwing out spur roofs at the angles but with these rising ever more steeply and sweeping up in the lines of the spire. A great number of these stone 'broaches' were built in Northamptonshire with its good freestone and many skilful masons. A study of these structures might enable one gradually to work up a knowledge of those earlier timber steeples many of the details of which may have been copied in stone.

These tall stone roofs are really rather remarkable achievements, with their eaves and corbel-tables all worked out in amenable stone. With the coming of lead the spire changed by dispensing with its angle features and surrounding itself with the usual parapet. Opportunities for angle treatments were seized with the usual enthusiasm of the medieval mason, until the High Gothic spire became one of the great features of historical architecture.

Most towers had built-in staircases leading to their ringing-floors. The later ones carried their stairs up to the leads. They were nearly always worked into an angle, usually an eastern one, of the thick walling, with a slight projection as required, but a series of Devon towers make a special feature of the stair turret by projecting it from the middle of a side wall. That the stair turret was regarded as an architectural feature of importance is shown by the fact that it is usually found on the south, or entrance, front. (Plate 16.)

Before the era of lead roofs the tower stair would have ended at the ringing floor. The existence of a short stair thus probably indicates that the tower was originally roofed with a timber broach.

By the end of the Gothic era the great towers have a turret at each angle, replacing the angle buttresses which had been the normal angle-feature of the tall tower. Such turrets rose high above the parapet and were often capped with little ogee domes.

When considering the problems facing the primitive builder one should remember that while the erection of a timber structure poses no very great difficulty, a request for it to be lifted up and set upon a wall is quite another matter. The 'close-couple' roofs of early days, brought up from a safe anchorage on the ground and perched upon the tops of walls, were far from stable, and to expect them to carry any weight such as a bell would have been unrealistic. Thus any timber bell-turret of those days would have had to be carried either on posts rising from the ground or on tie-beams passing across the building at plate level.

During the High Gothic era, in regions such as Somerset, blessed with fine freestone and a notable masonry school—probably based on the great abbey of Glastonbury—tower design reached considerable aesthetic heights. The development of tower architecture can be followed, in this region and others similarly engaged, in the same way as the student of today can be taught the elements of architectural design in any type of building.

A tower is aesthetically the most important structure to face an architect. It cannot be hid. However thoroughly an indifferent architect's elevations can hide themselves within the streets of a town, his tower rises visible to all. Yet nowadays as often as not a tower has become merely a pile of identical stories heaped up until a halt is called.

The medieval architects took the elevational presentations of their towers very seriously indeed. Mere height alone was not enough. The ground story being part of the church, it had to display the west window with a door below this for processions. These two features were often combined to provide a fine façade to the building.

The basic elements of the tower proper, that is to say the portion which rises above the roof of the main structure, are the two stories connected with the ringing of the bells. In the beginning we find just the small window lighting the ringing-floor and over it the larger one allowing the sound of the bells to ring out over the countryside. In low towers the ringing-floor may be kept low down within the roof level of the nave so that only the belfry rises above this.

As the outward indication of the bells within, the belfry windows always form the elevational focus of the deisgn. At first a simple Byzantine *bifora* (Plate 3) this is followed by a pair of lancets; eventually the belfry window becomes traceried to match the rest of the windows in the church.

We have noticed a tendency for large thirteenth-century towers to have their elevations divided into two bays by a medieval strip or embryo buttress. This practice continued into the High Gothic period, being followed where the masons were embarking on an elaborate elevation incorporating a buttressed treatment. Reaching the belfry story the medial strip or buttress split this into two portions with a window in each, thus greatly adding to the elaboration of the crowning story.

But all architectural students know that the central feature of an elevation should be an opening rather than a solid obstruction. Thus the last stage in tower design was to divide the elevation vertically into, not two, but three parts, resulting in a belfry stage with twelve windows ranged around it, a treatment providing a basis for considerable architectural embellishment.

Much of the architectural effect was produced by the buttresses. The normal form of the High Gothic angle-buttress projected diagonally but later towers, especially in the West Country, returned to a variation of the early form by setting the buttresses in pairs, leaving, however, a portion of the angle of the tower between them. (Plate 17.) Panelling spread over the blank spaces of walling and the vertical elements of this joined with the medial buttresses to accentuate the soaring effect. The pinnacles growing out of the summits of the buttresses and joined by lengths of pierced parapet helped to create a lively skyline. At the zenith of the High Gothic era, the tall towers of the English churches must have been among the finest achievements of their age. (Plate 28.)

Much of the glory of the tall tower vanished from church architecture with the passing of the Middle Ages. But the church tower—now always at the west end—continued to be accepted as an essential part of the building. It soon lost its unnecessary and aesthetically anachronistic buttresses. Its parapet became plain, with possibly urns or obelisks capping the angles. Its windows became simple round-headed openings in the style of the period. More often than not it was built of a pleasant brick, perhaps with stone quoins and a touch of stone here and there at windows or doorways. (Plate 23.) The English steeple was recalled in many ingenious Renaissance forms.

What would the countryside of England be without its church towers? They seem everywhere, peering shyly over the tops of great trees or soaring high above them. It is though they were mounting guard over the fields about them.

On many occasions they must have served as watch towers, especially during time of war. We can think of the mail-clad nobles of the Wars of the Roses struggling up the winding stairs to peer out from the leads in search of the sheen of enemy armour.

How many of our towers may have played host to Cromwell, Fairfax, Prince Rupert, or star-crossed Majesty itself? Reflect on the missions of accoutred colonels, attended by perspiring troopers, climbing up these rural observation posts, forever planning new battlefields.

The high bells did not always peal out so merrily.

There were times when the tenor was called upon to mourn.

15

Architectural Details

═══

As was explained at the outset, architectural history has for the past century and a half been studied in terms of aesthetic expression. Although Thomas Rickman was an architect, he was less concerned with the churches he was studying as buildings than as examples of an architectural style the aesthetic forms of which were at his time becoming of great interest to the élite. His successors have for the most part adopted the same approach and a very great many books, some of them elaborately illustrated, have been produced carrying on his work. But as very few of the writers have been architects they have been unable to study parish churches as buildings comparable in their way with houses or factories.

Yet architecture is composed of three elements, as Sir Henry Wootton and Sir Christopher Wren, at the beginning and end of the seventeenth century respectively, have both pointed out. First comes the purpose of the building and the efficiency with which it fulfils this. Then there is the form of its construction which will ensure its stability. And then, and not always lastly, is its ability to delight the eye with its dignity and charm. Indeed it is not really the architecture so much as its embellishment, which particularly delights the ordinary man.

The system of architectural ornament which sets the Gothic apart from all other styles is the moulding. The Classical architects formed their columns strictly in accordance with a recognized Order. The moulded Gothic pillar would have shocked their orderly minds by its infinite variety. Heavily-moulded 'architraves', also rigidly following an accepted ordinance, could be converted by the Roman architects for use in framing an opening. But no Classical moulding ever marred the plain soffit of the arch until its bleakness came to be softened by panelling.

Either through ignorance, or simply because they would have considered it barbaric, the Romans made no use of the 'ordered' arch constructed in expanding rings and thus economizing in timber 'centering'. This was left to the more practical and ingenious Byzantines.

But the elevational presentation of the ordered arch can appear rather crude and unattractive unless some kind of treatment should be given to the series of hard edges passing along each order. To this is possibly due the invention of the Gothic moulding.

It must have been the timber-builders who first employed the chamfer, the adzing away of the edge of the beam to convert a right angle into two obtuse ones. The principle of the chamfer was to play a large part in the later development of the moulding.

The medieval mason, however, approached his material from a different direction. His system was to take a chisel and cut a groove, called a 'quirk', on either side of the angle and work the stone between these quirks to form a 'roll'. (Fig. 24.) This is the second source of the Gothic moulding and that which brought it to its greatest achievements.

The first rolls, used by the pre-medieval masons, were six or eight inches across or more in the larger buildings. When they were used up the imposts of openings they could become worked up into colonettes with caps and bases. Above them the soffits of the arches were generally still flat, but sometimes had edge-rolls also. An ordered arch of this early period might have a half-shaft run up the face of the impost to meet it.

Once the orders began to creep into the arch soffits and be repeated in their imposts, rolls called 'nook-shafts' became formed to fill in the re-entrant angles as well as the salient ones. We can see the beginnings of the system of Gothic mouldings.

During the early-medieval period this developed with great rapidity. The rolls became more slender, the quirks expanded into deep channels. Rolls became triple, the hollows between them deeply undercut. Soon the actual arch orders became invisible, submerged, as had been intended from the start, in a riot of mould-ings. (Plate 13.) Some rolls were pointed like a keel, others had little flat ribs running down them. Some had their sections moulded to 'ogee' forms.

This was the period of the Cistercian colonization of Yorkshire. Their great tower-less churches, denied carved ornament, worked out their own scheme of non-representational ornament in the form of richly-moulded arches.

A good deal of the early-medieval moulding mystique rubbed off on the parish churches. On the whole, however, their treatment of orders inclined towards the humble chamfer. (Fig. 25.) Coarse-ness was somehow avoided, and the small scale of the architecture

Fig. 24 *Development of masons' mouldings*
(a) The initial 'quirks' forming the 'bowtell'. (b) The completed 'roll'. (c) By working up the section, undercutting and shaping, the complete profile of the Early Gothic period is achieved.

was probably less suited to the opulence displayed by the great churches. The chamfer continued in use right through the High Gothic, sometimes tending towards concavities or even quite broad hollows. But parish church architecture on the whole did not attempt the wilder extravagances of moulding systems.

Piers supporting arcades began as blocks of walling left between the openings. The Anglian pier of the pre-medieval period usually had rolls or colonettes at the angles and a single impost moulding marking the springing line. A half-shaft was sometimes added to carry an ordered arch.

The circular pillar came in at the end of the eleventh century as a rough copy of the Classical column. It continued into the early-medieval period by which time it had attached to itself four slender shafts to make it cruciform on plan. (Fig. 26.)

But a circular pillar, even if provided with a wide square capital, is hopelessly ill-adapted to carry an arched structure over. Despite encouragement from Continental Gothic influences, by the end of the thirteenth century it had vanished for good in favour of the traditional cruciform pillar with simply chamfered edges. This is almost certainly of timber origin and designed to fit in with the similarly chamfered struts and braces connecting with the timber posts as they rose. (Figs. 25 and 26.) In masonry a springing line would be marked by an impost moulding.

The attached shaft, however, retained some influence, appearing against or as a projection from the pillar, varying its own projec-

Fig. 25 *Mouldings derived from carpentry*
The timber posts of the early buildings are joined by lateral struts or braces having their edges 'chamfered' free of sapwood. As a refinement, these chamfers are hollowed out. As the section develops, the simple hollows adopt a wavy profile, while slender shafts are added to improve the appearance of the flat faces of the four projections. These are the parish church mouldings.

tion from half- to three-quarter round. In the former case the impost moulding might pass round the profile of the pillar. The bolder shafts would probably have their own caps.

The pre-medieval capitals, the 'coniferous' and other variations on the Corinthianesque, and the early Byzantine cubical caps, have been dealt with elsewhere in this book. The purely Gothic cap—there were no large 'capitals' in Gothic architecture—was a somewhat complicated feature which never achieved a proper ordinance and unless smothered in carving is seen as a rather ugly piece of design.

Its top member, the 'impost moulding', is a repetition of the form of the string-course of its particular period. Below this comes a curiously coarse kind of 'abacus'. Below this again is the 'bell' of the cap, a vague hollow cone of indeterminate profile. Separating bell and shaft is the 'astragal' or necking, the traditional member employed in all columnar architecture at this point.

The base of the pillar was derived from the 'Attic base', the Classical model from which all such features had sprung. This base had two roll mouldings separated by a hollow or 'cavetto'. The Anglo-Saxon base was of slight projection with its members hardly differentiated, but the bases to the later circular pillars spread themselves to match the capitals over and often had small 'spurs' filling in the angle between base and column. In these bases the hollow member became so deeply excavated that it began to collect condensation down the walls. These 'water-holding' bases were therefore abandoned by filling up the hollow with a third roll. The form of the impost moulding changed to match, becoming less undercut at the end of the thirteenth century and finally changing to the triple roll.

The development of the parish church pillar from the early-medieval through the High Gothic may best be described as a progression from the fully-moulded pillar with a continuous capping towards a 'cruciform' pillar with miniature caps to its four attached shafts. In any case the real finish to the pillar is the impost moulding marking the springing line of the arch.

The complete impost moulding as seen capping a pillar or respond is a combination of moulding and cap. Its upper member is the normal moulding which forms the string-course of the period. Below this comes a wide hollow acting as a sort of 'bell' to the feature ; this is sometimes carved. Below this the impost is completed by a small roll or 'astragal'. All these Gothic cap mouldings, never managed with the same skill as those running with the arch, appear wretched without the attentions of the carver who could fill the bell with foliage, as during the fourteenth century. (Plate 13.)

Arches were sometimes allowed to run their mouldings right down into the pillars without any indication of the springing line.

In single arches where the span was small, projecting responds particularly obstructive and the wall massive enough to take any thrust from the arch, as in the case of a tower arch, the arch orders were allowed to die away into the respond—the 'discontinuous impost'. Another way of avoiding obstructive responds was to let the arch spring from a corbel.

It is only from within a great church that one can receive the full impact of the richness of Gothic mouldings. But most old parish churches, even the humblest, will usually display an example or two of that other most characteristic aspect of Gothic architecture, the traceried window.

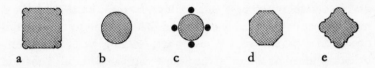

a   b   c   d   e

Fig. 26ᵣ *Pier and Pillars*
> (a) The heavy 'Anglian' pier of the eleventh century with its angle-rolls, derived from the Byzantine. (b) The plain circular 'Romanesque' pillar of the twelfth century, most common in the South and West. (c) The early Gothic pillar with attached shafts. (d) Plain octagonal pillars are common to Gothic parish churches of all periods. (e) The 'cruciform' pillar of the High Gothic.

Owing to our climate, the smallest aperture in the walling affects the comfort of those within the building to a degree far greater than in warmer countries in which architecture had been born and developed prior to its appearance in Western Europe.

In the small parish church of pre-medieval days the little windows are few and are often set so high up in the walling that they could not have been reached even to shutter them. They would not have been glazed, and had no drip-stones to prevent their collecting stormwater running down the wall-face over them. So they were set as high as possible to reduce the amount of this and perhaps find some protection from the overhang of the eaves.

Medieval glass was cast in diamond-shaped 'quarries' set in lead 'calms' and the panel sprung into grooves cut into the stonework. These grooves were set into a flat area of stone surround representing the exact sight opening of the window. In order to allow as much light as possible to reach the interior of the building this flat area was kept as small as might be and the stonework splayed away on both sides so as to expand the size of the actual opening as quickly as possible.

When it appeared, the mullion adopted the same system of chamfers, keeping as narrow a front as possible to the light. At first the chamfers were flat but they soon became concave, remaining so until the end of the medieval period. During the latter part of the sixteenth century the mullion became convex, to continue in that form as long as the feature survived.

During the early-medieval period, when the 'lancet' windows had been set in pairs with masonry forming embryo mullions separating them, it became the practice to extend this masonry upwards and provide there a quatrefoil light, the whole design being incorporated within the internal arched head of the window opening. In this way was invented the system of filling a window opening with bar tracery.

It was the multiplicity of patterns available to the ingenious mason with his 'compasses' which enabled him to raise the High Gothic to a degree of aesthetic excellence that has allowed it to become one of the great historical architectural styles. The introduction of the triangular 'cusp', which enabled the heads of all windows to be foliated, greatly added to the liveliness of the designs.

The heads of the windows could be varied in a number of ways. The shapes could be steeply pointed or depressed. An ogee head could be used. The drip-stones could be covered with crockets. Major mullions could be treated as aedicular buttresses. Running ornament could be spread over the stonework as fancy dictated. For as dressed masonry turned out by a mason of the highest skill, and unfettered by any rigid ordinance, there was no limit to the aesthetic possibilities offered by a large Gothic window.

There were the two main schools of tracery, the curvilinear and the rectilinear. The former was best suited to tall openings, the latter to broader ones. In the normal course of events, windows became wider, their arches correspondingly lower in pitch, and their tracery tending more and more towards the rectilinear. But there is no doubt that the two styles were interchangeable, appear in the same buildings at the same period, and were more dependent upon circumstances and taste than upon historical period.

Tracery spread from the windows of the High Gothic all over the structure. It covered wall-faces and intruded itself into vaulting. It developed its own systems of 'orders'—primary, secondary and so forth—as its complications increased. The major orders of tracery produced small rolls to their mullions and bars. In large treatments such as the Somerset bell-towers the elaboration of the members grew until each had a series of mouldings almost going back to the riches of early Gothic days. One may well ponder on what might have been the end of such brilliant excursions into masonry if progress had been allowed to take its course.

But parish church architecture quickly collapsed at the Reformation, the skill of centuries has in an instant of time to be thrown on the scrap heap while the disorganized remnants of medieval freemasonry strive to assimilate a new ordinance and try it out on a new type of building. It is only in special features such as arcades, which adopt Classical forms, and windows which are larger than the domestic, that the details of the Renaissance church differ from those of the mansion of the period.

16

Ornament

———

All architectural styles employ ornament, sometimes purely for embellishment, more frequently with some architectural purpose in view, such as to emphasize some particular feature or to disguise some defect or awkwardness in its character.

The most interesting type of ornament is that which is purely architectural, such as the moulded arch or its imposts, of the form of columnar architecture's most important feature, the capital.

The legendary origin of the Corinthian capital is always worth recalling. Of the sculptor of ancient Corinth who placed upon the grave of his infant daughter a basket containing her toys, with a flat stone on top to keep out the rain. And how, returning later, he found that the acanthus fern he had planted on the grave had climbed the sides of the basket and curled under the stone in a manner which he was able to capture and perpetuate for ever as the Corinthian capital.

His capital formed the crowning glory of the mighty temples of Hellenistic days and spread through Rome and Byzantium to our shores. Even in its most primitive forms its spirit seems to haunt in particular the churches of the twelfth and thirteenth centuries, linking rustic England with the seas Odysseus sailed.

Prior to the introduction of the first 'Corinthianesque' capitals into this country the early designers used Doric forms, either the Rhenish 'cubical' cap for completing the various types of edge- and nook-shafting, or the curious Byzantine 'cushion' capitals for heavier work. It was the effect of the Corinthian type of capital upon the latter forms which produced the typically English 'coniferous' capital and later endowed it with the uncurling fronds of the Corinthian volutes.

There is something particularly charming about the miniature twelfth-century Corinthian cap. Though so different from its Classical prototype it seems nevertheless to have completely captured its spirit and converted it into a feature as gracious in its Nordic way as the opulent Mediterranean capital of antiquity. This is especially true of the smaller varieties employed on the shafts attending upon columns and imposts.

The full-scale capital of Classical origin does not pass into the thirteenth century, its place being taken by a system of mouldings such as was becoming the hall-mark of the early-medieval period. But the small capital or cap remains upon the shafting and continues to do so until the end of the Middle Ages. Always retaining the basic Corinthian form, its bell absorbs the volutes and formalizes their shapes. Then these shapes develop into magnificent carving based on English naturalistic forms, all this finally disappearing altogether in the general austerity of the later period and leaving the bell bare.

The weakest item of the Gothic ordinance is due to its failure to agree upon the proper form for a capital. The Corinthian, filtering down the centuries through the long distances from its homeland, reached this country retaining its three main elements, the abacus or impost moulding, the spreading bell, and the small astragal separating this from the shaft. The frond-like volutes continued for a while to endow the bell with its peculiar distinction, but if carvers were lacking to provide these items the bell might have to be left unadorned, leaving the capital forlornly incomplete, a poor substitute for the crowning features known to antiquity.

As a capping to a large pier or clustered pillar the three elements of the capital could be utilized, in typical Gothic fashion, to form a band of moulding, with the bell portion extended to provide a broad hollow. In first-class work of the fourteenth century this cove could be filled with carving (Plate 13), but in the parish church it might have to remain bare, looking particularly crude when exposed above a simple, as opposed to a compound, pillar.

During the fifteenth century all three parts of the capital were merged to form the typical profile of the period with its broad upper splay, the dullest, but at the same time the most confident form achieved by this troubled feature. From the fifteenth-century capital is derived the large cornice-type moulding which is the sign-manual of the end of the Gothic era. (Fig. 27*d*.)

In addition to the architectural ornament one finds in association with structural features such as capitals, there is a great variety of ornamental devices which are purely decorative. The pre-medieval churches were full of such. The zigzag or 'chevron' is a prolific motif (Plate 10), so is the 'billet' moulding of simple rolls sawn into pieces and with each alternate one removed. In antithesis to such barbarous ornament is the appearance of Classical floral scrolls winding along some wide roll. Again we revert to paganism with the beaked heads of Nordic mythology paying no tribute to any known style of architecture.

Another interesting form of pre-medieval ornament was the 'battlement'. This would certainly have nothing to do with the military feature as this did not come into use in this form until centuries later. The motif is probably allied to the Hellenistic fret and represents ornament copied from clothing, probably round the neck. An indication that ornamental features of clothing were copied in stone is seen in the diaper motif, clearly representing smocking, frequently encountered among these rich displays of ornament.

It is this array of repetitive ornament, displaying a great diversity of motifs, which has come to be called 'Norman'. It is however peculiarly English; that it continues to develop despite the Norman invasion is evidence of its vigour. Anyone who has come upon the tremendous turbulence of the chancel arch at Tickencote in Rutland, or the riches displayed by the whole church of Elkstone in Gloucestershire, must surely realize that art of this ebullience is native and never the product of imported carvers forced upon the local craftsmen. (Plate 29.)

A feature appearing everywhere throughout English architecture is the running motif of a system of small items of carving set along a hollow moulding. In pre-medieval days it was the little pyramids known as 'nail-heads'. Later these became cut into until

they were remodelled as a pile of four narrow leaves which antiquaries, seeing in them some resemblance to violets, have come to
call 'dog-tooth'. (See Plate 10.)

At the end of the thirteenth century the motif changes completely, being replaced by a curious little bud called a 'ball-flower'.
The broad hollows of the fifteenth century which replaced the
original deep channels required different treatment in the form of
square paterae formed of groups of oak-leaves.

The models for the semi-representational floral carving of the
medieval era cannot always be determined with accuracy. While
by the High Gothic period accurate representations of leaves and
flowers appear, as in such lovely achievements as we may find in
Exeter Cathedral or Southwell chapter house, the early-medieval
'stiff-leaf' with its crudely-carved leaves of clover-like form may
be nothing but a symbol of the Trinity. The 'crocket' which climbs
the sides of pinnacles and even spires is certainly derived from the
Corinthian 'volute', but does its English form represent any particular native plant? The Gothic finial or 'pommel' with its pair of
half-open cabbage-like leaves flanking a central one appears everywhere on buildings and bench-ends. Has it, too, some forgotten
legend to explain its origin?

Carving has always played an important part in the ornamentation of the medieval churches. While schools of carving must have
existed, the shaping of soft stone, such as clunch, with the aid of a
chisel, or even a knife, is a natural occupation and much of the
carved ornament of the Middle Ages must have been amateur,
enthusiastic if not actually inspired. Beautiful statuary may be met
with in churches, though of course by far the majority of such
achievements perished after 1539 or at the middle of the next century. But there are many smaller portraits to be found in corbels
and the like, especially heads of kings and queens, bishops and
abbots, which may well be true portraits. The accuracy of such
botanical studies as those of Exeter or Southwell suggest that the
sculptors of the Middle Ages were far from being all amateurs.

There appears to be a wide division between art of this degree
and the vigorous, irrepressible productions of the carvers of the
medieval grotesques. The pre-medieval corbel-tables formed the

first playgrounds of the amateur carver, for the corbel is always watching you as you pass—seeming always to be tempting you to glance up at it as it pokes its medieval fun at you. Nor did the stately architecture of the High Gothic venture to abandon the traditional grotesque from its art. Still the writhing dragons spew out the stormwater upon our heads while the funny little medieval peasants play their obscene japes to tease the ladies. As we look up into the vaulting of the porch we can never be sure whether its central boss will be some lovely wreath of foliage or a hideous mask putting out its tongue at us. Generally, however, the vaulting boss was a site for the more gracious forms of sculptured art.

Generally speaking, the masons and carvers of the early-medieval period strove to abolish the crudities of previous centuries and achieve an effect of refinement and delicacy. In the more important buildings this resulted first in the development of mouldings to lighten the structural features, then, with the coming of the High Gothic, in the use of fine carving to embellish them. Neither of these phases really penetrated deeply into the sphere of the parish church for lack of skilled masons and sculptors to carry them out.

The last phase, however, was the replacement of grace by a more disciplined approach to architectural embellishment represented by panelled designs. This was more in line with the capabilities of the parish church mason and during the fifteenth century, when his activities became more and more sought after, mason-made panelling, not sculptured ornament, became the keynote of the decorative system of his architecture. Under this influence pillars tended to become panelled piers as masons co-operated with the screen-making joiners who were increasing their architectural activities at this time.

While in antiquity the carver's art almost certainly developed from experiments upon soft stone, English carving is much more likely to have been first employed upon timberwork, as seen in the prows of ancient ships. After England had profited from its excellent supply of freestone to become a land of masons, the carvers followed their efforts in the new material. But the English 'wright', far from relinquishing his efforts to the mason, extended these until

by the fifteenth century he was producing magnificent achievements, both in the carpentry of his roofs (Plates 19 and 20) and
in the intricate joinery of his screenwork. (Plate 22.) Once again
the carvers followed the material, and many of the old masonry
forms—such as fan-vaulting—were translated into joinery, while
the masons were retaliating by copying the panelled motifs of the
joiners on their wall-faces. But the carpenters were winning, and
all the old masons' motifs, such as vaulting bosses, were appearing
as ornaments to mask the junctions of roof-timbers. (Plate 18.)

The Tudor era saw the use of badges as ornamental motifs,
perhaps the beginnings of political publicity in architecture. The
stylized five-petal wild rose of the Tudors took the place of the
earlier naturalistic achievements. During the sixteenth century
Spanish influence resulted in the open pomegranate with its cluster
of pips.

Heraldic emblems had been in use for a long time. The names
of our country inns—the Red Lion, the White Hart—remain to
remind us that during the Middle Ages such heraldic charges were
familiar to all. In an illiterate population the main features of local
heraldry—the sheaves of Hungerford, the bleak chevrons of the
great House of Clare—would be familiar to all the inhabitants of a
district living in the shadow of some noble landowner. Again our
inn-signs testify—the Beauchamp Arms, the Duke of Suffolk.
During the High Gothic phase, heraldry plays a large part in the
carved ornament of churches, often indicating some part of the
building built by the person thus commemorated. Roof-bosses, in
stone and wood, are the usual sites for heraldic displays. And the
shields are scattered thickly about the arcaded biers upon which
the knights and their ladies sleep down the centuries, where—

> 'for past transgressions they atone,
> by saying endless prayers . . . in stone!'

The early Renaissance ornament of the late sixteenth and early
seventeenth centuries exhibits two main characteristics. First come
the plain forms derived from the use of framed panelling with
moulded edges, the panels themselves being filled in with crude
geometrical forms such as flat pyramids. The other is the elaborate

carving which took many forms and was mainly derived from the Spanish 'Plateresque' or 'Silversmiths'' style of ornament which reached this country as a spate after the Reformation by way of its refugees. The architectural forms of this post-Reformation decorative style consist mainly of ill-digested Baroque shapes translated into a form of strapwork with the ends turned up.

The carving was in low relief, contrasting in this respect with the medieval work which knew nothing of such treatments. At the mid-sixteenth century roundels displaying imaginary portraits of Roman emperors were in vogue. The joiners who had been engaged upon church screenwork continued their efforts without a check. Existing parish churches continued to employ them to make not only screens but such items as pewing and the new pulpits. The first half of the seventeenth century saw a riot of sculpture spreading through parish churches, until it was all stopped with dramatic suddenness by the far more serious Reformation which removed the new Head of the English Church.

Important features to note during the Elizabethan/Jacobean era are those derived from Baroque architectural motifs converted, for lack of lathes, to a squared form. Of these the most important is the baluster, the bulbous colonette found everywhere in such situations as the king-posts of roofs. The most curious feature of all is the finial of the period, appearing as a kind of square onion, sometimes hollowed out like a pumpkin ghost. The same device appears as a drop, perhaps recalling in a somewhat shamefaced fashion the glorious pendants of the High Gothic twilight.

The Civil War which occupied most of the fifth decade of the seventeenth century was not the political revolution of a century earlier but a religious upheaval which put an end to all vestiges of the medieval Church. Architecturally its effect was to eliminate all ornament, not only omitting it from new churches but attempting to obliterate it in those already existing. In such Puritan districts as East Anglia the destruction was very considerable, windows in particular being deprived of their painted glass. It is fortunate that the chief architectural glories of the region, its angel-covered roofs, were too far off to be reached by the iconoclasts.

The Classical elements in Renaissance architecture, however, were at this time becoming acceptable provided they were austere and inclined towards the Doric.

After the zeal of the Puritans had faded and the more comfortable churches of the Georgians had replaced the preaching-houses, the Corinthian Order began once more to cast its spell upon the architecture of the churches. In this Order the cornices are most elaborate. Amongst its standard ornaments are the 'dentil course' cut into small square teeth and the rows of shaped brackets or 'modillions' which help to support the overhanging 'corona'.

As early as the twelfth century the walls of churches were being decorated with paint. The colours used were red and ochre and the designs were based on contemporary carved motifs such as the zigzag or billet. During the early-medieval period when so much attention was being paid to the excellence of masonry wall-faces, walls were sometimes whitened over and a system of jointing painted on the surface. Various representations of the 'stiff-leaf' motif may also be found.

The Byzantine churches were alive with mosaic portraits of the Deity and attendant saints. The greater English churches reproduced the same kinds of portraiture in paint. But it was not until late in the medieval period that representational art appeared in the parish church. As the decorator became artist the church wall became covered with life-size figures, certain parts of the building having their special assignment. Across the nave from the main door, usually that on the south side, we may often find a huge St. Christopher carrying Christ as a boy across a river. Over the chancel arch was a favourite situation for a 'Doom'. So much of this medieval art was removed during the whitewashing of Puritan days that it is difficult to appreciate today the extensive use of church walling as picture-books for the instruction of congregations.

Post-Reformation churches also had their wall-paintings, for the most part representing Baroque scrolls; lettered texts may be incorporated. Among the less attractive features of church ornament are the boards displaying the Mosaic Law and the Creed set beside the altar during the eighteenth century, an appeal to morality taking the place of the medieval threat of Hell Fire.

Ornament

The chief glories of the parish church will always have been its carved ornament. No other historical style—except possibly the Hellenistic in its latest manifestations—employed the carver to the same extent as the Gothic.

For the students of art there are the lovely forms of fourteenth-century capitals or the incredible richness of the screenwork of the following century.

And for everyman are the portraits. So many of them one feels assured are true to life, and one longs to know who they were. And as amusing as ever are the caricatures. Grinning and mowing, telling lies and plagued with toothache, our ancestors are still there, laughing at us down the centuries, caught for ever by the chisel of the medieval carver. The England that was, helping us to endure in our turn the England of today.

17

Furnishings

===

When one compares a cathedral such as Salisbury, gone through and swept out like a long-neglected attic by a late-eighteenth century 'restorer', with its neighbour Winchester, still packed with the accumulated history of eight centuries, one begins to appreciate the manner in which any old church, even the parish church of a small village, may contain within its walls a museum of historical objects quite independent of its architectural structure.

While down the centuries there have doubtless been occasions when some forward-looking individual has removed some despised feature and replaced it with something more fashionable, there are still plenty of items left over from all periods each of which adds to the history and interest of the village to which it has served for so long as a focus of parish life.

Some of these features are part of the structure, or semi-permanent partitions such as screenwork. But there are a number of movable items, decorative features or even furniture, moved about from time to time within the building as circumstance dictated. And notwithstanding their significance as memorials of the dead beneath, some of the objects which time has shuffled about the building are its tombs.

Beneath the paving of the village churches sleep the village forefathers, their bones turned over from time to time to make way for crowding successors.

Only in the great churches do we find early tomb-slabs with inscriptions. During the illiterate Middle Ages the indication as to who lay beneath had to be left to the skill of the engraver in brass.

From the thirteenth century onwards we find the memorial brasses, each with an inscription and usually a portrait of the deceased in helm and chain-mail, let into a matrix cut in the tomb-slab. By the Tudor period the brasses were no longer being set into the flooring where they were getting worn by the passage of feet, but were fixed to the sides of tombs or the architectural treatments above these. A large number of brasses have been worn away or removed so that only their matrices remain.

Not until the seventeenth century do we find many tomb-slabs bearing inscriptions. The lettering of these is usually crude, but during the next century it may become very fine, both capitals and script.

Figure sculpture has always been a popular method of indicating the nature of the occupant of a tomb. During the twelfth century the tomb of a bishop often had his portrait effigy set lying upon it, incised into the tomb-slab. By the early-medieval period the life-size effigy was finding its way into many parish churches where it is found lying in low-arched niches formed in aisle walls and tran-sept ends to accommodate it. Mail clad-knights and their ladies, however, have far too often been shunted about their churches to make way for the re-planning schemes of the centuries since their deaths.

During the High Gothic era the so-called 'altar tomb' became the fashion. The feature represented a tall bier, arcaded about and often embellished with sculpture and heraldry, upon which lay the portrait effigy of the deceased. They are found everywhere in our old churches, some of them surprising examples of medieval furniture. Seeing them, one may be tempted to muse upon the lost loveliness shattered to ruin beneath the tumbling vaulting of the great monastic choirs.

The parish chancel had originally been reserved for the burial place of priests but during the Middle Ages important lay folk found sepulture there. By the end of the sixteenth century the Reformation had finally released these now somewhat discredited sanctuaries for them to serve as mausoleums for the new rich now denied tomb-room in the vanished minsters.

In life, the Elizabethan magnates advertised their riches in their raiment, in death they displayed it, in lieu of the plate-armour of their quarrelsome predecessors, on their impressive sepulchres. With the curious ill-taste of the age they abandoned the dignity of the medieval bier for the livelier setting of the four-poster bed. Many were the ponderous monuments they set up it this form, with themselves and their wives lying, fully clothed in ruffs and all the sartorial paraphernalia of the Elizabethan, upon these mighty couches, and arranging about them the kneeling figurines of their obedient offspring in attitudes of worship to God and their parents.

One cannot make mere mention of these and other Tudor tombs without drawing attention to the very fine artistry of many of the portrait effigies themselves. From the time of the Wars of the Roses onwards many of these effigies, especially those sculptured in alabaster, are breathtakingly beautiful. Little attention however is paid to them as their recumbent position allows them to be viewed only in a foreshortened aspect and it is usually impossible to see them properly without erecting some kind of scaffold. All the more glory to their sculptors who well knew that only Heaven would see in eternity the portraits they created.

So when one is feeling shocked by some monstrous Elizabethan sepulchre it is often pleasant to draw aside the curtain of the architecture and try to obtain a glimpse of perhaps some fine portrait statue lying serene amidst the meretricious nonsense about it.

Fortunately for the development of English sepulchral art the chancel of the parish church could not go on finding room indefinitely for such monstrosities. So lesser memorials came into fashion, fixed to the walls, depicting the Jacobean gentleman and his wife kneeling opposite each other in a pair of rounded-head niches ornamented in the curious sub-Renaissance of the period.

The change-over from floor to wall marked the trend of future sepulchral monuments in churches. The portrait statue remained, but now it was set in an upright position and surrounded by a Renaissance frame. Some of the noble dead of the Civil War were thus remembered. The standing figure remained until the end of the next century, but the tendency was for less expensive treatments with a bust of the deceased instead of the whole figure. Simple urns and sarcophagi appear in the eighteenth century. Some of the baroque monuments of the Georgian era are magnificent achievements, crowned by pediments and attended by cherubs, the whole in a setting of scrolls, swags, and here and there a skull.

In addition to these huge monuments we find a great array of simple wall memorials, slabs and cartouches, with a lettered inscription and a baroque surround to scale. At the end of the eighteenth century the Carrara slabs begin to appear, simple and austere with lettering which soon turns to ugly type. The sculpture remains, some of it bold but much of it in low relief. The loveliness of Flaxman's work sometimes shines in a village church.

Amongst the memorials of old parishioners are the 'hatchments' carried at the funerals of armigerous gentry and their wives or widows. These square canvases display the arms of the deceased, the divisions of the black and white backgrounds indicating his or her marital status and whether or not spouses were alive at the time. Accoutrements such as helmets and gauntlets, some made up specially for the purpose, may be found associated with late-medieval and Civil War monuments.

Once King Henry VIII had announced his title as head of the English Church in place of the Pope it became obligatory for the Royal Arms to be displayed in every church. Many of these still remain from the seventeenth and eighteenth centuries, far too often banished nowadays into some dark corner of the building.

Though usually far less prominent than the parish church's monuments, the font is often by far the oldest item of furniture in the building. Many a pre-medieval font, scene of the baptism of every villager for century after century, has survived the rebuilding of the church without having been replaced by a more fashionable successor.

This is surprising in view of the extreme crudity of many of these early fonts and indicates the veneration in which they must have been held in medieval days. The pre-medieval fonts were usually mere circular tubs of stone. The more primitive the shape of the font, the greater the likelihood of its being carved with lively sculpture of Anglo-Saxon type.

Twelfth-century fonts are often formed in the manner of coniferous capitals, mounted on a squat shaft and given a base similar to that of the contemporary pillar.

The tendency of the font was for it to grow in height so as to facilitate the act of immersion. The early-medieval design was to support the edge of the bowl with a ring of the slender shafts typical of the architecture of the period. The bowl was usually octagonal and often surrounded by simple arcading.

The High Gothic font was a sophisticated piece of furniture. Of what is known as 'chalice' form, it was octagonal and arranged so that bowl, stem and base were part of a complete design. It was often a fine piece of work with buttressed stem and sculptured figures and emblems. In its simpler form the sides of the bowl were ornamented with incised quatrefoils. The base is heavily moulded and often raised upon a step.

The post-Reformation font was far removed from the sturdy medieval form. Often formed in marble, it nearly always took the form of a baroque baluster of the more monumental type used not for balustrades but singly for a garden feature such as a sundial.

A font cover to keep dust out of the bowl was one of the features turned out by the splendid woodworkers of the High Gothic. It is usually fashioned as the aedicular representation of a very fine spire. Some late-medieval font covers are probably the finest creations of the Gothic Age. Post-Reformation font covers are plain boards supporting a fretwork finial formed out of crude baroque scrolls. During the eighteenth century they became small ogee domes.

While the sermon has always played a part in the parish Mass, no architectural provision for its delivery appears to have been made until late in the Middle Ages. The pulpit built into the wall and approached by steps formed in its thickness was generally to be found in the monastic refectories and there are a few examples to be seen in parish churches. One late-medieval example known to the writer is on the north side of an aisle-less nave immediately to the west of its lateral wing, a position which corresponds approximately with the monastic arrangement, though it is generally understood that in medieval days the sermon was delivered from the chancel arch.

Confirmation of this is suggested by the appearance, at the end of the fifteenth century, of the occasional tall slender pulpit, as at Holne in Devonshire, forming part of the elaborate timberwork associated with the rood-screen and elevating the preacher above the heads of the congregation in a church possibly still unprovided with fixed seating.

In view of the fact that after the Reformation the pulpit was the most important item of church furniture and that existing ones would presumably have been retained, one is forced to the conclusion that the pulpit was not a normal feature of medieval churches. Neither the great preaching naves of the friars' churches, nor the hall churches of the West, seem to have had them. But of course the medieval monastic pulpit built into the wall could hardly have been constructed in an aisled building, so that had pulpits been used in the average church it would have been necessary to build them up as a piece of detached furniture, presumably in wood.

The pulpit as an item of furniture comes in without warning during the sixteenth century and by the Stuart era it was to be seen in every church. The seventeenth-century pulpit is an interesting piece of furniture with its sides ornamented in Renaissance motifs and provided with a stair and balustrade. The usual rather crude fretwork scrolls carry it, and above is an acoustic device comprising a back-piece joining with an octagonal 'sounding-board' spreading out over the whole pulpit. Many of these huge pieces of seventeenth- and eighteenth-century joinery seem to have vanished today, their moorings to pillar or wall having become unsafe, threatening with extinction the preacher beneath.

During the eighteenth century the pulpit with its ever-expanding sounding-board remains the most prominent feature of the interior of the parish church. With the era of the 'horse-box' pews it had to be raised still higher above the congregation, becoming 'three-decker' and having incorporated into its lower stages a reading-desk for the lessons and a box for the 'clerk' who led the responses to the Protestant prayers.

As has been noted earlier, it was the emphasis upon the sermon, indicated by the introduction of the pulpit as a standard item of church furniture, which brought about the provision of a proper seating system within the parish church. Throughout the Middle Ages, congregations, when not kneeling in prayer, were forced to stand. In some churches, however, stone seats were provided around the walls of the building—giving rise to the saying 'let the weakest go to the wall'—and round the bases of pillars. Even as late as the last century some humble churches were still unprovided with enough pitch-pine pews, or even benches, and stone seating survived as the only form of furnishing. Worshippers forced to use these brought with them straw or bracken as insulation against the chill of the stone.

The introduction of fixed seating during the fifteenth century gave the joiners and wood-carvers of the period a full measure of experience. The seats themselves were ordinary benches formed of boards set at either end into heavy timbers called 'bench-ends'. As these lined the passages between the seated areas the bench-ends had to be embellished with some form of carving. The bench-ends of the fifteenth century were covered with carved ornament, often incorporating figures. Each bench-end was swept up into an ogee and crowned with a 'pommel' finial. By the sixteenth century the bench-end was still being richly carved but the Gothic pommel had gone and the top was square. Most of the finest examples are in the West Country. Elsewhere the interest in such costly furniture had been for some time on the decrease. In a Will of 1449 we find the testator providing for the re-furnishing of his parish church at Stamford in Lincolnshire; he particularly specifies *plain* desks, a *plain* rood-loft, and pewing 'not curiously, but plainly wrought'.

Throughout the history of parish church architecture in England, it will be noted that the South-West was always a century or so behind the times. Its parish churches date from a period at which the rest of England was already well equipped with buildings of all periods. The belated but vigorous burst in church-building was maintained right up to the Reformation and the arts of joinery and wood-carving continued unabated until the heavy hand of the Puritans came down upon them once and for all. During the Civil War the South-West was the staunchest in support of the Old Order, constrasting in this respect with the disloyalty of East Anglia and Yorkshire, older and more cynical regions.

The bench-end died out with the coming of the Renaissance when pews came to be framed up in sophisticated style and the ends were reduced to a panelled frame. Finials were sometimes introduced, either the 'square onions' of the Jacobeans or the rather charming acorns which succeeded them.

The next revolution in the seating of parish churches appears during the Georgian era and is concerned with the important consideration of bodily comfort. The monastic choirs had been warmed for the night offices by huge braziers set in their midst. The village churches presumably had no such amenities. Possibly the medieval congregation kept warm by stealthy movement; the introduction of fixed seating would however have put an end to this. The length of the Puritan sermon must have added to the discomfort of congregations sufficiently disciplined during the seventeenth century to sustain them but a century later becoming restless.

Among the many elaborately-carved items of furniture introduced into the parish churches of the first half of the seventeenth century were 'box-pews' seating two or three people, enclosed within waist-high screens and complete with doors, symptomatic of the middle-class attitude of the post-medieval era. This kind of display being of course anathema to the Puritan victors of the Great Rebellion, little of it can have survived this into the latter half of the century. But the idea had been established as a panacea to offset the hardships of winter sermons, so the intelligent Georgians completely re-seated their parish churches, providing a system of box-pews, almost man-high and provided with doors, to keep away draughts and perhaps allow worshippers in strategic positions to slumber undetected. The squire's pew sometimes had a fireplace set in an outside wall. Over all towered the panelled three-decker with its menacing sounding-board.

A great many of these 'horse-box' interiors were swept away during the restoration mania of the Victorian era. In their day the

Georgians probably destroyed a vast number of magnificent medieval bench-ends, only to have their own pews swept away to be replaced in their turn by feeble imitations of medieval pewing. Is it possibly due to the kindlier climate of the South-West that so many beautiful church interiors have been suffered to remain in their medieval form?

It was fortunate for Victorian congregations re-medievalizing their churches that they could now be warmed with piped hot water.

During the previous three centuries a considerable number of chancels appear to have become derelict or mutilated beyond hope of 'restoration', or simply to have disappeared altogether. A large number of new chancels were built during the Victorian era. In them, and in all the ancient ones as restored, lateral seating was provided, in imitation of cathedral stalls, to accommodate a surpliced choir brought thither from the demolished west gallery. With them came the pipe organ, to be re-sited in an 'organ chamber' extruded from the chancel wall and combining with a new 'vestry' to confuse still further the plan of many an ancient church.

The installation of some form of heating in an old parish church presents a problem which is however as nothing when compared with the provision of an appropriate form of lighting. One wonders what artificial lighting they had in medieval days when only the priest needed to read. Probably a simple boat-shaped oil lamp with a floating wick. Some of the isolated corbels found here and there in an old church may have been provided to carry such lamps.

Fortunate is the parish which has managed to keep its eighteenth-century 'spider' chandelier still scintillating above its chancel. In parenthesis it is pleasant to report that excellent reproductions of these charming features can at the present time be obtained; their lighting value may not be up to contemporary standards but their aesthetic properties more than make up for this deficiency.

On a summer Sunday the bells ring out over the English countryside. But how many of us think of the activity which fills the ringing-floors as the captain of each tower grunts his strange commands while the 'sallies' lift and plunge? How many people, admiring the pinnacled belfry stories of such glorious towers as that of Huish Episcopi in Somerset, think of the ancient machinery hidden behind the tracery of its windows, framing the lively bells which the whole magnificent structure was raised to carry?

Many of our bell frames are as old as their towers, their massive timbers solidly mortised together to hold firm against the tremendous whip of a ring of perhaps ten or more bells swinging in all directions in a great roar of sound. Each bell is strapped to a 'headstock' by a series of iron bands, the stock itself swinging in iron-bound 'gudgeons' strapped to the timbers of the frame. Attached to the headstock is a beautifully-framed wheel in the grooved rim of which the bell-rope is housed.

At rest, the bells hang down. In this position they may be 'chimed' by pulling on the rope and letting the bell rock to and fro. But before ringing a peal, the bells have to be 'pulled up' in a great clangour of sound until each is at rest mouth upward, held by a stay fixed to its headstock. A slight tug on the rope, and round goes the bell, sounding as it goes and coming to rest again at the other side of its swing. Then a tug on the fluffy 'sally' and round she goes again.

England is the only country with a tradition of 'ringing' church bells. In other lands bells are either chimed or sounded like a ship's bell by a rope secured to the clapper. In this country the tradition is of ringing bells in 'changes', each individual bell passing in turn through its companions until the original scale has been regained and the bells are once more 'in rounds'. This involves considerable skill, yet all over the country women as well as men continue to maintain one of the few genuinely traditional customs of medieval England.

Under the sound of the bells lies the parish churchyard. During the Middle Ages, and into the last century, the families of the squires were buried inside the building. The villagers went to the churchyard, and had no memorials other than the churchyard cross which most parishes seem to have raised on the south side of the church. These crosses vary considerably in the quality of their design, some being very humble and others fine monuments in the highest Gothic tradition, and are mounted upon a stepped base.

Furnishings

In the illiterate Middle Ages the poor had no epitaphs. No stones marked their graves. Not until the seventeenth century do we find churchyard memorials. But the great period of churchyard tombs was the Georgian, when the baroque 'table-tomb' came into fashion. Most of our village churchyards can show some of these impressive monuments with their panelled sides and balustered angles. The tiny church of Winson in the Cotswolds owns a fine series of these, the finest of all churchyard memorials.

Few churchyards seem to be without an ancient yew tree. As children we were solemnly told that these trees were grown in churchyards to provide timber for the manufacture of long bows. But a moment's thought will expose the improbability of such a theory. Farmers will tell you a different story. The churchyard yew is an insurance against defective churchyard fencing. For the foliage of the yew is fatal to cattle.

The parish churches played an important part during the Civil War. As public buildings of permanent construction they were used as armouries, magazines, and prisoner-of-war cages. Often they were actually garrisoned, usually in an emergency such as during a retreat, and many of them endured stern sieges. A surprisingly large number of them still show traces of battles fought around them: shot-holes in their towers, bullet-scars round their doorways. Perhaps the most dramatic incident was at Alton in Hampshire where Royalist cavalry under Colonel Bowles, trapped by a superior force, galloped to the churchyard and defended it behind a rampart of their slaughtered horses. Driven at last into the church, they died to a man, their colonel making a last stand in the pulpit. To recall this gallant episode in English history makes it difficult to enter Alton Church today without a sensation of awe.

The character of the parish church must have been strangely transformed to suit the cult of Puritanism which for a decade submerged them. And how glad they must have felt when they reached the year 1660 and they could once more display the royal heraldry upon their walls. To this day the 29th of May, birthday of King Charles II, is welcomed by the tall towers of Cornwall, each displaying above its battlements the branch of an oak tree in gratitude for the sanctuary it afforded him after a lost battle.

18

Notes on Dating

========

Visitors to an old parish church may view it through different eyes. To many there is the human interest presented by its memorials with their inscriptions and epitaphs. Aesthetically there are many aspects of old churches to delight the eye—the splendour of some fine late-medieval building has a different appeal from that of the humbler church in its setting of towering elms. Within, one may discover a narrow shrine of unknown antiquity or watch the play of light and shade in a pillared interior full of artistry in its sculptured memorials.

To the architect the interest lies in the variety of planning concepts and the ingenuity of structural devices of other days. But to the antiquary—who in order to study buildings should possess more than a smattering of architectural knowledge—the building presents a problem in historical detection. What are its origins, visible or conjectural, and what is its subsequent history of development?

It is hoped that among the foregoing chapters the student may discover observations which will help him with his research. But the writer thought it might be as well if he should recapitulate some of the items more particularly concerned with attempts at dating an old parish church.

Beginning with the building masses themselves, an interesting start can be made if the church should have a central tower. This may have started as a pre-medieval tower-nave. Crossing arches may be insertions of later date. Blocked-up arches in an old west tower may suggest that this began its existence as a tower-nave.

Signs of the lateral wings which indicate a pseudo-cruciform church of about the time of the Conquest may be looked for. These may be scars on the nave walls marking vanished roofs or walls. One may find signs of the actual arch which led into a wing. A difference in the form of the easternmost arch of a later arcade is often an indication of a vanished wing.

Timber towers rising at the west end of a nave, especially if they appear to have been built inside it, may be suspected of being the remains of an early timber church which has been absorbed within later walling. A half-bay at the west end of a nave arcade seems generally to indicate the site of the vanished eastern aisle of a timber church, absorbed by some westward modification of the nave built on to this.

Up to the end of the thirteenth century, aisles were narrow, eight feet or so in width. Many have been subsequently widened, but traces of the old spreading roof which once covered in one span both the nave and its aisles may often be found at the east end of the nave, on the tower, or on the west wall of a wing or transept. The new aisle may have been accompanied by the erection of a new arcade or, more rarely, a clearstory might have been raised above the old one.

Often in a Gothic church one may see traces of small round-headed arches above an aisle arcade. This is probably the remains of the high-set windows of a pre-medieval nave.

While one can find many old features in unexpected places within a church, one must not be misled into believing them to be in their original positions. A fine pre-medieval doorway in the wall of a wide aisle has certainly been carefully taken down and rebuilt. Such features were often more treasured than we might believe; it is no uncommon thing to find the early-medieval triplet of lancets which once formed the east window of the chancel re-sited in the east wall of a transept or even an aisle.

While one may thus find early features in a late wall, one is still more likely to find the reverse. Few early churches escaped being at least in part re-fenestrated during the High Gothic era. Inserted features can often be detected by the fact that the dressed stone-work surrounding them is out of course with the walling about them. This is not however a certain clue as some of the early builders ordered ready-made windows from the quarry instead of having them made by a banker-mason on the job, as would have been the case with first-class work, the point being that both the walling and the dressings should have been raised course by course as the work proceeded.

The masons of medieval days were too concerned with their reputation to build with 'straight joints' when adding one wall to another. Thus one hardly ever finds straight joints to indicate a change of building period. On the other hand the new work would probably have its own course system so that the junction, however properly bonded, would be bound to show.

Changes in roof pitch are nearly always clearly indicated by the remains of water-tables on tower walls and above the chancel arch. Vanished additions can be detected by the vertical lines made by alternate quoin-stones left in the remaining wall. The actual internal angle of the vanished building can be seen as an absolutely vertical line of stone edges.

Dating stonework becomes more difficult when one cannot associate it with contemporary architectural features such as windows which by the pitch of their arches or the form of their mouldings give a fairly accurate date. There are, however, quite a number of clues to the date of walling visible in the arrangement of its stones.

Rubble stonework set 'herring-bone' is always an indication of pre-medieval date. The same is generally true of squared rubble set uncoursed or 'random'. After the twelfth century the mason would set his facing properly coursed.

When one comes to dressed stonework dating is helped by several factors. The first is the size of the stones. Until the early-medieval period these were squarish on the face but the medieval mason used stones about twice as long as their depth, typical of the neatness of the period. The High Gothic was raised with much larger stones, deeper in the course and up to considerable lengths. (Plate 31.)

The angles of a building can be most helpful in dating. Roman brick gives an early date. As the thirteenth century was coming in, quoins were often doubled, giving quite a smart-looking angle in conjunction with rubble walls. With the fifteenth century ashlar appears, stone which is laid in slabs set upright instead of flat. This appears in the angles of the building and is easily recognized. From then onwards, the properly-laid quoin disappears from all but the best-quality work. In rubble or brick walling the upright quoins becoming particularly noticeable, indicating all too clearly the deterioration of masonry.

During the seventeenth century the 'drafted margin' in which the face of the stone is heavily tooled along its edges, is often found. This is later developed until the face of the stone is left 'rock-faced' and not worked at all except along its margins. In Georgian days comes 'rustication' in which the joints are marked by square or V-shaped channels. At the end of this period one finds 'vermiculation', a raised pattern of flat strips wriggling across the stone. It is by looking for indications of this sort that one can date otherwise featureless additions such as buttresses.

Sometimes one may be surprised to find that the quoins of a building are not plumb but follow a wavy profile. This is an indication that the stone building was originally built against a timber one and that this has been destroyed.

Angle-buttresses give a useful clue to date. The 'French buttress' set diagonally does not make its appearance until the fourteenth century. During the thirteenth century appears a pair of buttresses set at right angles; prior to this we have the 'clasping pilaster' of pre-medieval days. (Fig. 21.)

If the west gable of the nave has a buttress-like pilaster passing up its centre it is likely to be of thirteenth-century date.

Any dressed stonework can be roughly dated if its tool-marks have not weathered away. Thus the pre-medieval stones, left off the axe, show its unmistakable uneven diagonal strokes. This rough-hacked finish is in complete contrast to the early-medieval bolster-work which is beautifully neat and is run dead vertically up each stone. The bolster continues in use throughout the medieval period (Plate 32) but after the thirteenth century its strokes are seen running in careless fashion diagonally across the stones.

The Renaissance masons seem to have exchanged the light bolster for a rather heavier tool which leaves coarser and much more untidy marks except where the margins are 'drafted', when more care is taken with the marks left along the edges of the stones.

One of the easiest ways of dating a portion of a building is to examine horizontal mouldings such as string-courses or dripstones which follow a recognizable profile which remains more or less constant for each period. (See Fig. 27.)

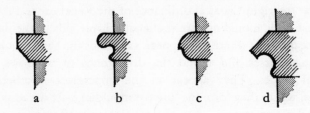

a   b   c   d

Fig. 27 *String-courses*
The standard profiles of string-courses and impost mouldings. The upper members of the caps of pillars; the top moulding in any horizontal system of ornament. Useful as an aid to approximate dating. (a) Pre-medieval. (b) The deeply-undercut early-medieval moulding equating to the water-holding base. (c) The fourteenth-century moulding equating to the triple-roll base. (d) The heavy 'cove' of the fifteenth century and onwards as long as masonry mouldings survive.

In the pre-medieval period the moulding was a square projection with its lower edge chamfered off. With the approach of the Gothic in the early-medieval period it changes completely to a rounded section, either a simple 'torus' or a slimmer roll deeply undercut and with a still smaller roll below. This is the moulding which accompanies the richly-moulded architecture of the thirteenth century and goes with the 'water-holding' base. During the mid-Gothic which follows the early medieval the hollows are filled up and disappear from both string-course and base. The basic moulding becomes a 'torus' with its upper radius greater than its lower and a small break where the two join. The last

Gothic period is marked by an unmistakable moulding which is a kind of coarse version of the early medieval in that it has a deep hollow with a small roll below it; the top however is a thin projection with a wide splay on its upper edge to throw off water. In all it forms a kind of Gothic cornice moulding but with a concave 'cove' instead of the projecting 'corona' of the Classical cornice. Incidentally, it is of interest to note that during the seventeenth century a large 'cove' is often found under the eaves of buildings. Usually run in plaster, it takes the place of the standard Classical cornice and appears to be a Gothic survival retained to mock at the rigid Classical ordinance of the Renaissance.

These basic mouldings are the most reliable aids to the dating of those portions where they appear. One finds the basic moulding in string-courses and round the drip-stones of windows and internal arches. They appear in the uppermost members of capitals, where they form the 'impost moulding'. At the responds of arcades and single arches the moulding is often compound, having below it a wide concave band representing a 'bell' as in the capital—often carved in the same way—and finished off below with the small 'astragal' roll.

The sizes of bricks can be a help in dating otherwise featureless walling. The Roman bricks, rather more than an inch thick, found in the rubble of walls and employed as quoins, suggest a very early date. From the thirteenth century—in the eastern counties only— to the sixteenth, one finds the 'two-inch' brick which from the end of the fifteenth century has a firm hold on the larger buildings of the day. During the sixteenth century 'Tudor' bricks are quite common. The seventeenth century uses rather wider bricks but still not quite running four courses to the foot as today. The standard two and five-eighths inches of the modern brick dates from the Georgian period.

Until the end of the sixteenth century bricks were laid as though they were rubble, without any pattern of coursing. There are more 'headers' than 'stretchers' showing in the walling. During the seventeenth century the 'bond' is 'English' having alternate courses of each; after this the 'Flemish bond', which alternates headers and stretchers in the same course, finally takes over. A feature of Georgian brickwork is the use of over-burnt headers called 'chuffs' to form patterns in the bonding.

Graffiti are often interesting and may help with dating. Geometrical 'doodles' made with a mason's compasses are medieval. If one of the primitive 'mass-dials' is found on the north side of a church the stone has been re-used. One may speculate on the significance of situations where one can see that men have gathered and gossiped while they sharpened a blade on some piece of ancient architecture known to serve as a good whetstone.

Initials and dates of the seventeenth and eighteenth centuries may be found. Earlier dates may be suspect, for Arabic numerals did not reach this country until the sixteenth century and were presumably unknown to the rustic vandal until the next.

While some of the additions and alterations to an old church will be connected with the improvement of its accommodation, others will be due to attempts to improve its stability, nearly always connected with trying to check distortion due to inadequate abutment.

The progressive widening of chancel arches led to spreading abutments and cracked gables. The eastern angles of new bell-towers damaged the western responds of the nave arcades and distorted the tower arch. New arches cut into transepts were cut without regard for abutment. Large windows were inserted without regard for the spread of their arches or the quality of the surrounding walling. Above all, an old 'close-couple' or cradle roof continued to spread and thrust against its walls while each generation watched the list increasing until at last it was decided to try to stop the trouble.

This kind of thing was going on all through the Middle Ages, as today. And it is of interest to see the measures taken to maintain the buildings of the parish churches against the stress of time. One can find old walling rebuilt in a new and more efficient fashion. And after the thirteenth century the real buttresses begin to appear, each generation adding its own, in its own fashion, as the old church calls for aid, to keep it standing still.

19

The Troubles of Old Parish Churches

========

Buildings grow out of the wants of men and are the embodiment of their wishes. In a parish church which leads a life prolonged through many centuries, its walls carry along with them memories not only of past worshippers but of those among them who strove to keep its stones alive and hand them down from generation to generation.

And as it was a thousand years ago, so it is today. Sturdy walls may defy the forces of disintegration while ancient roofs hold fast against the tempests of the seasons. But here and there the signal cracks begin to creep, on plastered walls faint stains are taking shape. Once more we are reminded that buildings, too, are mortal.

The student who takes pleasure in the store of history and art gathered by the centuries within the walls of an old parish church might once in a while give a thought not only to the men who built it but also to those who have undertaken the less impressive task of maintaining its condition. He might also remember that these same devoted guardians remain with us today, more often than not struggling with depleted congregations to scrape together the funds necessary for the never-ending programme of restoration.

How often at holiday-time the visitor to the country comes upon a village fete? He may even pause to study the efforts being made by the villagers to gather in funds from amongst themselves, their neighbours, and with luck the passer-by. Perhaps after many hours of effort in arranging and carrying out the day's programme, the profits may be small. But it is by these means that the parish-ioners—not all of them worshippers—are able to keep their old church in being.

The visitor to an old parish church may see for himself what needs to be done. As he searches for breaks in the level of a plinth let him take note that he is being hindered in his search by an over-growth of vegetation which will cost money to eradicate. When he has noted with interest a settlement crack which indicates some change in the span of an arch the stability of which has as a result been threatened by centuries of cumulative strain . . . let him go on to wonder whether the rector has noticed it and whether such a small parish will be able to find the cost of restoring the situation.

The day is past when the study of old buildings was being considered only in the light of their aesthetic interest. It behoves the architectural historian of today to note the construction of a building and then go further to appreciate it as a living structure. He should teach himself to sympathize with the problems it encounters with the passing years. For someone has to, or there will be no more old buildings.

Very few of the guardians of our old parish churches are really amateurs of architecture. They simply have to try to keep their charges going. Their ignorance is an unfortunate handicap, and indeed traps them into situations which need never have been encountered.

They are actually helped in no small degree by the fact that the wilful jerry-builder was unknown in medieval days. Moreover his materials were natural and not synthetic, had been well tested by time, and could last for ever if given proper care. Their great enemy was the climate, especially the humidity due to too much rain and too little sunshine to dry things out quickly before deterioration begins.

There is an ancient saying concerning 'cob', that now-forgotten material of which so many houses have been built, to stand today after perhaps two centuries. It is said that all cob needs to stand for ever is a good hat and a good pair of shoes. This means that if you can keep the damp from rising through it and seeping down into it from above there need be no other reason for it to deteriorate.

Settlements due to foundation failure or structural thrusts excepted, the same saying could be applied to any wall of rubble, masonry, or timber.

Of the two deficiencies mentioned, the most serious would be absence of footgear. For while a wall might take some time to deteriorate downwards, let its base begin to disintegrate unchecked and its doom is sealed.

Some of the troubles of an old parish church are of a nature very easy to detect and remedy. Of these, the encroachment of vegetation around the base of the walls constitutes an assault which can hardly escape notice and which is easily remedied without expert assistance. A jungle of this sort keeps the base of the wall wet, prevents its drying out and leads dampness into the interior of the building.

Sometimes the encumbrance reaches a stage where the actual material of the walling is being attacked and its jointing being gouged out. Ivy is the great enemy in this respect as its sap will actually dissolve the mortar. Every scrap of ivy should be removed from walling and its roots treated with corrosive.

Another protection against damp walls is the ground gutter, often formed in brick, run at the base of the walling and drained by short lengths of pipe. Far too many of these gutters are allowed to deteriorate and become smothered with vegetation.

The graveyards surrounding many old parish churches have risen through the centuries until the lower part of the church walling, through which it needs to 'breathe', has become buried deep in the ground. Conservers of the last century often excavated a trench called a 'dry area' round the church to remedy this, but in many cases the purpose of this feature has been forgotten and it has been allowed to fill up.

So much for the 'shoes'. The 'hat' is more difficult. A most common source of trouble, however, is the rusting away of eaves, gutters and down-pipes for lack of paint, a defect which should be easily detectable and soon remedied. The inside of the gutter must not be overlooked.

In addition to the problems presented by the protection of the tops and bases of walling, one has to keep the wall-faces sealed against driving rain which in winter will freeze in the joints and burst the wall-faces asunder. A little attention with the pointing-trowel—neatly done so as not to offend the masons of old—will keep the wall-faces sound for ever.

In Chapter 12 the writer called attention to the disastrous aesthetic results of covering church walling with Portland cement rendering. Apart from its dead colour, it has no texture of its own, and will never weather, as other renderings do, by growing algae. Roman cement is nowadays difficult to procure, but an admixture of lime with the Portland cement will help to improve the colour to some small extent. The 'pebble-dash' used by the builders of cheap houses does help to give the rendering a texture but this is quite foreign to any existing in historical days. The stuff used during the eighteenth century was road grit washed by rain into the sides of the water-bound turnpike roads of the period. Today one can make do with crushed stone chippings, but these should not be larger than three-sixteenths of an inch in gauge.

The proper way to deal with damp walling is to remove internal plaster, apply a bituminous membrane, and re-plaster. But external rendering has a tradition behind it and is acceptable provided it be done with care for its appearance.

The most important part of the head-covering of church walling is of course the roof. While leaks in this may appear here and there above the building, the accumulation of stormwater is at the eaves, so that it is the walling, concealed from view, which bears the brunt of any seepage. Tiles of stone or burnt clay form a very good covering, but the iron nails which hold them to their battens, or the battens to the rafters, will not last for ever. The day comes when sagging lines appearing in the tiling indicate that the roof is due for re-covering if a tile-slide into the churchyard is to be prevented. But for the time being the annual replacement of missing and broken tiles costs little enough and keeps the 'hat' sound.

In this connection the writer would like to call attention to the insensitive way in which some church roofs are being patched. It is not so difficult to obtain second-hand old tiles. If however concrete tiles have to be used, they should be collected in at least two, preferably three, tones, approximately similar and mixed together before laying. A square patch of brown concrete tiles staring from the most prominent part of an old church does little to assist its aesthetic presentation.

Many post-medieval churches, and some ancient ones, have roofs covered with blue-grey Welsh slates. The traditional method for replacing slates is to hook the new one over its batten with a lead clip. The weight of the slate, however, opens out the soft lead clip and down it slides once more. Stout copper wire makes a much more reliable clip.

Churches with lead roofs have the best covering. But even lead will not last for ever. If the pitch is too steep the lead sheets will creep and slip. Over-large sheets will split themselves with the seasonal changes of temperature. The 'welts' joining the sides of sheets will crack. Spalls of stone will fall from the tower and hole them, and a lead sheet once broken can never be satisfactorily repaired, certainly not by solder which has a different coefficient of expansion. (Lead-burning was until recently believed to be the answer, but even this is now found to place too great a strain upon this somewhat pernickety material.) And lead eventually oxidises and loses its pliability, so that then there is nothing for it but removal and replacement.

Medieval lead was laid in much heavier sheets than are used today. It contained a certain amount of silver, and was more valuable than modern lead. It used to be possible to re-cover an old church for the salvage value of the old lead. Even today this asset must not be disregarded by those faced with the renewal of old lead roofs.

One occasionally sees preserved in some part of the church lead panels containing inscriptions recording a date and the names of two churchwardens. Such panels were cast into lead sheet at the time when a roof was being re-covered and were salvaged and preserved with the next re-covering.

The earliest dates are usually mid-eighteenth century and continue at intervals as successive parts of the church were dealt with. It would be interesting to know whether these dates represent replacements of the original lead of perhaps the fourteenth century, implying that this may have lasted for four centuries. Nineteenth-century lead is not lasting for half as long.

An important part of the leadwork of a roof is its gutters, for these collect the whole of its stormwater and quite a small fracture may discharge a large proportion of this into the building or its walling. Such gutters need to be constantly inspected, kept clean and examined for cracks. And cracked lengths should be replaced, and not patched with solder or asphalt.

The damage which can often be traced to a leaking gutter can be desperate indeed. The ends of main roofing beams or the feet of magnificent trusses can rot away unseen within their walls. The repair of such features is expensive, difficult, and frequently necessitates complete replacement. So watch the gutters!

A nice damp beam makes a desirable situation in which to found a colony of that scourge of old buildings, the death-watch beetle. This destructive creature has increased its depredations a hundred-fold since the fumes from oil-lighting were banished from the high crannies of the ancient roofs. Disinfestation is nowadays possible, but requires a desperate amount of scraping away of ruined timber before the beetle can be reached and destroyed.

The ironwork of doors, also—some of it maybe eight centuries old—is worth a dab of paint now and then. And the doors themselves, especially the unprotected west door, battered by the furies of English winters, will welcome a lick of varnish to bring back life to the grain of their boarding.

There are many qualities of stones. Some weather well, others decay all too soon. Sometimes a stone flakes or 'spalls' through settlement or through being burst by rusted ironwork. It is nowadays far from easy to discover a mason who will cut out and renew the defective stonework in a decent style worthy of an ancient building, but they may yet be found. Dabbing with cement looks squalid. The hard synthetic application soon pulls away, doing further damage to the old stone as it does so.

The key to the successful maintenance of an old building is found in regular examination—especially of the 'hat' and 'shoes'—followed by immediate repair of any defects discovered. Much can be done by a local builder provided he is willing to take pains not to contribute work of poor standard to that of his predecessors. Masonry work, repairs to glazing, and the renewal of lead roofing are of course the province of the specialist.

It is when structural failure occurs that expert advice has to be called in. The most common-trouble is foundation failure. This is often of recent occurrence, as from the digging of graves too close to the building. But many settlements are of long standing and have been very slowly developing as some thrust increases, walling disintegrates, or foundations subside.

The bonding system with which all walling is constructed enables any length of wall to carry the walling above it in a line of about forty-five degrees outwards from any point. Thus any diagonal crack indicates that the part of the wall below the crack is sinking. Vertical cracks denote not sinking but a tearing sideways about the line of the crack, as in toppling, or the breaking of a joint between two walls. It is interesting to find that the earthquake damaged buildings round Peldon in Essex show plenty of such cracks.

To deal with major structural disasters such as the disintegration of walls or the threatened collapse of roofs through rot or the depredations of the beetle, it is necessary to call in an architect. Foundations may be underpinned, loose walling may be 'grouted'. But once a large timber beam has been deprived of its bearing on the wall it may be almost beyond human aid.

So, guardians of old parish churches . . . look to your lead!

Returning from roofs to walls, we shall find one of the most troublesome items in the equipment of the medieval church and probably the most expensive to deal with is its fenestration.

The window glazing of a church needs care and attention, for the lead 'calms' perish and the wiring oxidizes so that the whole window becomes loose and subject to damage from tempest. This needs the attention of the expert. But it is a small matter to keep the window ironwork from rusting away by painting it now and then.

Glass does not fulfil to perfection the task of waterproofing openings in external walling, and church glazing is formed of a number of small pieces held together by very slender strips of lead, each panel being sprung into narrow grooves cut into the stone-work and thereafter secured by wire ties to the vertical 'stanchions' and horizontal 'saddle-bars' which together form the window's 'ferramenti'.

A broken piece of glass—or 'quarry'—can easily be inserted by working it carefully into the lead 'calms', but once these become decayed or fractured, repair is impossible without removing the whole panel and laying it on a bench where it can be re-set with new leadwork by a skilled craftsman.

Lead is the most temperamental of metals and any disturbance is apt to cause it to become fatigued. Thus the flapping of a loose panel of glazing may start the disintegration of its glazing through the decay of its leading. The sound of a window giving to the wind is an indication that its security is threatened and that immediate attention must be given to its wire ties.

Ferramenti rust and need permanent protection by paint. If the rust reaches the ironwork embedded in the window surround it will split the stonework and thus become a source of extremely costly masonry repairs.

The most troublesome part of the fenestration of a church is its movable ventilators. One sees them rusted into immobility and letting in the winter tempests as well as the fresh airs of summer. They should always be kept rust-free and painted, their hinges and pulleys oiled, and their cordage intact and ready for instant use. Such maintenance as this is very undemanding and is a great help to the comfort of the congregation as well as eliminating those telltale stains which mar the decoration of the wall below the window-sill.

Stained glass, even though it should be of nineteenth-century origin, is an important part of the ornament of a church and is nearly always a memorial to some benefactor. While some of the designs may be regrettable, for the most part it represents the skill and devotion of some craftsman and should not be lightly torn out and replaced by plain domestic glazing introduced on the plea of improving the natural lighting of the building. It must be confessed, however, that heavily-pigmented Victorian glass in the clearstory windows of a tall church covered by a fine ceiling often conceals much of its carved detail, an aesthetic disadvantage which cannot but be deplored. The removal of such semi-opaque glazing can have dramatic results by abolishing the lowering shadows and providing the building with a glorious canopy soaring above its paving and emphasizing its true height.

The coloured glass filling the large traceried windows of the High Gothic was intended to provide a religious picture-book. The work was carefully detailed and produced a jewelled effect which can still be enjoyed at Fairford in Gloucestershire. But the religious bigotry of the seventeenth century swept away most of our medieval glass. What remains of eighteenth- and early-nineteenth-century glass shows it to have been of considerable aesthetic value, the pictures based on the masterly achievements of the contemporary painter and set out in large pieces of material so as to break up the scene as little as possible. Most of this Renaissance glass was removed at the Gothic Revival. The Victorian glaziers aimed at re-creating the medieval effect but traditional skill having been long forgotten there were no longer men capable of the work. The result was for the most part amateurish, in colouring either gaudy or drab, and quite unlike the gentle but brilliant glass of Gothic days. During the last fifty years an inevitable reaction has introduced pallid sub-aqueous treatments, less obstructive to light but lacking all the ancient warmth and liveliness.

Coloured glazing for a large Gothic window is nowadays a costly venture. But the writer has noticed how the charm of some small churches has been curiously enhanced by the introduction of plain coloured glass in a small window, especially if it should be near the altar where one's attention is naturally focused. Sunlight is not as golden as the poets would have us believe, but it can be lent a golden radiance from carefully-selected glass, so that the light may bring with it not the hard sheen of metallic gold nor the synthetic pigment of aureolin but something more resembling the natural glow of lichen on weathered stone.

A good deal of thought is being given today to the subject of how to brighten our churches by the development of more open planning (to say nothing of 'hotting up' services by introducing 'pop' accompaniment!). But so many of our village churches could be relieved of dreariness by giving a thought to their interior decoration. So many splendidly-proportioned buildings—austere perhaps for lack of architectural ornament—could come into their own for the cost of a couple of coats of distemper.

There is no need to invite glare by thrusting out the painted glass which, however indifferent its artistic value might appear to the cognoscenti, has been for so long a treasured feature in the life of a village church.

Light can enter in the train of the distemper brush.

20

Churches in Dissolution

Throughout the length and breadth of the land the parishes stoutly maintain the struggle to keep their old churches sound and watertight.

But what of the churches which have seen their parishes fade into history and no longer have priest or congregation to fill them and maintain their structures?

What happens to them?

As a small boy the writer was familiar with an ancient church in Buckinghamshire which had been abandoned by its parishioners for a new church and left in the fields to decay. Beyond its twelfth-century chancel arch it was still roofed, but over the nave only bare timbers remained; through them one could watch the clouds racing past a tall tower of the seventeenth century. The doors were open and the interior had become squalid with the debris of decay. A few years ago he visited it again to find it gone, smothered in a brake of brambles through which here and there an ancient stone remained to testify that here was once a parish church. Upon inquiry he found that some adventurous child had fallen to its death from the tower. So the Army had been called in to demolish the whole building as a military exercise.

There is something disreputable about this history. The church had undoubtedly become, in the modern phrase, redundant. So, like a regiment abandoning a temporary war-time cantonment, its parishioners had just walked out of it and left it, after perhaps a thousand years, to sink into squalor and in the end fall a victim to the breakers.

The writer has seen a number of derelict churches. Most counties can show them. Some of them have had their doors only recently closed for the last time while others have gaping roofs and pewing befouled. And some have become heaps of stones from which rotting beams protrude while they wait for bramble and briar-rose to give them decent interment.

Sometimes the situation results from a temporary breakdown in parochial organization due to the presence of an unsatisfactory incumbent or even a protracted period of sequestration during which the parish has lacked a priest. And without regular mainte-nance, especially of roofs, an ancient building can quickly reach a condition when repair becomes costly indeed.

Neglect the structure of an ancient building, and decay will creep in and flourish with increasing speed until a day comes when the situation suddenly bursts into crisis. It may be that insurers will no longer accept the building and closure becomes essential. With neglect broadened by this, the time is not far distant when the parish church becomes officially a 'dangerous structure', unapproachable and possibly even meriting demolition.

The devotion with which some sparsely-populated parishes will strive to preserve an ancient church the upkeep of which is quite beyond their means is well known. But the time may come when even such gallant communities have to give up the struggle and decay begins to get out of control.

Some of the most beautiful of the High Gothic parish churches are to be found in areas of the country that were once wealthy from the proceeds of a flourishing wool trade which financed their erection, areas now given over to mechanized agriculture and no longer able to support a large rural population. Such parishes are sometimes grouped together as many as four to one priest, who may in consequence have a number of magnificent buildings to try to maintain with the help of a population scattered over a few farms.

There are places in this country where the parish has not just moved its population to a new site but has vanished completely, so that the old parish church has literally no one at all to care for it. That such churches could ever be used again would seem inconceivable (though one such, at Chingford in Essex, was rescued from roofless ruin and restored to full use with the expansion of the town).

Some parish churches which have lost their villages through changes in rural circumstances have long been maintained by farming squires, against the day when their heirs, plundered through death-duties, will have to abandon the old buildings to inevitable ruin.

Was it proper that an architectural and historical monument such as an old parish church should have been allowed to sink into a state of squalor until in the end it became a dangerous structure and had to be, with its architectural treasures and its memorials of village history, summarily destroyed.

Many persons in this country have fought for years to preserve from dissolution some of the finer of our old parish churches. But the struggle may in some cases have become hopeless. In the end it has been necessary to make a cold-blooded survey of the whole situation and decide upon a workable policy for the country's architectural treasures. This policy will need to be more honestly administered than that which obtains at the moment for secular buildings, where attempts at preservation may be countered by delaying tactics while the structure concerned decays into a state where it is no longer capable of being restored.

There are possibly cases where an old parish church is passing through a bad period in its history and must wait for a new incumbent or a more enthusiastic congregation—who need not necessarily be regular worshippers to take a pride in their parish church. But amongst the thousands of old churches in this country there may well be scores which have indisputably reached the end of their history and if merely abandoned will simply slide into squalor, desecration and miserable decay.

The problem of redundant churches is at last being given authoritative consideration under the provisions of a new Pastoral Measure creating an Advisory Panel which will investigate the architectural merits of a church threatened with closure, and suggest what might be done to preserve the building, in whole or in part 'in the interests of the nation'. A Redundant Churches

Fund is to be created. An authoritative body such as this has long been needed and it is to be hoped that with its support the Diocesan Authorities will at last feel able to cope with the agonizing problem of the derelict churches of England.

Many of these buildings will contain features which are not only of considerable historic and aesthetic interest but may be of material use elsewhere. Furniture such as pews or screens might be acceptable to the congregations of other churches, especially those in the old Dominions or even the U.S.A. Better export than oblivion. Bells would certainly be welcome. Fonts also might take their history with them to other lands.

Many old churches suffer aesthetically from a lack of atmosphere owing to the absence of features of interest normally found in an old church. This is often due to a too drastic tidying-up during some 'restoration'. Valuable monuments such as medieval tombs or particularly fine Renaissance monuments, instead of being allowed to decay, might be moved to neighbouring parishes glad to add to the interest of their churches by preserving them. It is pleasant to record that the medieval effigies of Imber Church in Wiltshire, its parishioners driven from their homes by the Ministry of Defence, have been given a new home in neighbouring Edington.

While items of furniture such as these, however, may easily be transferred from one building to another, the greatest care is essential when performing the same operation with features belonging to the sphere of architecture. For the danger lies in creating the impression of a *museum* of architecture. Thus any item, such as an arch or doorway, transferred from its original site to a strange home, must be given an appropriate setting. This does not imply that a medieval setting must be created for it, but simply that it must be accorded the courtesy of an atmosphere suited to its age and dignity. Any sensitive architect should be able to achieve this by using materials appropriate, by virtue of their colour, texture or finish, for association with the transferred feature. It is the achievement of atmosphere, not the accuracy of detailing, which should in such circumstances be the consideration of the architect.

Thus if an old parish church were to be officially declared redundant and an order for its closure issued by authority, the first stage in its dissolution would be the rescue of its treasures.

We shall then have to consider the actual building. It is to be hoped that its windows contain no valuable old glass, but any which may exist would have to be extracted and found a new resting place. Not long ago, the Dean of York asked that any persons investigating the sites of Cistercian abbeys in Yorkshire should send him any fragments of old glass they might come across. From the pieces he received he fashioned a window in his Minster.

All roofing materials are valuable. The restorers of old buildings are always seeking tiles of clay or stone and will pay good prices for them. Lead, of course, is readily saleable for melting down and casting anew. Thus an old church in dissolution can itself provide some of the funds needed for a possible preservation as a monument.

In the middle of the last century a Wiltshire rector was waiting for a train on an East Anglian platform and became interested in some medieval timbers stacked there. Finding that they represented the roof timbers of the refectory of a local Friary which had just been pulled down, he decided to buy them, reconstruct the roof, and build under it a new church for his parish. At the Dissolution of the great monasteries a number of parish churches were able to employ salvaged roofs when enlarging their own accommodation. The roofs of dissolved parish churches might well be transferred to other buildings, endowing them with an architectural splendour no longer available by any other means.

Even the lesser timbers of belfries and porches might be salvaged and passed to persons only too glad to make use of them in houses undergoing restoration.

With all furnishings and perishable structure removed the old church will become a shell of masonry which is capable of being preserved as an ecclesiastical monument in the same fashion as a ruined abbey or medieval castle.

There are architects, especially those working for the Ministry of Works, who are nowadays quite expert in the treatment of such ruins. The parish-less church of Knowlton in Dorset has been preserved as an ecclesiastical monument by this Ministry.

It is of course essential to aim at the creation of a structure which will require the minimum of maintenance. Stone is a permanent building material but when it is set in mortar to form a wall the result is not immune from disintegration. Thus it is essential to point the wall-faces against the depredations of frost. Most important of all are the tops of the walls upon which rain falls and freezes. A layer of asphalt will provide a permanent waterproof cap.

Architectural detail cannot always be preserved in a ruin unless a certain amount of periodic maintenance can be envisaged. Thus the window tracery might have to be sacrificed; the dressed openings will stand firm enough without it. Parapets, especially if they should be elaborate, might have to be removed to enable the wall-tops to be waterproofed and save the scaffolding without which such high places remain inaccessible. Any delicate ornament, such as pinnacles, which might become loose and dangerous, might have to be sacrificed.

While the loss of such architectural features as parapets and window tracery might be regrettable, the transformation of a derelict parish church into a rural monument might be considered as an alternative to its removal as a dangerous structure or its segregation within a wire fence to rot away into squalor.

Let it rise from the land untroubled by fencing. Its yard can be kept from the plough by mere-stones. Suffer sheep to graze its sward in summer, folded within an electric fence which should give no great trouble to the farmer who will supply it.

Keep weeds away from its walls by sterilization, and touch up its pointing or rendering once in a while. Surely no parish would grudge their ancient church a small annual budget.

There is no building in all England that knows our country and its history so well as a village church. Its lines may have been marked out on the ground at the time when the Greatest Englishman was hammering the Danes at Ethandune eleven centuries ago. Generations of farming squires have knelt in it to bear witness to their Faith.

The Saxon farmer sadly handed it over to the Norman ruffian who as the generations passed became the stern Plantagenet and later, perhaps, crossed with the army to fight at Crecy or Poitiers. The happy breed of the wool-rich yeomen followed in that Merrie England which was later to turn to mourning for Englishmen clubbed to death by neighbours in the Great Rebellion. Then the peaceful era of the Georgian farmers, and the austerity, mellowed by sunny afternoons, of Victorian England.

Behind the squires, as they enter the south door of the parish church, file the whole of Englishry. Ploughmen, herdsmen, smith and miller, and the women who cooked and cleaned, and reared the children who played their games and put away their toys and grew up to make England.

What is so remarkable—moving even—is that they are all still there, every man and woman of them, gathered together within the compass of that small plot . . . for ever.

As you follow the path of the sun along the old processional way round the walls of a village church you may one day catch the mood and begin to realize that a thousand years of England is beside you as you pass.

Should not every old parish church be suffered to sleep out an honourable retirement in the midst of its great congregation, lapped by those friendly pastures which down the long centuries have been its neighbours?

Notes on Plates

———

Holder of Copyright indicated by italics
N.B.R. National Building Record

1. STOCK. A timber church of the twelfth or thirteenth century.
Sheathing has probably been renewed many times but original
framing remains inside. Structure has been retained to serve as
bell-tower to later church, a practice met with elsewhere in stone-
less Essex. Note the timber 'broach' or spire. *N.B.R.*

2. WEST HANNINGFIELD. An interesting little timber church
illustrating the cruciform 'West Byzantine' plan. Probably
thirteenth-century framing; sheathing modern. Retained to serve
as bell-tower to later church. Note broach. *C. J. Bassham.*

3. BARTON-UPON-HUMBER. Stone tower-nave, probably of the
eleventh century. Ornamented with strips of stone arranged to
imitate timbering. Note the Byzantine *bifora* windows in each
storey, and the entrance doorway west of centre. A small 'west
nave' remains. The tower has been retained to serve as a bell-
tower to the later church. *N.B.R.*

4. BREAMORE. A turriform nave probably of the twelfth century.
The chancel has been rebuilt but the southernmost 'wing' can be
seen, and the long 'west nave'. Note the fourteenth-century 'reticulated' east window. *N.B.R.*

5. WORTH. A fine 'pseudo-cruciform' church of the eleventh
century, having the chancel arch and those leading into the 'wings'
of unusually wide span but very crudely fashioned. *N.B.R.*

6. WORTH. Typical 'pseudo-cruciform' church of the eleventh century but with unusually long aspidal chancel, possibly a successor to the original. A late Gothic window has been inserted in the south wing. Note the stone strip ornament representing timber posts and the Byzantine *bifora* lighting the nave. *N.B.R.*

7. HEATH. A twelfth-century church set out on the simple 'Celtic' plan of nave and chancel. Compare the rough rubble walling with the freestone 'dressings'. Note the 'clasping' pilasters at the angles and the provision for belfry openings in the apex of the west gable. *F. C. Morgan.*

8. IFFLEY. A twelfth-century church built on the so-called 'axial' plan in which the tower-nave has been retained as the nucleus of the design and the 'west nave' enlarged to medieval proportions. Beyond the tower is the small chancel. Note the slender angle-shafts beside the tower windows and rising up the angle of the clasping pilaster at the west end. The large buttresses are additions. *N.B.R.*

9. WHAPLODE. A twelfth-century interior illustrating the more massive 'Anglian' type of design. Note the heavy 'Doric' type of cap and its development into the 'coniferous' form. A typical twelfth-century 'impost moulding' crowns each cap. Note the early clearstory beyond. *Rev. Maurice Ridgway.*

10. STAPLEFORD. A twelfth-century arcade richly ornamented with zigzag and other repetitive elements. The pillars are of the circular 'Romanesque' type common to the Midland and Western regions. Their caps are based on the Corinthian and have bells tending towards the concave. Note the carved 'dripstone' band passing above the arches, embellished with an unusually early representation if the 'dog-tooth' ornament. *Bernard White.*

11. UFFINGTON. A cruciform church of the thirteenth century, possibly an attempt to emulate the form of a small monastic church. Note the chapel projecting from the east wall of the

transept. The octagonal tower was probably so transformed to facilitate the construction of a broach. Note the forms of the embryo 'buttresses', especially at the angles, and the fine 'reticulated' window inserted during the fourteenth century to improve the lighting at the chancel arch. *N.B.R.*

12. AMESBURY. A fine 'crossing' beneath a thirteenth-century central tower. Note how the compound piers are assembled. *Bernard White.*

13. STOKE GOLDING. A fine medieval arcade of the period when the early-medieval style of the thirteenth century, with its deeply-undercut mouldings, was turning towards the more restrained profiles of the High Gothic. The 'botanical' caps, with their impost mouldings formed of broken rolls, are typical of the fourteenth century. The pillars are seen as a compromise between the shafted early-medieval type and the plainer 'cruciform' of the High Gothic. *N.B.R.*

14. LOWICK. The fully-developed parish church of the High Gothic era with its large windows, in this example displaying 'rectilinear' tracery. Note the large 'wing' or transept provided to widen the nave immediately to the west of the chancel arch. Note the large north chapel flanking the chancel, and the octagonal corona at the summit of the west tower. *Rev. Maurice Ridgway.*

15. WALPOLE ST. PETER. A brilliantly-lit chancel of the High Gothic era displaying the maximum amount of glazing and the minimum of solid supports. Note the reduction in the rise of the arch spanning the east window, clear evidence of concern in the mind of the designer for the proportions of the opening. *N.B.R.*

16. CHIVELSTONE. The West-Country 'hall-church' with its nave and aisles independently roofed and the clearstory omitted. Note the arrangement of the tower buttresses and the presentation of the tower-stair as an architectural feature of its southern aspect. *Noel Habgood.*

17. LAVENHAM. One of the finest achievements of the East Anglian parish church architect. Note the brilliance of the fenestration with the clearstory an almost continuous range of glazing. Note the elegance of the tower buttressing, the detail of the parapets, and the carefully-designed façade of the south porch. *Noel Habgood.*

18. THAXTED. By the end of the High Gothic era the improvement in roofing systems permitted the provision of very wide aisles. The lead-covered roofs needed so slight a pitch that the undersides of their timbering could be embellished with carving and displayed as a ceiling. Note the carved 'bosses' masking the intersections of the timbers. *N.B.R.*

19. SOMERTON. The system of heavy roof trusses which forms the foundation of the High Gothic roof can be seen carrying the pair of longitudinal 'purlins' which in their turn support the rafters in mid-flight. The whole of the exposed timbering is framed together to display a panelled ceiling enriched with superb carving. *N.B.R.*

20. MARCH. Each of the principal trusses of this roof is constructed of an arched collar-beam carried at either end upon a pair of superimposed 'hammer-beams' the ends of which are masked by angels with their wings displayed. A pair of purlins pass along either slope of the roof. The brackets carrying the lowermost hammer-beams are taken down the walls to end in ranges of sculptured figures. *N.B.R.*

21. ST. ENDELLION. A wide-spread 'cradle-roof' of the West Country, formed of a series of primitive 'trussed rafters' strapped together with longitudinal timbers. The church is of the 'hall' type and has no clearstory. *N.B.R.*

22. MANATON. One of the West Country's superb rood-screens with its loft over. The delicacy of the woodcarving contrasts effectively with the grim granite architecture. *Rev. Maurice Ridgway.*

23. WOLVERTON. A post-Reformation church, its body trying to recapture something of the liveliness of the medieval, but its tower frankly of the Renaissance. Note the typical windows of the belfry, the emphasis upon the quoins, and the elaborate Classical cornice with its plain parapet above. *N.B.R.*

24. NORTH RUNCTON. A post-Reformation interior. Note the simple Classical columns with their rather ingenuous capitals, and the plaster ceiling which has replaced the primitive splendour of medieval joinery. *N.B.R.*

25. BURY. The typical English 'broach' which must have represented the almost universal method of roofing a tower-top prior to the introduction of flat roofs covered with lead sheets. The original sheathing of the broaches would have been of oak shingles. *Noel Habgood.*

26. SLAWSTON. The timber broach reproduced in masonry. The dormer windows are interesting features seen in connection with stone spires of all types. *N.B.R.*

27. SOUTHEASE. A bell-tower of early date reproducing the Byzantine campanile. Built, for lack of freestone, in flint nodules, such towers are found in scores throughout stone-less East Anglia. Note the shingled roof. *Noel Habgood.*

28. BOSTON. One of England's finest bell-towers, culminating masterpieces of the Gothic Age. Note the large belfry openings, the lofty windows of the ringing floor. In lieu of a stone spire, many of the later Gothic towers were finished with graceful octagonal coronas. *Noel Habgood.*

29. KILPECK. One can study this magnificent example of twelfth-century architecture without exhausting one's interest in the diversity of motifs available in the repertoire of the Anglo-Saxon sculptor. *Noel Habgood.*

30. CULLOMPTON. The stone ceiling constructed as a series of cones sweeping fan-wise to meet each other across the span was the final achievement of the Gothic masons and carvers. *Rev. Sumner.*

31. The sizes of stones, and their proportions, are a help with dating. In the pre-medieval period stones were small and nearly square, probably for carrying in panniers attached to pack-saddles. In the early-medieval they were slightly larger and very neat and regular, generally about twice as long as they were high. In the High Gothic era stones were often much larger and very long on the bed, transported on sledges drawn by ponies. *Author.*

32. The marks left on the faces of stones by the tools used by the masons are a help in dating. Pre-medieval stones have their faces roughly hacked with the heavy stone axe which left coarse diagonal scars cut irregularly into the face. The 'bolster' tooling of the early-medieval period was very carefully executed, the marks are neat and regular and always vertical. During the High Gothic period much less care was taken; the tooling was run diagonally across the face and no longer regarded as a decorative finish. *Miss P. Wynn Reeves.*

Glossary

═══════

abacus: uppermost member of a Classical capital

aedicule: a miniature reproduction of a structural feature used for ornamental purposes

apse: semicircular—or in some cases polygonal—end to a building

arcade: a row of arches

architrave: lowermost member of a Classical entablature (q.v.)

ashlar: freestone employed in thin slabs as a facing

aumbry: small cupboard in wall beside altar

baluster: miniature column of bulbous form supporting handrail of balustrade

banker: stone bench upon which a mason dresses stone

battlement: crenellated parapet alternating embrasures or 'crenels' with 'merlons' (q.v.)

bay: longitudinal division of a building

bell: spreading portion of capital (see also 'echinus')

'bifora': two-light Byzantine window

bolster: broad chisel used by masons

bond: method of arranging joints in walling so that no two appear immediately above each other

brace: a timber stiffener under tension

brattice: a boarded partition

broach: a spit, the medieval word for spire

buttress: masonry support against overturning pressure upon a wall

calm: lead strip holding window glass: pronounced 'came'

centering: temporary framework upon which an arch is turned

Glossary

chamfer: a bevelled edge

clearstory: a tier of small windows lighting the upper part of a building

collar: short timber tying a pair of rafters together near apex

coniferous capital: one having its bell fashioned to resemble a row of cones point-downwards

corbel: a stone bracket

corbel-table: a row of corbels carrying a tablement (q.v.)

core: the inner part of a masonry wall

cornice: the upper—projecting—part of a Classical entablature (q.v.) used in Renaissance architecture as a crowning feature

couple: a pair of rafters joined at the apex

course: layer of stones in masonry

cove: broad concave moulding

crocket: Gothic volute (q.v.) seen on sides of pinnacles, spires etc.

crossing: space under a central tower

cruciform: a church having a central tower flanked by transepts

cubiform capital: cushion (q.v.) having its angles cut away to reduce projection

cushion capital: Byzantine version of the Doric capital resembling half a domestic cushion

cusp: triangular tooth separating the 'foils' (q.v.) in Gothic tracery

dormer: window through a roof

dressings: dressed stone used in walling for lining openings and forming angles. Any worked stone as opposed to rubble

drip-stone: projecting stone band over window to prevent storm-water from wall overrunning down glazing

duplex bay: bay system having intermediate supports to main ones, often represented in English architecture by alternating character of supports in an arcade

eaves: the roof projecting over the wall-face

echinus: the projecting part, or 'bell', of the Classical capital

entablature: the principal feature of Classical architecture spanning the columns

fan vault: late-Gothic vault elaborately designed as a series of stone fans

flushwork: an East Anglian form of walling appearing as a pattern of stone tracery filled with knapped flint

flying buttress: an arch carrying a thrust from a wall over to an isolated buttress

foliated: having a silhouette divided into a series of 'foils' by cusps (q.v.)

freestone: stone—properly speaking limestone—capable of being dressed by a mason

frieze: the middle or flat portion of a Classical entablature (q.v.)

gablet: a small gable

gargoyle: water-spout draining gutter, usually carved as a grotesque

groin: in early vaulting, line where two vaults meet

hammer-beam: end of a beam carried by a timber bracket from wall after middle of beam has been cut away

header: brick showing endways in a wall

hood-mould: similar to a drip-stone (q.v.)

impost: springing line of arch, usually indicated by a moulded band

jamb: side of a door opening

king-post: central feature of a roof-truss (see truss)

lantern: central tower carried above surrounding roofs and there provided with windows for lighting crossing below

lierne: short decorative rib in Gothic vaulting

lights: the divisions of a window

lintel: horizontal beam bridging an opening

lodge: a lean-to structure, especially that occupied by masons

masonry: dressed stonework laid in courses, or any other dressed stonework

Glossary

merlon: the projecting portion of a battlemented parapet separating the embrasures. In medieval times 'cop'

moulding: running ornament formed of continuous lines of rolls and channels

mullion: vertical stone member separating lights in a window

ogee: a double curve

order: a line of voussoirs (q.v.) in an arch carrying another over it

parclose: screen filling an arch and enclosing a chapel

pediment: a low-pitched triangular feature, the Renaissance version of the medieval gable

pier: an isolated mass of masonry carrying an arch

pilaster: a half-pier projecting from a wall, usually employed for decorative purposes

pillar: a slender support

piscina: stone basin set in walling on south side of altar for washing sacred vessels

pitch: angle of roof with horizontal

plaster: lime mortar used to cover a wall or ceiling

plate: horizontal timber carrying rafters on wall-top

pole: unit of measurement, originally sixteen feet

pseudo-cruciform: early type of church with wings or transept but no central tower

purlin: horizontal roof-timber passing between trusses (q.v.) to help support rafters

quarry: diamond-shaped piece of glass

queen-posts: pairs of posts forming features of trusses

quoin: angle-stone

rafter: sloping roof-timber carrying roof covering

relieving arch: arch set in walling above an opening to relieve pressure on its lintel

rere arch: arch carrying core of wall over an opening

respond: end of an arcade or jamb of single arch

reticulated: window tracery arranged like the meshes of a net *reveal:* an opening through a wall

ribs: slender members carrying a stone vault

ridge: apex of a roof

rood-beam: beam passing across church at chancel arch carrying crucifix or 'rood'

rood-loft: gallery above rood-screen

rood-screen: screen passing across church at chancel arch

rood-stair: stairs giving access to rood-loft

rubble: rough stone, undressed

saddle-bar: horizontal iron bar set in window as an anchorage for glazing

saltire: the diagonal cross formed by two timbers passing each other

sanctuary: the part of the chancel containing the altar

scalloped capital: capital having its bell grooved in crude imitation of Corinthian capital

scoinson arch: arch carrying inner face of wall over opening

sedilla: stone seats set in walling on south side of chancel

shaft: diminutive of column

shingle: wooden tile for roofing

sill: horizontal timber of stone at base or feature

six-poster: timber church featuring six posts instead of the more usual four

sleeper: horizontal timber carrying posts

soffit: the underside of a feature, such as an arch

solar: an upper floor

spall: flake split from stone

spandrel: triangular space between arch and rectangular surround

squinch: an arch crossing an internal angle diagonally

stanchion: vertical iron bar in a window

steeple: the medieval word for a church tower; Renaissance spire

stoup: basin for holy water

stretcher: brick lying lengthways in a wall

string-course: horizontal moulding used for punctuation and for linking features together

strut: timber stiffener in compression

tablement: medieval word for system of horizontal 'planks' of timber or stone. The tablement is the plinth

tail: rough end of stone buried in wall

teazle post: post set root-upwards so that thick butt end may be used to seat beams

template: a profile for a moulding

tie-beam: heavy horizontal beam first used for tying plates (q.v.) together, later the foundation member of a roof-truss

torus: projecting rounded moulding. Today 'bull-nose'

tracery: the system of bars in a Gothic window, also in wall decoration

transept: a lateral projection from a central tower, or a central area, usually one of a pair. Wider than a 'wing' (q.v.)

transom: horizontal member of window tracery

truss: system of timbering spanning church and carrying purlins (q.v.)

tympanum: space between lintel and relieving arch over

vault: stone ceiling

volute: angle projections of Corinthian capital; in Gothic becomes a 'crocket'

voussoirs: the wedge-shaped stones which make up an arch

wainscot: boarded ceiling

wind-bracing: system of timber arches beneath roof purlins (q.v.) to prevent roof from becoming distorted from wind-pressure upon ends

wing (ala): a small projection from the eastern end of the side wall of the nave

Index

Index